APOSTOLIC AUTHORITY by

MW00901136

There is such an obvious void today in leadership in the church today. Strong, determined, visionary and ethical leaders who are willing to step up are still in demand, but so hard to find. Can leaders be taught; is it caught? How do we encourage the next generation to take the authority?

May I dare say, who will take up the apostolic authority necessary to face the challenges of the 21st century?

In this, Dr. Spake's latest book Apostolic Authority, she exposes the strengths and weaknesses in present leadership models and practices, and present with clarity and conviction esential principles desparately needed for today's church and society in general. She also presents keen Kingdom insights which will indeed prepare and encourage present and future leadership.

All real, biblical leadership sees and builds from a Kingdom perspective; generationally.

I am honored to endorse this needed book for our generation, presented by Dr. Kluane Spake - who is a leader of leaders and a gift worth receiving.

Dr Stan DeKoven
President
Vision International Education Network
Vision International University

by Dr. Kluane Spake

Why Godly Authority is missing

INTRODUCTION:

The NUMBER ONE problem in the church today is this issue of authority.

There is no subject in the church or the world more controversial than who (if anyone) should be in authority. Because of the controversy, this subject is usually avoided. But now, because of escalating times, there is a hastening necessity for us to think Biblically and to redefine AUTHORITY in the church in Biblical terms.

Leadership authority is weakening and often missing. Effective apostles must emerge in this hour to regain, demonstrate, and release true authority.

The restoration and functionality of the apostolic global Church emerges with Kingdom velocity. The Lord waits for leaders to establish their God-given authority and restore His INTENTION and plan upon this earth.

Apostles must establish a functioning apostolic community of believers who are effective, empowered, and skilled. Apostles have the authority to equip believers to engage in Divine purposes. Apostles guide by giving corporate vision and strategy to mature believers who impact their homes, their cities, their nations, and the world.

It is the season of change, velocity, and momentum.

This New Season of Migration

God's Authority is missing because

We need to MIGRATE!

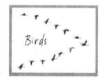

Before delving into the issue of authority, we must first understand the season we live. In the seventh century B.C., Jeremiah the prophet taught a poignant spiritual principle based upon his observations of storks. Have you ever seen storks flying overhead? What can we learn from them? Over 600 thousand migrating birds fly over Israel every spring and autumn! Even people who could not read were able to learn from the birds.

That means whichever Bible character you choose to read about, you can be assured they often watched birds flying overhead. And that's why Jeremiah taught difficult spiritual principles by using physical examples.

"Even the STORK IN THE SKY knows her APPOINTED SEASONS and the dove, the swift, and the thrush observe the time of their migration. But MY PEOPLE DO NOT KNOW THE REQUIREMENTS OF THE LORD."
(Jeremiah 8:7, NIV)

The verse above provides us with a big key! Jeremiah compares the believer's ability to know what to do next with how migrating birds observe the season of their journey. That means – if we know how to observe the time, then we will know WHEN we must migrate. But how? Where? When? If a stork can know... then DOES THAT MEAN WE CAN KNOW?

We live in an incredible moment of time – it's a new day. Of all the people ever born, the Lord selected us to be alive during this appointed SEASON. The Hebrew word for "season" is *mowed* which means a fixed time or season. The Greek word for "season" is *kairos* (set-time) or the "due season" (Gal. 6:9). This new SEASON is full of expectation.

NATURAL SEASONS CHANGE WITH TEMPERATURE CHANGES

I was raised in Northern Alaska where winters are cold, long and dark. Most of my life, I watched the Northern Lights dance in the crisp arctic sky. Then, we moved to the South Pacific island of Guam where summer never ends. The only way we could tell the changing seasons in the tropics was by the browning of some of the leaves on certain trees and the winds blowing. Regardless of how we have been acclimated in the past, the Lord comes into this new season in a new way. And, this new apostolic hour demands re-defining and re-adjusting our mind-sets.

Temperature variations cause the seasonal changes. Temperature is one of the main ways that birds know when to migrate. Winter is over. The changing TEMPERATURES in the Spirit realm determine that "set TIME is here to favor Zion" (Ps. 102:13). And, if it seems like just the opposite is happening in your life, then you're probably ready for corporate shifting, personal repositioning, and dimensional unpredictability. We can certainly say, as Joshua of old, "We've never been this way before" (Josh. 3:4). The Holy Spirit of God causes the unfathomable Glory of HEAVEN to dislodge and break free into our environment.

Right before migration, birds experience a fascinating activity called "Zugunruhe" (German for migratory RESTLESSNESS). This analogy seems more than clear. Many believers have felt an almost unexplainable restlessness and a sense that "there must be more!" Even indoor cage-raised migratory birds that have no indication of climate or temperature changes experience *Zugunruhe*. When life-long caged birds are released, they *know* how to join the migration.

QUESTION: Do you experience restlessness in the realm of the Spirit? Do you long to fly with those who carry the same spiritual DNA? It is imperative that we locate those with whom we are to migrate.

DIVINE DISCONTENT

RIGHT NOW there is a DIVINE DISCONTENT and restlessness – it is a MAGNETIC pull toward the Lord's intention. It is a pull to be with those who are going in the same direction that we are going.

Reformational leaders must move past the frigidity of static doctrines. It's almost impossible to birth young leaders in times of winter when nothing grows. Reformers must minister from the heart of a lion. It is time to press the envelope of what is now thought and practiced.

There's a change in the season of government. In each *kairos* SEASON, the Lord "downloads" to His selected leaders His concise intentions that will launch the global Church into revelatory advance. The Lord speaks a Preceding Word that reveals Himself within the relevancy of this oncoming SEASON! This newly modulated and upgraded message of apostolic leadership fine-tunes us into this new dimension.

 We're –heading toward God's intention for His Church rather than expecting Him to do it our way.

We need to be ready for recognizing the "SEASONAL" changes. The Scriptures are being illuminated. There is an increased shedding of light upon what we thought we understood in the past. The Day Star is arising in our heart (Jn. 5:39-40; 2 Pet. 1:19) with focused enlightenment.

Have you noticed that for many, what is happening now in the Western Church is becoming stale and stagnate? That's because THE OLD MUST GO! NOW! Old mentalities, cultural preferences, outdated theologies, religious rituals... all of that must be left behind. It's time to move from emotional shouting without content to accurate Biblical theology. Unfortunately, most believers do not understand that the time for this new era is already here – NOW. We must reposition ourselves for the new day! We have entered the final Feast of Tabernacles and the last trumpet.

We begin to see some of the "Old Guard" type leadership being replaced by a passionate new breed who focuses on the King and the advancing Kingdom. New comprehensions surge through apostolic and prophetic voices. The revolution of Present Truth (2 Pet. 1:2) enlivens us once again. New technologies enable us to present the Gospel in creatively fresh ways. Each believer is being equipped to accomplish more than ever before.

Our future success depends upon knowing our "appointed seasons" and MOVING rightly at those times.

That means we must get into position to MIGRATE into unknown dimensional passages. This hour is defined as an Apostolic reconfiguration – it is a globalization of the KINGDOM. Because of these changes, we must let go of many of the past understandings. We migrate to effective articulation of a new vocabulary, to understanding PATTERNS and to discovering an awareness of increased dimensions of Glory. Leaders must observe the changing of this time and become ACUTELY AWARE of where we are now... and where we are going. Only then can we EXTEND DILIGENCE to maximize our influence.

First, the LEADERS of the apostolic Church must come into their rightful place. Then, they can lead the Church into a migration of this next dimension of dominion rule and reign.

MIGRATING TO THE NEW ORDER

Migration allows for vast re-colonization and expansion of all that has been reformed.

The temple is in us.

The writer of Hebrews talked about this new season, "But only the high priest entered the inner room, and that only once a year...The Holy Spirit was showing by this that the way into the Most Holy Place had not yet been disclosed as long as the first tabernacle was still standing. This is an illustration for the PRESENT TIME, indicating that the gifts and sacrifices being offered were not able to clear the conscience of the worshiper. They (gifts and sacrifices) are only a matter of food and drink and various ceremonial washings. (They are) EXTERNAL REGULATIONS APPLYING UNTIL THE TIME (KAIROS) OF THE NEW ORDER" (Heb. 9:7-10).

The writer of Hebrews was obviously not referring to the physical temple in Jerusalem because it was still standing. The "NOW" began 1920 years ago or so... this principle was initiated then but never fully accessed. The reality of the New Order appears once again in greater clarity.

Sacrifices are symbolic *until* reformation of the NEW ORDER (season) comes to us. When the existing systems no longer meet demand, when the external regulations cease, the NEW ORDER arrives. And guess what? That time is NOW. Finally, the external regulations are over.

 We must come into the "New Order" of apostolic government – and that doesn't just mean to change the name of our church and the title on our name badge at conventions.

The one true Body (the spiritual house of living stones) that assembles in diverse gatherings now must move in her understanding. The cloud of His presence is moving! THE CHURCH IS SHIFTING! It's a time of acceleration and divine alignment and re-FORM-ation! Right now, the Lord is releasing new plans of action for His leaders. God has given them His most important task. Their assignment is to facilitate this season of transition that will ultimately reveal the Lord's Bride coming face to face.

This transition is a re-ordering of people in their calling.

There is no ONE right way (assembly line) for each church to migrate. Just like no creation of God looks like another, each snow flake differs, and each voice print is unique. Likewise, each expression of a local church will be original for their need. Each Flock must be led individually by the quickening Holy Spirit – but we will all arrive at the same destination. And, there are some standard basic principles necessary to understand.

Imagine! You and I have been selected to live at the brink of time – the *kairos* moment of the new order. This is NOT more of the same; it is NOT an expansion or changing of what has gone before us. This is the NEW DAY of re-FORM-ation and new beginnings.

How can we describe this new order? It is the reformation, restoration and renewal of the Church. What's next? Entering fully into the Kingdom while we live on this earth. Kingdom living is now. Jesus is ruling and reigning now. If we want to live in the Kingdom, we must live in it NOW.

If you desire a greater impact of apostolic authority, you must migrate in the right season to the correct LOCATION! That doesn't mean a new geographical address – it means you acquire a new NOW mind-set! Are you ready for MEASURABLE MOVEMENT? Then we must take a moment and understand more about migration.

The Kingdom of Jesus is wherever He can fully rule without resistance.

Ask yourself, "Where are we going?" To defeat? Are we waiting "to fly away" or suddenly "escape" from a dreadful nuclear war? Or are we discovering how to FLY INTO and along with a migration of like-minded believers who will bring the Kingdom onto this earth? Fly out of the wilderness and into the Promise? From man pleasers to God pleasers. From outdated hierarchical models to the restoration of apostolic team government. From faith to Faith. From victory to Victory. From glory to

Glory. The goal is to migrate to where believers represent and re-PRESENT Christ to this world.

 Our success in finding true *authority* lies in the degree of migration and transformation we experience right now!

"We will never be qualified to rule nations until we have first brought into subjection the "nations" that reside within us." Wade Taylor

It's time to move out from just the "church with walls" and into reforming and transforming the nations. It's not changing our jobs, our friends, our income, or our spouse. It's a change in our perception! That's what's needed. From teaching to training. From information to activation. From encouraging to equipping. From being a child of God to being a grown-up heir. From waiting for the "ol' rocking chair in the sky" to coming into the "Time for the saints to possess the Kingdom" (Dan. 7:22).

 When the seasons change, birds migrate. After they change locations, their feathers get ragged and fall out. This is called "molting." If birds didn't molt, they would not be able to fly well. Each bird species has their own molting sequence. Molting occurs symmetrically (on each side equally). This system of molting allows the bird to retain balanced flight. Sometimes, when the new feathers appear, they are a completely different and brighter colors.

We believers need to SHED the old so that our flight can be enhanced with new feathers. Are you ready?

The migration of our attitudes determines how high and far we fly.

The Intended Destination

God's Authority is missing because

we haven't known where to go

"You see, He is making the birds our school-masters and teachers... In other words, we have as many... preachers as there are little birds in the air." (Martin Luther 1521, Commentary on Sermon on the Mount)

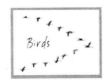

Jeremiah describes a startling relationship between birds and leadership. He specifically refers to the migration of storks. Storks rarely fly; they prefer to glide through the air. The flapping of their wings takes so much stored energy that they would never be able to reach Africa without gliding. Just like with glider planes, warm air currents (thermals) provide the lift storks need to glide over 1,800 miles of water in 80 hours.

Gliding (soaring in the Spirit) causes us to go farther, conserve energy, rest from work, move quickly in rest, and travel greater distances.

The Bible is a book about the phenomenon of migration. It greatly affects our lives and is, in fact, a global issue. People migrate for basic survival, for hope in a better future, or to search for dignity in a new place.

'The wind blows (breathes) where it wills; and though you hear its sound, yet you neither know where it comes from nor where it is going. So it is with everyone who is born of the Spirit' (Jn. 3:8, AMP).

BIRDS TEACH US

When geese and storks are born, they bond with the first thing they see. Scientists call this phenomenon "IMAGING!" Imagine... even birds try to develop into the IMAGE of that to which they are bonded. When the first human was created, Adam looked right into the Lord's eyes. God was the *first thing seen*! And God saw His reflection in the eyes of Adam!

In much the same way, we find deep within the recesses of our mind the desire to IMAGE our creator! Humanity longs to be like God - to be in HIs image and likeness.

Entering into God's INTENTIONAL direction means leaders no longer frantically flap their wings until they get somewhere – but we soar to migrate into God's image and INTENTION. Soaring birds like the stork wait for the winds to be blowing in the direction that the birds need to go. They always wait FOR THE RIGHT WIND. They don't migrate until favorable weather conditions exist. Hello! The application to us is clear here. Birds know how to connect into the trade winds and fly immense distances.

The Guinness book of records says that birds choose to fly higher because it enables them to reach their destinations more efficiently. Radar studies show us that birds frequently change altitudes to find the best wind conditions. If the wind opposes their direction, the birds fly low, near the trees that slow the wind. If there are strong headwinds, the birds will need more strength to travel the same distance.

Birds wait to utilize strong tailwinds going the right direction in order to fly as high and as fast as possible. Some broad-winged birds such as Jeremiah mentioned, rely on thermal columns of rising hot air to soar.

 The *kairos* time has come to fly higher as we migrate beyond our previously predetermined ideas about achieving and leading. Those who possess the ability to share key information with key people at these strategic *kairos* moments will make significant impact upon the world. Let's catch the wind of the Spirit and soar to new spiritual frontiers.

Yes, the Lord would have us migrating toward our destination in this *kairos* moment. And the Lord would have us affect cities and release His intention trans-regionally, on a national and global scale. We can accomplish this best by soaring and not flapping!

MANY ANIMALS MIGRATE

Caribou, wildebeests, bison, African elephant, American Buffalo, Gnu reindeer, and zebra.

Deep sea ocean fish and shark migrate daily. Dolphins migrate far distances. Each species of whale has its own migration routes. Stingray, manatee, and crabs.

Some insects and butterflies. Earthworms. Frogs and snakes. Birds and bats.

Lobsters migrate into warmer waters. Hundreds move together in single file, clasping pincers to form a living chain of lobsters walking together.

Bible MIGRATION

The Spirit of God hovered and MOVED across the earth at creation (Gen. 1).

Migration is purposeful movement!

Cain killed his brother, Able (Gen. 4:8-16) and as a punishment, God makes Cain a wanderer on earth.

Noah and his family migrated in the ark to a new location where God repeated the mandate, "Be fruitful and multiply, and fill the earth." The only way to fill the earth is to migrate to new territories. Genesis 10 gives the account of the migration of Noah's sons, "From these the nations spread abroad on earth after the flood."

Out from the Tower of Babel, new languages spread (Gen. 11:9).

Abraham was "called out" of Ur, out of Babylon (Gen. 12:1, Heb. 11:8) and migrated to Mamre in Hebron (Gen. 13).

Hagar and Ishmael migrated into the Middle East.

Israel was "called out" of Egypt and its world of religion.

Joseph was sold into Egyptian slavery. His family migrated there for help during the famine.

Jacob traveled to find a wife and then returned (Gen. 25-37).

Moses migrated to Egypt and then later wandered for forty years.

JOSHUA and CALEB had to wander THROUGH WILDERNESS TOO – because of the unbelief of everyone else.

Jews were taken captive into Babylon (Kings, Chron., Jer., etc.).

Ruth and Naomi left the Moabite lands and came to Jerusalem.

Judah was "called out" of Babylon to restore the Temple (1 Cor. 10:6,11).

The New Testament begins with the migration of Joseph and Mary.

Magi left Persia and traveled by the direction of a star (Mat. 2:1).

Throughout His life, Jesus moved from place to place and called the disciples to "follow Him."

 Evangelist Arthur Blesset says that conservatively speaking, Jesus walked 21,525 miles in His lifetime. The distance around the world at the equator is 24,901 miles – so Jesus nearly walked the distance around the world! Mary the Mother of Jesus walked at least 12,187 miles by the time she was fifty.

Jesus SENT FORTH (*apostello*, out on a mission) the twelve (Mat. 10:5). Jesus was *sent* from the Father (Mat. 10:40). Jesus *sent* disciples

(15:24, 21:1, Mk. 9:37). Gabriel was *sent* (Lk. 1:26). Jesus was *sent* to heal (Lk. 4:18); He was *sent* to preach the Kingdom of God and heal the sick (Lk. 9:2); God *sent* His Son (Jn. 3:17); John the Baptist was *sent* before Jesus (Jn. 3:28); Jesus *sends* us to reap where we have not labored (Jn. 4:38). We see migration in other ways as well, such as being "called out."

- The Jewish believers were scattered (*Diaspora*) after Pentecost.
- Believers are called to move from where they were and come INTO Christ.
- Believers are "called out" of darkness and into the light (1 Pet. 2:9).
- We are called away from the world, the flesh, and the pride of life (1 Jn. 2:16).
- We are called into hope (Eph. 4:4).
- We are called to the heavenly Kingdom being aliens to this world (1 Pet. 2:11-12).
- We are called into a holy calling (2 Tim. 1:9).
- We are called by a heavenly calling (Heb. 3:1).
- We are called to eternal Glory (1 Pet. 5:10).
- We are called to His Kingdom (1 Thes. 2:12).

Like a diamond, the principle of migration releases spectacular truths that join together and shine forth with composite brilliance of what apostolic authority is all about. We'll be intertwining this idea of migration with our learning about how to discern the times of New Governmental Order.

ABRAHAM AND SHECHEM

Genesis 12:6-7 tells how Abram traveled through (*evar*, CROSSED OVER, migrated) the land as far as the site of the great tree of Moreh at Shechem. That name of *shékém* —(shoulder) appears to have come from the configuration of the hills.

Shechem means two shoulders - see photo. (This is where it all started in the 1st place. Shechem means INHERITANCE–SHOULDER, or GOVERNMENTAL AUTHORITY).

From this definition, we see the typology that Shechem pictures how the government of the church rests on the shoulder's of God's leaders.

The Lord told Abram, "To your offspring (that's us) I WILL GIVE THIS LAND." Abram built an altar there to the LORD, who had appeared to him.

> 1. We must rise beyond natural inheritance. God gives us a blessing of destiny and then calls us to migrate to His inheritance.

> 2. Kingdom GOVERNMENT is our inheritance. SHECHEM is the inheritance of Abraham's offspring – it's about partnering with God in Governmental authority.

Migration brings an explosive understanding of government and divine order.

We all know that not everything that happens in church has been good. In fact thousands are leaving the present structure because of faulty government. Many leaders have misused their authority and caused much pain and disappointment.

In parallel, we notice that DINAH was raped in Shechem (Gen. 34:1-7). This unfortunate story is similar to how many church members have felt abused and ravaged by their church leaders. Why is it that often the ones most trusted have been the ones to cause greatest abuse.

But... just because we have been hurt doesn't mean we should abandon Shechem. We need to discover what the Lord God intended when He gave this LAND to Abram and his children.

Joshua's wanted his bones buried in Shechem (Jos. 24:32). Likewise, we must return to Shechem and take vengeance against injustice. WE CAN'T THROW AWAY GOVERNMENT – WE MUST RETURN and FIX IT.

Shechem is situated between Mount Gerizim and Mount Ebal, about 65 miles north of Jerusalem. This is the location of Jacob's Well. It is also were Jesus met the Samaritan woman (Jn. 4). The Jews would walk an extra three days to not cross the land of hated Samaria (Shechem). Correct governmental (Samaria, Shechem) concepts have been misunderstood and lost to most of us. Just as the woman from Samaria longed for living water, we long for the correct discovery of how to function governmentally.

In like manner, many believers today stay far away from anything that might have to do with a local church. But, Jesus said that He must "by need go to Samaria." And we must return to find those who still hurt.

But, those who question the status quo are viewed as an illegitimate women. At last, Jesus comes again as our 7th man (she had five husbands and the one she was with was not her husband). He appears sitting on the ancient well of Jacob in Shechem – offering us LIFE.

For those who have been left in the ditch of disappointment, the Good Samaritan comes along to pour out the oil and wine.

Hebrews "crossed over" from death to LIFE.

 Going back to our original thought about Shechem, it was here in that Abram was first called a Hebrew (Gen. 14:13). Notice that this is the first time this word HEBREW (*evar*) is used to designate a people. Amazingly, EVAR means "to CROSS OVER, to PENETRATE INTO, to IMPREGNATE."

> Migration is the central and most powerful metaphor in the Old Testament.

The chosen of God (Hebrew) are those WHO HAVE CROSSED OVER (migrated) from the OTHER SIDE.

 Migration moves the pioneering church beyond the traditional mentalities into the dimensions of apostolic reformation and corporate destiny where God meets us with renewed authority.

Your talent and ability is released when you are properly mentoring.

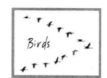 Birds *choose* their migratory routes. Many birds are unable to fly across vast bodies of water, deserts, or mountains, so they fly around them.

Birds always return home after migrating. It's always a two way trip. After giving birth to their young, they return back to where they came from. People need to learn from the homing instinct of this avian behavior and come back to gather those who need to go forward with them the next time. We are not elite because we have progressed further. We return home because we need to mentor and guide others to greater heights and depths of truth.

Connecting to your assignment raises the capacity of your anointing and authority.

MOSES

Moses rescued the Israelites from Egypt and they CROSSED OVER to the OTHER SIDE of the Red Sea as IDENTIFIABLE TRIBES following LEADERS having identifiable ensign flags. They followed the cloud of God (Num. 9:17-23) to new locations. There was no choice or opinion. The only way to survive in the desert was to migrate. Move or die.

God requires US to MOVE into His SEASON of fruitfulness.

Moses ushered the Israelites to the outskirts of the Promised Land. They could see the land. Moses sent spies in to Canaan (Num. 13:17-24). He told them to check out the land and the soil, and to bring back the fruit of the land, because it was "The SEASON for the first ripe grapes."

Ancient Israelites demonstrates a "type of the church" progressing toward the Promised Land and destiny. Changed from bondage to freedom. From limitation – to identity and conquering

Being FAT in the RIGHT SEASON!

God's Authority is missing because

We need to KNOW THE SEASON!

Did you know that hungry birds DON'T MIGRATE. Instead, they MOVE TO A NEARBY SOURCE of food. Many birds feed together gaining strength for the long trip ahead.

A bird needs a reserve of fat within its body to be able to travel the long distances. Fat deposits store the energy necessary for the bird to survive migration. Storms require even more energy to endure. Smaller birds may even have to double their body weight before migrating to a new location. Many feeble birds die along the journey, unable to overcome hardships.

Birds can't fly to a new location when they are hungry.

We're talking being spiritually ready (fat) to travel! It's all about how there is a necessity for the present church to mature in order to be able to migrate into this NEW ORDER (SEASON) of leadership. We need to fatten up and get strong in order to survive this journey to the New Order. The question is, how do we break out of past oppression and wrong teaching in order to arise and influence the Kingdom?

Three times a year, Israel was commanded to keep the FEASTS! They always knew the SEASON.

Hebrews 9:10, "They are only external regulations applying until the time of the new order." The Message Bible translates this verse, "Under this system, the gifts and sacrifices can't really get to the heart of the matter, can't assuage the conscience of the people, but are limited to matters of ritual and behavior. IT'S ESSENTIALLY A TEMPORARY ARRANGEMENT UNTIL A COMPLETE OVERHAUL COULD BE MADE."

It is the TIME OF THE NEW ORDER. The word "order" is *diorthosis* which means, "to reform, to straighten thoroughly, to rectify." The "TIME of the New Order" literally means a time to bring forth a restoration and reformation of Christ (Greek word meaning Messiah).

Jesus introduced this New Order as He died and resurrected. At that moment, He gave the world everything that we needed to bring it forward. Much of these truths were lost in the Dark ages and Middle Ages. A sequence of covenantal restorations has continued up to our lifetime. Now, we stand at the fullness of time at the dawn of a new day, chosen to be used in this apostolic order. This is an order of wisdom, knowledge, and stability (Is. 33:6). It ushers promise of the revelation that we are ALREADY FULLY ARRAYED WITH ALL THAT we NEED because Christ is IN us. That's the re-FORM-ation of Christ.

Our assignment is not to find fault or criticize what has gone on before. We only need to understand it, so that we can move forward. We can appreciate the value of each passing renewal that brought us here.

WHEN?

"Look at the birds of the air."
(Jesus at the Sermon on the Mount, Mat. 6:26)

WHEN DO BIRDS MIGRATE??? They look for the best conditions, right temperatures, and strongest winds.

The church is moving. We know that. Things just aren't the same anymore. We didn't expect it to look like this. We forgot that the Jewish day begins at night – and it's dark out! We've entered the new day expecting it to be much different than it is. Like the ten virgins we have been awakened at the midnight hour not quite ready for morning. At the darkest hour, the watchman cries, "Wake up!"

WHAT TIME IS IT???? It's NOW. The winds are blowing and giving us lift. We've come to the acceptable fullness of time. Psalms 90:12 says, "So teach us to number our days that we might have a heart of wisdom." Did you see that? The heart of wisdom is in knowing the TIME when we live.

This isn't some weird doctrine... just a fact. The time we live in right now is the *kairos* time of God. Each of us is hand selected to move through this change and into the fullness of all that has been waiting.

Remember... it is NOW. Too many are stuck in a time warp and still preaching, shouting, and spitting like in the 50's. Listen... if you stay standing on first base you'll never run to home! It's time to RUN – to Migrate to the next stage. Remember, time is an illusion. The past is not precious – the NOW IS PRECIOUS. The past is gone. Our concern must become for the NOW. God only SHOWS UP IN the NOW.

Leadership is being revamped. All that we have learned so far (the "temporary arrangement") is being exchanged for a higher and more effective result. NOW.

Ask yourself, "Am I willing to discern this new hour and learn how to walk within the new levels of delegated authority that will release the power of God?" The Scriptures foretell this new order.

GOD'S PROGRESSIVE KINGDOM OPERATES ONLY BY AUTHORITY

WHAT SEASON IS THIS?

A twelve year old boy can earnestly pray and make declarations for his beard to grow long... but it won't happen until it is TIME. He may become discouraged because nothing has happened. Perhaps this young boy hasn't fully grasped that for the time being... he is in a different SEASON. What season are you living?

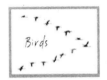 Birds migrate SEASONALLY. Many migrating bird species fly to the north and find nesting places in summer, while other birds remain stationary. Learning what causes birds to know which SEASON to travel is a fascinating study.

We are in a new Renaissance SEASON concerning leadership development. We know that traditional methodologies aren't working well any more. We must discern the correct SEASON we live in now and discover how to release authority in order to facilitate the advancement of the Kingdom.

Seasonal weather patterns determine the migration of birds. Our text verse in Jeremiah 8:7 says, "EVEN THE STORK IN THE SKY KNOWS HER APPOINTED SEASONS." And right now, we are alive and live in a NEW SEASON for the church. It's a *kairos* time of continuous learning and readjusting our mind-sets. There's a change in the season of government.

* The Kingdom of Jesus (Who has all authority in heaven and earth) consists of the Kingdom within each individual believer, civil governments, and the church.
* In order to experience the Kingdom, Christians must invade all three areas and bring them under His Lordship.

SOME DON'T WANT TO FLY ALONG. Many prefer their comfortable routine to anything new. Any huge change done too abruptly will cause damage and potentially divide a church. Convincing and leading people into change takes time. Change takes time. For the hesitant, great leaders design various times of inspiration and motivation within the transition of change.

Beloved Loved One of the Lord, the TIME has COME. This is the HOUR! All of previous history has occurred to get us to this SEASON. The glorious Church is a product of progressive MIGRATION toward this ultimate *kairos* SEASON of the Lord.

S.E.A.S.O.N. – an apostolic acronym

S - Shift in ministry capacity and levels of authority and anointing

E - Earnest integrity and morality re-established.

A - Acceleration of an apostolic company aligns and arises into greater authority.

S - Strategic victory.

O - Observable demonstration of God's Power and authority.

N - New national and Global view of the Kingdom.

A CHANGE OF SEASONS

A NEW SEASON and time for the saints to possess the Kingdom (Dan. 7:22).

A NEW SEASON on earth as it is in heaven (Mat. 6:10).

A NEW SEASON OF FOCUS - From strictly the local setting to the global Kingdom of God.

A NEW SEASON OF LEADERSHIP - from man pleasers to God pleasers.

A NEW SEASON OF STRUCTURE - from outdated hierarchical models to the restoration of apostolic team government.

A NEW SEASON OF BELIEF - from faith to the FAITH OF GOD (Rom. 1:17).

A NEW SEASON OF CHURCH MEMBERSHIP - from immaturity to victorious believers.

When the season changes, we must align to that season.

Trumpets sound the time of migration – into vast re-colonization, establishment, and expansion of re-form-ation.

Great leaders design within the seasonal transitions, various traditional times to help accommodate the preferences of those who are hesitant to change.

IT IS THE SEASON OF APOSTOLIC AUTHORITY

"To punish me for my contempt for authority, fate made me an authority myself." Albert Einstein

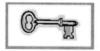

One of the major obstacles to growth into this new SEASON, is our current idea of "spiritual authority." For the most part, we've misunderstood and misapplied it.

Understanding authority did not come naturally to me. That's for sure! As a teenager, I remember thinking how unbearable rigid authority figures were. But in reality, I was intimidated by authority and usually rebelled against those who seemed to have authority – so that they couldn't control me. Most of us have experienced this! And, it is why it is difficult to grasp Biblical authority.

Many people distrust authority. There are several possible reasons that could create distaste for authority. Obviously, we all know of many accounts of excessively abusive leadership. Lots of preachers claim scriptural "authority." They simply appoint themselves into positions OVER others and expect certain responses. They expect and demand that members obey them. Usually, that's how they were taught.

Many believers are convinced that the leaders (who represent authority) haven't given them what they deserve. Sometimes that may be true. Many have been hurt or disappointed by someone in authority. It's not too difficult to see misuse of authority. It's impossible to overlook how many believers have left the safety of their local assemblies.

We must find answers! Today, the Lord calls us to stretch the tent pegs of our understanding. We must press beyond the habit of filtering ongoing Truth by our previously formed world view (our own culture, past experiences, and theologies that formed how we respond to the world around us). As we search together for greater Truth that supersedes our own present thought, let's remember that our conclusions determine how we view God and how we live our lives.

There's a difference between God's authority and operating in authoritarian-ism.

The church desperately needs to discover the truths about effective leadership. So far, we've copied far too many models that have failed. The present day church should function out of an apostolic GRACE (1 Cor. 3:10-11) that provides accurate patterns of spiritual authority. We must endeavor to discover what God's "PRESENT TRUTH" church should look like. Then, we must also begin to realign ourselves within this process of Apostolic/Prophetic restoration and reformation.

Apostolic government must come into order. When we talk about the *apostle* and the *apostolic* in this book we are referring to the leaders in this NEW SEASON who are shifting into an apostolic Leadership style.

The time has come for us to MIGRATE. Major cultural and theological changes must occur as the Church shifts into the emancipation of God's liberty. Massive changes face us as the Church redefines herself and becomes the accurate structure that images the intentions of our Great Designer. We must take heed how we build upon the foundation of

The key to success in ministry is to learn how to rightly implement Biblical authority.

Christ (1 Cor. 3:10-11). Old paradigms, archaic modalities, meaningless tradition, and empty religious ritual will be dismantled. The church no longer benefits from a rigid pyramid of hierarchy... but rather, it must become correctly re-structured into a loving community that respects individual dignity and distinctiveness.

 "The word *hierarchy* in Greek (*εραρχία*) is derived from the word *hieros* which means 'sacred', and *arkho* which means to 'rule.' It is an organizational system of ranking things or people, where each element of the system (except for the top element) is a subordinate to a single other element." (Wikipedia) We commonly call this a "pecking order." Improper leadership causes lack of direction, chaos, anarchy, and confusion.

As we leave hierarchy behind, we find that the Church will no longer benefit from controlling leadership – and must come into a place of building and redirecting God's Kingdom. Modern apostles discover His ways to live out honest leadership, relationship, and stewardship!

The Lord gives us proportionate responsibilities according to our reliability and talents. We reach out and influence our sphere.

"If your actions inspire others to dream more, learn more, do more, and become more, then you are a leader!" John Quincy Adams

INTENTION - Ruling in Dominion

"In that day that God created man, He made him in the likeness of God. He created THEM male and female, and BLESSED them and called them "mankind" in the day they were created" (Gen. 5:1-2).

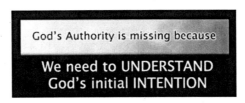

God invested His authority in humans in order to build His Kingdom.

The Edenic garden wasn't an idyllic primrose park where the first humans just skipped around with flower garlands in their hair while dancing around a maypole. God commanded THEM to RULE.

Dominion started with one couple.

> Having the authority to rule is a matter of apprehending what was already theirs (and ours!) Gen. 1:26

This garden principle of dominion rule was given to THEM, (Adam being both male and female).[1] It was God's intention for THEM to share authority and tasks by successfully engaging in the five commands from God to tend the earth (be fruitful, multiply, fill the earth, subdue, and have dominion).

Having authority is not a singular activity.

- The Lord God gave them a decisive principle of Rulership which was a revelation of governmental *authority*. The RULERSHIP was given to both of "THEM."
- It was God's intention for THEM to rule in authority by tending and guarding the garden. Notice that there was initially given a PLURALITY of leadership (them).
- Their mandate of RULERSHIP (*radah*) was all inclusive (Gen. 1:26-31) and totally apostolic in principle.

"Then God BLESSED THEM, and God said to them, 'Be fruitful and multiply; fill the earth and subdue it; have dominion over the fish of the sea, over the birds of the air, and over every living thing that moves on the earth'" (Gen. 1:28, NKJV).

Notice here that the dominion mandate was/is a BLESSING of the Lord that was wrapped in a command about how to gain that blessing, "Be fruitful, multiply, fill the earth, subdue, and take dominion."

---

1. THEIR NAME WAS ADAM! (The first woman was not named differently until after the fall.) See my book "From Enmity to Equality" for details.

This assignment to rule over ALL -- still remains.

This command to be a blessing is a non-negotiable issue. We must begin to maturely use our apostolic authority within the parameters of God's great design.

The Message Bible puts it this way: "Prosper, fill the earth, and take charge!" We are to have dominion over:

- OVER the fish of the sea—the depth downward and penetration of dominion
- OVER the fowl of the air—the height and extent of our dominion
- OVER cattle—the animals and natural world of dominion
- OVER all the earth—the expanse and breadth of dominion
- OVER every creeping thing – the microscopic extent of dominion
- OVER every living thing that moves — the completeness of dominion

AS you know, Adam lost dominion. But, Jesus came to seek and to save what was lost (Lk. 19:10). He now awaits our apprehension of all things lost (which is the restitution of His Kingdom, Acts 3:21). Jesus is held in the heavenlies *until* the restoration of "all things." He remains there until dominion is regained!

The Second Adam regained (ransomed) what was lost in the Fall. Galatians explains that before faith came, we were kept under guard by the Law (2:23). Jesus fulfilled the Law, defeated Satan, and gave us the KEYS to regain the GARDEN OF GOD. He redeemed and restored humanity's full authority upon planet earth.

 Jesus came to this earth AS A HUMAN in order to return our full AUTHORITY over the devil and over this world.

Ruling in the Edenic template of dominion, power, and AUTHORITY defines the <u>original</u> <u>intention</u> of God.

You ought to be in holy conduct and godliness, looking for and hastening the coming of the day of God... (2 Pet. 3:11).

Believers are supposed to be hastening the coming of "that day" and restoration (*apokatastasis*, which comes from another word meaning "to restore back to the original and better"). This is why the Church must migrate – to arrive at completion, maturity, and dominion. We must keep moving toward this destiny.

 The word "dominion" in the Old Testament is the New Testament counterpart for "authority." Notice that this is the first blessing and first command given!

Dominion Rule is GOVERNMENT!

TO TEND & GUARD:

Adams' (pl) revelation of God's WORD qualified him (them) to function in the *authority* necessary to TEND and GUARD the garden (Gen. 2:16). (The principle of "tending and guarding" will be one of the themes of this book.) As God's chosen representative(s), we are given authority as a SEED TRUTH. This SEED is calling us to GROW, break through, and take us to the next place. But we must tend and guard it.

> This five-fold garden commission is our assignment of AUTHORITY.

Please note the theme throughout this book of "tending and guarding." We TEND and GUARD by operating in our five-fold mantle. To "TEND" is the Hebrew word *awbad* and it means to "dress, work, bring to pass, or husbandman (farm)." It also means "to till, to serve, or to execute." This term is particularly relevant to the purposes of this book. Proper leadership "tends and guards."

Amazingly, this word "*awbad*" is translated five times in the Old Testament as WORSHIP! Did you get that? TENDING our lives is worship! The apostolic leader must always remember that in order for Adam to tend the garden, he had to work worshipfully. Taking care of our responsibilities is worship – "presenting your body as a living sacrifice, which is spiritual worship" (Rom. 12:1, NIV).

Taking care (tending and guarding) of our garden is a form of worship.

The word "GUARD" is *shawmar,* which means "to guard, hedge about, protect, to watch, to retain or care for" (see Gen. 18:19 – keeping covenant, 2 Kg. 2:14, Job 2:6, Ps. 121:4). This principle applies to us today as we still must tend and guard the garden of our heart as well as the garden of the world. Leaders are supposed to watchfully protect what is placed under their care – and that can be ourselves, other people who are assigned to us, and our sphere of geographic regions.

Even the name "Adam" meant "ruddy GROUND" (from where he was formed). Adam was given charge over the garden (the sphere of authority). The job was to TEND and GUARD. Because they did not do that, they no longer had any legitimate authority.

When Adam fell, God didn't get weaker!

The consequence of the fall was to lose total access to the Garden of God and a cherubim kept them from returning. The consequence was that man had to "till the GROUND from which he was taken" (Gen. 3:23).

* The emphasis shifted – an internal working had to be accomplished within Adam, himself – tilling our carnal nature, soul, and clearing the ground of thorns and thistles.

- We give the enemy NO GROUND. We tend our garden to restore ourselves to that image of Christ.

LEADERS GUARD. Just as Jesus told the Father, "Those that you gave me, I guarded and not one of them perished" (Jn. 17:12). We guard over those we are given.

"Keep watch over yourselves and all the flock of which the Holy Spirit has made you overseer. Be shepherds of the church of God... BE ON YOUR GUARD! Remember that for three years I never stopped warning you night and day with tears" (Acts 20:28-31, NIV).

THE AUTHORITY OF HUMANITY

If we violate our assigned domain, then we totally forfeit our sphere of authority.

Believers have an obligation to RULE in authority. It is the dominion mandate. Adam's assignment was to protect and guard that which the Lord had given. That assignment has never changed. Now that we have partaken of the tree of Life, we must "tend and guard" our garden.

> No force is stronger than the authority that Jesus gives His believers.

Authority is given by God -- and is ALWAYS given to individuals... not to orgainizations, denominations, or institutions.

- God's plan to extend His RULE was given by words.
- The function of NAMING the animals allowed Adam (pl.) to use words to give them identity, meaning, and purpose for existence. Their name defined their behavior.
- This creative naming becomes a significant role of the apostolic leader. Our words release Godly authority into those who receive.

"For every sort of beast and bird and every living thing on earth and in the sea has been controlled by man and is under his AUTHORITY"
(Jms. 3:7, BBE).

This is the age old problem with authority! The Serpent confronted the woman asking, "Has God indeed said?" The first woman listened to the voice that offered her something that would cause her to be "like God." BUT... she was already "LIKE GOD." She didn't realize what was hers.

Believing the lie against the authority of God in your life is living in fallen existence.

- The first couple didn't understand their own authority.
- The prophet Miriam and Aaron had a big problem acknowledging God's authority in Moses "because of the Ethiopian woman whom he had married" (Numb. 12:1).
- Samson lost his *authority* when Delilah cut his hair.

Humanity was created morally innocent. Yet, they had the free choice. Adam, by an intentional disobedient act of his will, forfeited humanity's

authority to the devil. It was all about authority at the beginning! Satan became the God of this world. Adam (pl) had the authority to make decisions and the right of free will; and even the choice to make wrong decisions! By making the wrong choice, Adam forfeited authority.

The first couple had the God-given authority to make that wrong choice.

It's the age old message: Adam lost the stewardship AUTHORITY of this earth and Jesus regained this AUTHORITY back for us. The Kingdom has already been given. We have everything we need. All our inheritances are here for us. God's intentions for our dominion never changed!

The passage in Psalm 8:3-8 explains how humankind was created to have dominion even over the "heavens, moon, and stars." The works of God's fingers were all designed for us to enjoy, discover, and rule. The book of Revelation tells us that each one of us was created to help fill the earth with His presence (the image and likeness of God), to tame and master every living thing, and to continually exercise that mastery.

 Dominion was given so that humanity would use their creativity and innovation to develop this cosmos. Our future is the blank canvas which awaits the incredible potential of our discovery of our *authority* in this world.

No force is stronger than the authority that Jesus gives His believers!

Remember carefully the significant inheritance to the OVERCOMER: "AUTHORITY over the nations" (Rev. 2:26). There will be those of you who will say, "This promise will occur after Jesus returns." But... is it possible for us to believe and take it now? Many believers have been able to exercise authority over their nation. The early church was not an infant church. They were able to turn their world upside down (Acts 17:6). Luther influenced Germany. Wesley greatly influenced England.

You have authority over what you overcome (Rev. 2:26).

MANDATE: In order for us to apprehend this re-acquired authority, we need a clear understanding of this first Edenic mandate. The assignment of the first couple was to establish God's Kingdom upon the earth through dominion rule. But, they failed.

Just like this first couple, Apostolic leaders are "sent" with a *mandate* to activate these specific five functions of the Garden commission. All other understandings about authority are directly connected to this dominion command. This ruling authority produces the Kingdom of God.

- A *mandate* is the authoritative command, formal order from a superior court or official to an inferior one; an authorization to give a commission to a representative.
- Our apostolic mandate is to rule with dominion and authority. The consequence of ruling in authority is God's POWER.

This mandate pertains to leadership today. We see this as we overlay Adam's pre-fall five-fold commission blessing over the five-fold leadership ministry. This comparison helps us understand more about the job of the five-fold ministry today:

BE FRUITFUL[1]

The apostle brings forth FRUITFULNESS.

> Apostles carry authority and wisdom to the church. They are empowered with insight concerning the true nature and image of God's initial intentions. (Micah 5:2)

The first assignment from the Lord was apostolic. He said, "BE FRUITFUL." APOSTLES are the first ones in (*proton*) and they produce FRUITFULNESS. This ministry brings into existence the reproduction and replication of God's likeness and image. (The husbandman patiently waits for fruit (Jms. 5:7) – the produce of the Tree of Life).

Apostles are builders who harvest the PRODUCTION of the FRUIT. They reproduce the mind-set of FRUITFULNESS and ABUNDANCE. The apostolic believer rejoices in ABUNDANT LIFE (Jn. 10:10).

The ROD: The rod illustrates a *type* of FRUITFUL apostolic authority. The ROD of Moses symbolized authority (Ps. 2:9; 89:32; Is. 10:24; Ez. 20:37). God said, "Lift up your rod!" Be confident in who you are. "Cast it down" (Ex. 4:3), don't hold too tightly to that which belongs to the Lord).

* Moses confronted those who represented Pharaoh's authority. They threw down their rods (symbols of authority) and the ROD of Aaron ate them (Ex. 7:12).
* This rod accomplished signs and wonders (Ex. 4:16-17).
* The ROD released the rivers in the wilderness (Ex. 17:5).
* The ROD secured victory (Ex. 17:9).
* His ROD divided the sea (Ex. 14:16). The word "divided" means to burst forth, opening what was shut, the forcefulness of breaking into a walled city. God's authority causes us to break through every problem.

Later, Aaron struck the waters of Egypt with his ROD and they turned to blood (7:15-20). Aaron's ROD (authority) came to life (budded and became FRUITFUL) and brought forth flowers and almonds (Num. 17:3-8). Aaron's ROD OF FRUITFUL APOSTOLIC AUTHORITY was kept in the ark of the covenant.

* The rod provides food (Micah 7:14).

1. This five-fold command to the first couple compared with the five-fold office concept comes from my book "Understanding Headship."

- Jesus rules the nations with a rod of iron (Rev. 19:15).
- Perhaps we can establish a new ministers' creed – "Walk softly and carry a big stick!" (One that buds and flowers!)

Jesus told them (Luke 9:3-6) that they didn't need luggage, or food, or extra clothing. Notice that they were instructed to: "take nothing for their journey, except a mere STAFF (or rod, representing fruitful authority) – no bread, no bag, no money in their belt... (nothing they needed or earned). This may be the reason why certain Bishops of certain "apostolic succession" carry a staff.

Wilderness surrounds the perimeters of the Garden. God's intention is to create EXPANSION and habitation. It requires stewardship to EXPAND and replenish the earth and bring "fruitfulness."

MULTIPLY

The five-fold elders particularly involved with MULTIPLICATION are the Apostolic-PROPHETS. God particularly released into the prophet the ability to increase, multiply, and call into being.

> Apostolic Prophets motivate, direct, and activate the saints into migration and advancement (Joel 2:11).

"Surely blessing I will bless you, and multiplying I will multiply you" (Heb. 6:14, NIV).

The prophet reveals Divine direction into the assemblies that activate and motivate the saints to advance and multiply (Joel 2:11).

FILL THE EARTH

> Apostolic Evangelists release the REALITY of the living God through POWER GIFTS to the unbeliever.

The five-fold elders involved with FILLING THE EARTH are the EVANGELISTS! Apostolic evangelists operate differently than the evangelists of the past. There will be no more knocking on doors with the Roman Road tract. No more notches on a Bible. Character will convince!

When unbelievers encounter those who are fully walking in their inheritance, they will want what we have. Evangelists in this new day have a profound MISSION of manifesting the tangible substance and reality of the Lord and His Kingdom purposes.

Evangelists relase the reality of the living God to "Fill the earth" with believers.

SUBDUE

> Apostolic Pastors nourish and care for the local assemblies.

The five-fold ministry greatly involved with SUBDUING is the apostolic PASTOR. Their main and most difficult job is to stabilize believers until they can conquer and subdue the soul realm and every incorrect and limited mind-set.

The PASTOR nurtures the babes and feeds them until they are able to subdue their own surroundings. Pastors nourish and care for the believer and insist that they learn to overcome.

Subdue is the word *kawash* – which literally means to grab the "life force" (or throat) and cast down. Subduing is the true and only warfare of the church – God mandates that we take charge. (The manchild will subdue the dragon.)

Today's apostolic pastors should have the authority to subjugate all opposition and strategically rule over their assigned territories.

AND HAVE DOMINION

Dominion is a BASIC fundamental truth that every believer needs to learn. The new breed of TEACHER brings the believer into dominion.

Notice that the Scripture doesn't say, "take" dominion – but rather, "have" dominion. This concept of dominion is the overall umbrella that incorporates the rest. The Hebrew for "dominion" is *radah* which means to "subjugate, tread down, dominate, conquer, violate, or bring into subjection." It means to rule with a sphere of authority and reach of influence.

> Apostolic Teachers unveil truth so that others can apply it to their lives.

The Apostolic TEACHER particular instructs the Body how to take DOMINION. Under true dominion we find tangible BLESSINGS.

One of the principle messages of the Apostolic Teacher is about the Biblical principles about "possessing the LAND." Land provides influence and brings stability.

"The saints shall possess the kingdom and the kingdom and DOMINION and greatness of the kingdom... shall be given to the saints of the most High" (Dan. 7:22,27).

The bottom line here is that nobody is supposed to take dominion OVER another person. DOMINION RULE has nothing to do with DOMINATION and control of people. We must use our authority rightly. The massive misuse of authority explains why there's such a resistance and a "don't tell me what to do" attitude in the church these days towards authority figures.

THE COMPARISON:

These five initial charges to humanity (both male and female) are also the five ministry giftings that enable us to fully RULE in the Kingdom.[1]

APOSTLE	PROPHET	EVANGELIST	PASTOR	TEACHER
Fruitfulness	Multiplies	Fills the earth	Subdues	Has Dominion
Productive reproduction	Energizes the seed	Gathers seed	Nurtures & matures the seed	Plants seed
	Motivates			Determines the soil
Abundance	P			
Harvest				
Brings forth in the NOW	Speaks what happens in the future	Gathers the new supply	Establishes and waters the seed	Subjugates and "puts under" wrong mentalities
Accomplishes	Activates	Gathers and presents	Trains and cultivates	Instructs & waters

This five-fold garden commission is our assignment of AUTHORITY.

Five-fold ministers with various capabilities must come together and cooperate as a team to build the Kingdom.

Let's repeat it! God never changed His mind or altered His plan for humans to subdue, conquer, guard, defend, and take dominion authority over the world and the enemy. Nothing can stop the unstoppable.

SUMMARY

God is all about authority. The amazing thing is that when God created humanity, He decided to give them a soul with the ability to CHOOSE. To choose what? That's it: AUTHORITY! God gave them RULE over this creation, which means they had to TEND and GUARD it. Deeply woven within this command is the discovery that our stewardship is an ongoing extension of creation itself. Now, believers can function in the "powers (*dunamis*) of the age to come" (Heb. 6:5).

At our new birth, God gives us the unseen and unfelt gift of authority. This gift grows with realization and use. Authority is the channel through which the POWER of God operates. God operates His Kingdom through authority.

---

1. Some would like to reverse this list! But, the Scriptures say, first (*proton*) the apostle.

God gave both the man and the woman the dominion to RULE OVER earth with authority. Dominion is a active process of what God does within us.

Our response today to having the dominion of AUTHORITY is the determining factor of our future.

Apostolic leaders need to teach believers to become the stewards of God's intention. We need to learn to manage our lifestyle to have greater impact, mobility, and access to future potential. The nature of Christ brings forth the FORCE of truth that resonates within us as we take up the charge upon humanity to RULE in the Kingdom.

> Having true authority is the consequence of the revelation that allows us to apprehend God's Word.

Our lives provide the workshop (with all of our victories, trials, and difficulties) that develops our growth in authority. Ruling over present circumstances propels us into future levels of responsibility. As we grow in authority, God's ruling purposes naturally follow.

 We live in the circumstances we permit. If we're unhappy with these circumstances, we must adjust what we say. Jesus gave us the ability to create what we say according to His Word. It requires action on our part. We decide to rule and have dominion. We decide to walk in greater authority by our choices. We cultivate the Kingdom culture. We determine the course of our world.

Apostolic leaders must cause believers to move forcefully out into the cities as anointed equippers that will take over the worldly kingdoms. The earth is their inheritance and all of creation anxiously longs and groans for the revealing of the grown up SONS of God who will release this authority and dominion (Rom. 8:19-20). Humans are the stewards of the earth that waits for us to repair and liberate it. It's our job!

Differences Between Power & Authority

The chief priests and elders challenged the teaching of Christ in saying, "By what *authority* do You do these things? and who gave You this authority?" (Mat. 21:23-26). Still today, one of the most common misunderstandings in the church is about authority. The misuse of authority is at the core of every issue that causes religious division.

"Sin against power is more easily forgiven than sin against authority, because the latter is a sin against God Himself. God alone is authority in all things; all the authorities of the earth are instituted by God. Authority is a tremendous thing in the universe—nothing overshadows it. It is therefore imperative for us who desire to serve God to know the authority of God" (Watchman Nee, SA, p.10).

The chief priests and elders challenged the teaching of Christ in saying, "By what *authority* do You do these things? and who gave You this authority?" (Mat. 21:23-26). Still today, one of the most common misunderstandings in the church is about authority. The misuse of authority is at the core of every issue that causes religious division.

This question about authority is still the question of the hour. One big reason we continue to have misunderstandings is that the Greek word for "authority" is often mis-translated. There are two words – *dunamis* and *exousia* that have very different meanings; yet many of the most popular Bible versions translate BOTH of these words as POWER.

 The difference between *"dunamis"* and *"exousia"* is that *"dunamis"* signifies power itself TO GET THINGS DONE. *"Exousia"* means we have the legitimate authority, claim. and RIGHT TO USE GOD'S POWER.

DUNAMIS - Power

"Our deepest fear is not that we are inadequate – our deepest fear is that we are powerful beyond measure." Nelson Mandella

The Church seeks for God's POWER. But, we must have the RIGHT to use His power!

Seems like everyone wants the "power" of God - the problem is that first we need to apprehend His "authority." There are three words in Greek that mean "power." The one that has been confused in translations is the word *"dunamis"* from which we get our word for dynamite. *Dunamis* power belongs ONLY to God, (humans don't possess *dunamis* power – but they can use His power within His limits). Dunamis is energetic power, explosive power, or a demonstrative power that can reproduce itself. It is a demonstration of God's force.

Dunamis operates only through God's authority.

Here are a few examples of *dunamis*:

- *Dunamis* universally signifies physical power (energy or force) needed to create, raise the dead, and work miracles, etc.
- "The Gospel is the power (*dunamis*) of God unto salvation, because by it God exerts His power (force, energy) to save" (Rom. 1:16).
- "While on earth, Jesus healed all manner of diseases, for there went virtue (*dunamis*, power), out of him and healed them all" (Lk. 6:19). The POWER was IN Jesus.

With great POWER comes great responsibility." 1st Spiderman movie.

EXOUSIA - Authority

Exousia is the mis-translated word. *Exousia* signifies the authority and liberty to operate and govern in God's power and anointing. The Bible continually talks about authority – but we miss it.

- Jesus is the (*exousia*) authority of God (1 Cor. 1:24).
- The Gospel is the *exousia* of God (Rom. 1:16).

A few years ago, my son was a policeman. He was given the *authority* to stop huge aggressively moving semi-trucks on a freeway. They had to recognize the authority of a young policeman on a motorcycle – and they had to stop and obey him. My son didn't have the "power" (*dunamis*) to stop the semi-truck. He couldn't even stop the smallest of cars by his own strength! But, even though he doesn't have the physical strength (power) to stop traffic – he is given *authority* by law to commandeer traffic. He could literally stop traffic by his *exousia* – that is his right by delegated authority. He does not and can not stop traffic by his POWER.

> True AUTHORITY is DELEGATED POWER. Its strength depends upon the force behind the user.

*Authority is the permission given to do something.
That permission to use authority is given to us by God
– the One in control of that right.*

- The more of His authority we have, the more of God's power is released and revealed through us. We don't need more power; we need God's authority to move in His power.
- AUTHORITY (*exousia*) is our legal right to do something.

Biblical church government clearly establishes a theocratic type of rule, in which God gives leaders the authority to RULE – according to His will.

Jesus expanded the idea of ruling when He said that "ALL POWER in heaven and on earth" was given to Him (Matt. 28:18-20, KJV). This is an example of the wrong translation in the King James Version, and others. The word "power" is "*exousia*" – which really means that ability, privilege, force, capacity, competency, freedom, mastery, magistrate, and delegated influence was given to Him. This verse should read, "All authority in heaven and earth was given to me."

Apostles are given a particular realm of authority.

 Jesus gave that same incredible *"exousia"* to His disciples (Matt. 9:8, Lk. 9:1). That means that authority is for each of us – whether we are church leaders or not, bond or free, male or female, Jew or Greek. Now, we must activate that quality we ALREADY POSSESS!

Sometimes *exousia* and *dunamis* are used together. "For with authority (*exousia*), and power (*dunamis*), He commanded the unclean spirits, and they came out" (Lk. 4:36).

WHAT IS AUTHORITY?

"Freedom is about authority. Freedom is about the willingness of every single human being to cede to lawful authority a great deal of discretion about what you do and how you do it." Rudy Giuliani

Simply speaking, AUTHORITY IS THE RIGHT to INFLUENCE with POWER. It is the right to rule. The *New Standard Dictionary* defines authority as: "The right to command and to enforce obedience." It is the authorization or right to act for another. It is the confidence and assurance to influence with knowledge and experience.

Thayer's Dictionary defines *authority* as 1) power of choice, liberty of doing as one pleases, permission; 2) the ability or strength with which one is endued, possesses, or exercises.

Leading with authority demands that you discover new ways to uniquely motivate.

The word authority is derived from the Latin word *"auctoritas"* – a word often used in Roman law. In Weberian sociology, authority is defined as the right to RELEASE POWER which is recognized as legitimate and justified by both the powerful and the powerless.

> Authority is the WEIGHT (measure) of God's INFLUENCE upon a person's life to function in specific assignments.

You will have the authority that is in proportion to the gifts delegated to you.

* Your authority is also dependent upon who you believe you are in Christ. Your Godly authority will never supersede your concept of who Christ has made you. As you by faith walk further into your assignment, more authority comes.
* No one else can walk in your specific assignment or arena of authority.
* It is easy to flow in your correct assignment.

Government - Other Delegated Authority

All authority belongs to God and He delegates His authority to us (Rom. 13:1).

Our lives are protected by authority. Ultimately all derived authority reverts back to God, who gave it (1 Cor. 15:24-28). Jesus has all authority in Heaven and earth. There are several major realms of government in the universe. There is a Government of and in Heaven, the universe, the realm of angels (Ps. 145:10-13). The Lord delegated some of His authority to each of the following four distinct groups:

- The Social (National, State, and human) government (Rom. 13:1-8).
- Academic, social, governmental, political, creative, etc.
- The family, the Church (1 Cor. 12:28; Heb. 13:7, 17, 24).
- And the individual.[1]

SOCIAL and CIVIL GOVERNMENT OFFICIALS HAVE AUTHORITY

"Obedience to lawful authority is the foundation of manly character."
Robert E. Lee

> Social government is defined as people who are given authority to accomplish certain tasks and functions in society.

The Lord established spheres of civil authority. Romans 13:1-2 clearly explains, "Everyone must submit himself to the governing authorities (*exousia*), for there is no authority (*exousia*) except that which God has established. The authorities (*exousia*) that exist have been established by God..."

- The governor of Judea had authority (Lk. 20:20). Pilot had the "authority" of judicial decision; he could release or bind (Jn. 19:10). Jesus answered, "You have no POWER over me if it were not given to you from above" (Jn. 19:10-11).
- A ruler or magistrate is one who possesses authority (Col. 1:15-16).
- The kings of the Gentiles exercise authority over benefactors (Lk. 22:25).
- The Ethiopian eunuch had great AUTHORITY under (delegated by) Queen Candice and was in charge of all her treasury (Acts 8:27). (Notice that his *authority* was over all her money!)

(Please note that this huge subject of the civil authority is only briefly addressed here.) For this purpose, let's say that a governmental agency

---

1. The angels also function under divine authority (Luke 1:19-20).

is set up with a particular competence to deal with the matters pertaining to its function.

The United States Supreme Court is an example of a governmental institution with authority. They are given authority with LIMITS to assure that the responsibility assigned is accomplished while still allowing for the essential protection of the free rights of the people.

> Political authority is POSITIONAL, meaning that their authority is derived from the office they occupy.

Some people inherit governmental authority as a birthright (Kings, Queens, etc.), while others gain it gradually.

AUTHORITY IN THE BUSINESS WORLD. The failure or success of a business is directly determined by how well the administration of authority is received. If the authority of the organization is not clear, many problems develop. At many work places, the employees avoid responsibility.

THERE IS AUTHORITY IN THE ACADEMIC WORLD. There is a constant struggle and competition in every field of academia. Determining who is the greatest expert is an ongoing battle.

THERE IS AUTHORITY IN POLITICS. The most successful politicians are those with the greatest positions of influence and authority.

HOW SHOULD THE CHRISTIAN INTERACT WITH CIVIL AUTHORITY?

"Everyone must submit himself to the governing authorities, for there is no authority except that which God has established... Do you want to be free from fear of the one in authority? Then do what is right and he will commend you. For he is God's servant to do you good... This is why you pay taxes, for the authorities are God's servants, who give their full time to governing" (Rom. 13:3-4, NIV).

> Submit (voluntarily yield) yourselves for the Lord's sake to every *authority* instituted among men... who are sent by him to punish those who do wrong and to commend those who do right (1 Pet. 2:13-14). See also Titus 3:1; Heb. 13:17; 1 Pet. 2:13-17.

WHEN NOT TO OBEY CIVIL AUTHORITIES: Peter encourages disciples of Christ to submit to governing authorities (1 Peter 2:13). However, when those governing authorities commanded Peter to stop preaching, he refused to obey (Acts 5:29). Therefore, we can surmise that the limit of civil government is when it encroaches upon our liberty to obey the commandments of God.

- But Peter and John answered, "You yourselves judge which is right in God's sight, to obey you or obey God" (Acts 4:19, TEB).

- Peter said, "We gave you strict orders not to teach in this name..." And the others replied; "We must obey God rather than men!" (Acts 5:28-29, NIV).

PARENTAL AUTHORITY: The fourth commandment tells children to honor their fathers and mothers that the children's days may be prolonged in the land which the LORD gives them (Ex. 20:12; see also Eph. 6:1; Col. 3:2). Families are a vital part of the establishment of His Kingdom on this earth. Nobody likes to be ruled and neither do kids. Humanity has a built in inclination to self-rule (garden failure) and satisfy selfish desires. Godly parental authority makes cooperation desirable.

Parental authority over their children gives them the responsibility to provide practical guidance, instruction, and protection to equip children for adulthood. Practically, this means that parents carefully help guide their children into correct decisions. Children need parental authority. Children who are taught respect authority grow up to be more productive adults.

Gods gives us His authority to BLESS.

Parents who are overly authoritarian don't allow their kids any freedom. No child can "respect" this kind of parent – but obeys only because of fear. Overly strict authoritarian parents cause children to become discouraged, unable to be optimally creative, and/or to feel rejected. Being overly permissive leads to chaos and lack of self-discipline.

QUESTION: How do you run your home? By authoritarianism or permissiveness? Discuss.

THE FIVE MAIN FORMS OF GOVERNMENT ARE:

ANARCHY. Government is bad. No government.

CAPITALIST. Free market. Government provides education, health, and welfare services.

COMMUNIST. Government owns everything and provides it's people as they decide.

DEMOCRACY. Government rulers are elected by the people. Everyone can vote and run for office to make decisions.

DICTATORSHIP. A country is ruled by a single leader who is not elected. This leader may use force to control.

KINGDOM GOVERNMENT is a **THEOCRACY**. A theocracy is a form of dictatorship. However, a Theocracy is a government by a Divine loving guidance delegated to officials who are regarded as divinely guided.

The government of God brings believers into His divine nature and purpose. God gives His people authority to rule in dominion under His guidance.

"It is absolutely necessary to have government, even in the things of God. Therefore, someone must be given authority by the Spirit. But authority is dangerous, unless the person with it has a heart full of compassion for others." ("Then Dangerous Possessions" Bill Britton)

GENERIC AND SPECIFIC AUTHORITY

GENERIC *AUTHORITY* is a generalized authority for everyone. It can be illustrated by general commands such as, "Go ye therefore, and make disciples of all the nations ..." (Mat. 28:19). They were to go, but how were they to go? They could walk, ride a horse, or sail a boat. Everyone in the global church has authority to "GO."

SPECIFIC *AUTHORITY* specifies what God wants a certain person or group to do.

Both generic and specific authority are derived by one of three ways – by direct command, by observation of a leader, or by the inference of necessity. Those in authority are given responsibility, duties, and assignments associated with function or position. Several things must be defined:

> Authority gives a leader the legitimate right to use resources and exercise discipline to move a group to a certain objective.

Who is in authority in this instance?

What exactly is that position?

Why is this authority needed?

What are the duties and abilities required?

Which Spiritual Gifts are needed to accomplish the objective?

What is the scope and/or the limits or boundaries of this authority?

> *"Nothing strengthens authority so much as silence."* Charles De Gaulle, 1890-1970, French President during World War II

SECTION 2

What is Authority?

Migrating to Spiritual Authority

The preeminent source of all authority is the **WORD** of **GOD**, inspired by God Himself (Mt. 22;29, Mk. 12:24, 2 Tim. 3:16; 2 Pet. 1:20-21) and therefore is our authority. The apostle Paul set forth the principle that the *authority* of the Word of God is binding as long as this earth remains (Mat. 24:25).

The authority of Scripture is derived from its intrinsic nature as a communication from God to man - it is an authority independent of the translators and people's opinions.

"*Forever, O Lord, Thy WORD is settled in heaven*" (Ps. 119:89).

The authority of God and the authority of the Bible are inseparable. Paul clearly told us, "Every scripture inspired of God... that the person of God may be complete, furnished completely unto every good work" (2 Tim. 3:16-17).

On many issues, the Scriptures are silent. But we must realize that silence does not authorize permissive or deviant behavior. The question is not "where does the Scripture prohibit an action?" But rather, "does the Scripture authorize an action?"

JESUS HAS ALL AUTHORITY

It was revolutionary! Jesus stated that **ALL** *authority* (*exousia* – the ability and the right to exercise power) in heaven and on earth was given to Him (Matt. 28:18-20).

There's no limitation to the authority of Jesus.

> We have been given the name of Jesus and His AUTHORITY to act in His behalf.

The inspired apostle Paul declared, "And whatsoever you do, in word or deed, DO ALL in the name of the Lord" (Col.3:17). The do(ing) "all in the name of the Lord" SHOWS that we respect His authority.

Jesus spoke with AUTHORITY, and not as the scribes (Mat. 7:27). A scribe's work was highly respected and required rigourous accuracy. Being a scribe was an exacting, time-consuming, and painstakingly job. No mistakes were allowed. Mainly, they were in charge of copying the precious Torah. The difference is huge. Jesus initiated the spoken message from God; scribes just wrote it down and copied it.

Colossians 1:16-17 says that ALL THINGS are made by Jesus – the structure of the powers and AUTHORITIES in both heaven and earth were created by and for Jesus. And in Him ALL THINGS consist (meaning are glued together). Without Him, everything would fly apart. Nothing exists by its own design. Jesus created a superlative and complex infrastructure of "thrones and dominions and principalities and authorities." NOTHING exists without Him – to this day, the moon still shines at night and the tides still respond to schedule, all because of His *authority*.

- Jesus had the *authority* to give eternal life (Jn. 17:2).
- The winds and the sea obeyed His voice (Mat. 8:26, 27).
- He had *authority* over the Sabbath (Mt. 12:8).
- He had *authority* over temporal matter – He could multiply loaves and fish (Mt. 15:34-38).
- Jesus had *authority* over the creation (like when the fig tree withered away, Mt. 21:19).
- Jesus had *authority* over devils and with authority he commanded even the unclean spirits, and they obeyed him (Mk. 1:27; Lk. 4:36; Mk. 5:7).
- He had the *authority* to forgive sin (Mk. 2:10-12).
- He had *authority* over sickness and death (Mk. 5:41, 42; Jn. 11:43,44; Acts 2:24). As many as touched Him were made whole (Mk. 6:56).
- Majesty, power, and *authority* is through Jesus Christ our Lord, before all ages, now and forevermore (Jude 25).
- Jesus had *authority* over gravity and walked on the water (Mk. 6:49). He was carried up into heaven (Mk. 16:19). He walked through walls.
- Jesus had *authority* to execute judgment (Jn. 5:27).
- He taught as one having *authority* (Mat. 7:29, Mk. 1:22).
- "Then I heard a loud voice in heaven say: 'Now have come the salvation and the power and the Kingdom of our God, and the *authority* of his Christ'" (Rev. 12:10).
- At His name everything must bow (Phil. 2:9-11).
- "For by Him all things were created that are in heaven and that are on earth, visible and invisible, whether thrones or dominions or principalities or powers. All things were created through Him and for Him" (Col. 1:16, NKJV).

Jesus will RETURN this authority BACK to the Father.

WHY JESUS HAD AUTHORITY

1. His Father delegated authority to Him (Mk. 1:11).

2. He lived under an open heaven (Mk. 1:10).

3. He never "tried" to make things happen.

4. He prepared thirty years for three years of ministry

5. He overcame the wilderness test with the devil (Mk. 1:12-13) and never allowed demons to hinder his assignment (Mk. 1:33).

6. He knew His timing and SEASON (Mk. 1:15).

7. He preached the Gospel of the Kingdom and nurtured new believers (Mk. 1:16-20).

8. He spent "alone time" with His Father (Mk. 1:35).

9. Compassion filled His motivations (Mk. 1:41). He focused on the down-and-out and the sick.

10. He stayed within His geographic assignment (Mk. 1:38).

THE AUTHOR (SOURCE)

The Greek word for *authority* is "*exousia*" which comes from the preposition "ex" that means "out of" and the verb "*ousia*" which is a form of the verb "to be." Literally, *exousia* means, OUT OF THE "I AM."

All legitimate spiritual authority stems from the great I AM (the name of God given to Moses, YHWH, I AM who I AM). God is the I AM and the SOURCE of authority. Spiritual authority refers to "essence" or PRESENCE that comes from God.

> The source of AUTHORITY is "Out from the I AM!"

Jesus (the issue of the Great I AM) had ALL authority (Mat. 10:1). He gathered together twelve disciples and gave them His (I AM) authority (Mark 3:14).

Not only does the word "authority" comprise this meaning of "out of the I AM," it is also understood to come "from one who originates or authors, the one who stands before others with dignity and provides an example."

- An "author" is the one that originates or creates: the SOURCE, or the original designer of a project. Our AUTHOR-ity comes out of The SOURCE of all things.

- An "author" or SOURCE gives His authority to do what He says.

God set up the church system to have leadership and "authority" in Biblical matters.

- Those in "authority" were understood in the Hebrew language to be: "The author, maker, creator, nourisher, teacher, the one who carries a weight of dignity."

God is the SOURCE of all authority which is unconditional and absolute (Ps. 29:10; Isa. 40:1).

We see this "source" concept illustrated in Hebrews 12:2, "Looking unto Jesus, the AUTHOR (#747 chief leader, from #756 the beginning (originator, source) and finisher of our faith..." (NKJV). Jesus is the AUTHOR. He started it and He will end it all. Jesus is the chief leader and the SOURCE of all.[1]

We must migrate to where our governmental church authority ONLY comes from God – our SOURCE. It seems Biblically clear that the Lord allows us to become under-shepherds and to minister WITH Him. He allows us to replicate His authority. Any rights we have to represent the "government of God here on earth" must be carefully and respectfully handled.

THE AUTHORITY OF JESUS WAS QUESTIONED

Many challenged the authority of Jesus. "And when he was come into the temple, the chief priests and the elders of the people came to him as he was teaching, and said, 'By what AUTHORITY do you do these things? AND WHO GAVE THEE THIS AUTHORITY?'" (Mat. 21:23 KJV).

It was an issue of *authority* when Jesus was accused of blasphemies (Mk 2:6,7), and when His own family said HE was "out of His mind" (Mk. 3:21). The Pharisees made lying accusations, calling him a gluttonous man and a winebibber (Lk. 7:33-34). The authority of Jesus was often challenged (Lk. 6:6-7). The scribes and pharisees provoked Him to speak of many things (Lk. 11:53-54). They laid in wait for Him, "seeking to catch something out of His mouth that they might accuse and discredit Him" (see also Lk. 7:39). They were angry that He healed on the Sabbath (Lk. 13:14) and that he ate with sinners (Lk. 15:2). They derided (sneered at) Him (Lk. 16:14).

> The unrighteous scoffed. They "hoped to catch Jesus in something He said so that they might hand Him over to the governor..." (Lk. 20:20). They condemned Him because they "did not understand the authority that He held" (Lk. 23:2).

> JESUS ANSWERED these accusations simply, "If I honor myself, my honor is nothing: it is my Father that honors me..." (Jn. 8:53, 54). And, He explained, even if I told you (the source of my authority), you would not believe (Lk. 22:67).

---

1. Also see my many books and articles on "source."

"GREAT FAITH" IN AUTHORITY

It's important to not skip over familiar stories just because you've read it before. Let's look at it a little differently. Jesus exercised His *authority* in response to the faith of the Centurion (Lk. 7:1-10) who understood authority.

Most of us have heard the story about the Centurion told as an eternal edict as to how church members are to "submit to leaders" - but there is MUCH MORE.

The Roman Centurion had authority over one hundred soldiers because of his relationship and submission to a higher authority – which was the rule of Augusts Caesar. The *authority* of Caesar sent the Centurion to Israel.

When we are sent by one in authority, that same authority flows through us.

When the Centurion gave an order, he did so under Caesar's authority, not his own   Caesar, the Roman emperor, was universally known by this word "Lord" (*Kurios*) as his TITLE – and everyone else was subservient to him... particularly everyone in Judea.

The Centurion made a request of Jesus, "LORD (*Kurios*), my servant lies at home sick of the palsy, grievously tormented." By calling Jesus "LORD," this Centurion indicated that he recognized the AUTHORITY of Jesus to be equal to or greater than Caesar! This was a treasonous comment for a Centurion to make.

The Centurion's "FAITH" THAT JESUS RECOGNIZED was being called *Kurios* – the LORD of all – greater than the mightiest ruler of the known world. Recognizing anyone else as *Kurios* was forbidden by this Roman Emperor.

The recognition of AUTHORITY (exousia) releases the POWER (dunamis).

Furthermore, the Centurion knew that the Jews were forbidden to enter the house of pagan Romans. Knowing that forbidden custom is why the Centurion said to Jesus, "I am not worthy that You should come under my roof."

He said, "Just speak the word (he understood that authority could operate from great distances), and my servant will be healed. For I know how authority works..." From this statement, Jesus recognized his FAITH.

The Centurion operated through HIS WORDS: "I say to one man 'Come!' and he comes, to another man 'Go!' and he goes, and to a third 'Do this!' and he does it." The Centurion's words had the authority to cause people to do what he said. That's why he knew that disease would submit to the authority of the WORDS of Jesus. The words of the Centurion came into line with the WORDS of JESUS – who only needed to send His Word.

Notice also that the Centurion wasn't searching for the power of Jesus. He understood that Jesus had authority OVER all things including disease. Sickness is subservient to the authority of the Word of the Lord.

The POWER to heal comes from His authority over ALL THINGS.

> Faith = the practice of expressing our confidence in the total AUTHORITY of God.

It is our FAITH in the *authority* of Jesus over sickness, the devil, sin, and death that saves us. Faith is not wimpy or uncertain! His authority has no limit – ALL authority in heaven and earth was given to Him (Mat. 20:18) It is infinite, never ending, immutable, and sure. Jesus gave His Church the same potential for this kind of authority.

- Our use of POWER depends upon our authority from God.
- Ministering with God's delegated authority is dependent upon our relationship, cooperation, and submission to God.

THE TWO METHODS OF OBTAINING AUTHORITY:

"My people (not sinners, not the world) are destroyed for lack of knowledge" (Hos. 4:6).

1. PRIMARY AUTHORITY belongs to those who have the initial right to command.

2. DELEGATED AUTHORITY is the right to command and to enforce obedience which was given to someone by the one holding primary authority. (Deputies are given authority to make arrests for the sheriff.) The first delegation of authority was from the Father God to His Son.

- "God appointed His Son to be heir of all things, through whom also He made the worlds" (Heb. 1:1-2, NKJV).
- "... Suddenly a voice said, 'This is My beloved Son, in whom I am well pleased. Hear Him!'" (Mat. 17:5, NKJV).
- "... The word which you hear is not Mine but the Father's who sent Me" (Jn. 14:24).
- "For it pleased the Father that in Him all the fullness should dwell" (Col. 1:19, NKJV).
- "For I have not spoken on My own *authority*; but the Father who sent Me gave Me a command, what I should say and what I should speak" (John 12:48-50). Notice that Scripture teaches us to do the same thing. (Phil. 2). We are to have the same attitude as that of Christ – and speak like God.

The AUTHORITY of BELIEVER

*"Blessed are they that do his commandments, that ،
(exousia, the authority) to the tree of life, and may ente،
gates into the city"* (Rev. 22:14, KJV).

Every believer needs to learn about their own authority. This topic is
incredible concept and a whole book in itself. However, this book
considers mainly the apostolic authority of the leader and our
relationship as leaders and with other leaders. Leadership authority in
the church is not to replace the authority of the believer.

Before we can find out about
leadership *authority*, we have to
unmistakably understand the
intrinsic *authority* of every
believer. From creation until now,
God purposed to give humans the
ability to have Dominion. It is our
job is to activate that initial
mandate.

> **Authority belongs
> to us –
> whether we
> realize it
> or not!**

It's ours! Already. Think about
this... Even though I hid $10.00 in
my purse and forgot it – it was still mine. I may have carried it around for
a year, but I couldn't spend it. We can't use what we don't discover!
People unnecessarily perish. They lose when they should win.

First we "tend and guard the Garden" of our soul. When we become
mature, we can "tend and guard" the garden of this earth and expand
the Kingdom. Maturity is the discovery of what God already gave us.

Jesus TOTALLY ushered in an incomprehensible revolution of *authority*.
The Resurrection of Jesus placed the *authority* of God (which had always
exhibited externally), INTO THE VERY HEARTS OF THE BELIEVER – to
USE! This central insight can potentially be the most significant Truth
you will learn concerning success.

*The only way humans can protect God's authority is to
ensure that they take no credit. God is the only
SOURCE of the power operating in their lives.*

* The *authority* that Jesus operated in was NOT HIS OWN (John
  14:10). He gave that same authority to us.
* All *"authority* belongs to God and He allows us to use it."
* Jesus defined our authority when He said, (Jn 13:20) "Truly, I
  say to you, he that receives who I send receives Me; and he
  that receives Me receives Him that sent Me" (also see Mk.
  9:37, Lk. 9:48).
* John tells us about the promise of salvation (1:12) and how we
  are given (according to the Greek) the *"authority"* to be called

the sons of God. That means that we have the right, the freedom, the honor, and privilege of a son.

- Jesus also spoke parables about gaining *authority* over cities, "A good servant who is faithful in very little has *authority* over ten cities" (Lk 19:17).
- Overcomers are promised "*Authority* over nations" (Rev. 2:26).
- Divine *authority* empowers us to overcome everything that hinders or should not exist in His Kingdom.

How the Lord delegates Spiritual Authority

TO our SPIRIT ◄━━ | ━━► TO our SOUL

The Holy Spirit speaks *Rhema* to your spirit.	Sovereignly selected leaders train your soul.
Gifts of God.	By LOGOS Word
	Civil Government
Impartation	Family & friends

All authority resides in Jesus. No authority exists except that which He delegates.

In order to relate properly to authority in our lives, we should ask, "What are the specific responsibilities of each person in my life?" The Holy Spirit can and will reveal to your mind concerning the will of God for you.

The Lord can speak to our human spirit and to our soul. The Holy Spirit speaks to us through people who use the Gifts of God to bring us an impartation. God can also use leaders to speak to us.

Authority is everywhere. It exists in every aspect of our lives. And, like we said, nothing stirs up the flesh more than the controversy over authority. However, the Lord delegates His authority to other human authorities to train your SOUL (mind, will, and emotions) to come into alignment with the will of God.

The issue facing contemporary Christians today is how can we exercise THIS authority in this earthly realm NOW? At this exciting SEASON of time, through us, Jesus will subjugate every other kind of rule (*archee*), authority (*exousia*), and power (*dunamis*) (1 Cor. 15:24). Every knee will bow to Him (Phil. 2:10).

- There is no authority except that which comes from God (Rom 13:1). God gave Paul the right (*exousia*) to preach the gospel (1 Co 9:18).
- The concept of *authority* refers to the ABILITY OR CAPABILITY to complete an action. Jesus had the authority to forgive sins (Matt 9:6-8) and to drive out spirits (Mark 6:7). Jesus gave seventy-two the authority to trample on snakes and scorpions (Luke 9:1, 10:19).

* Authority is delegated from God as a license, or authorization, to act in His behalf. God gave the apostles license to build up the church (2 Co 10:8).

JESUS GAVE HIS APOSTLES HIS AUTHORITY

The selection of these twelve was not random. Jesus by-passed all those educated men who had studied at the fine schools of religion. He went out of His way to choose unschooled fishermen and a (known to be) dishonest tax collector. He took time to explain revelation to them (Mat. 15:15-18). Jesus sent them out in pairs (Mk. 6:7-13, Mat. 10:5-42, Lk. 9:1-6) to various towns in Galilee. The major assignment of the Apostles was "to be with" Him and to declare the Kingdom.

Jesus expected each of them to come into a personal closeness with Him. He called them "apostles." At this point, Jesus did not tell them the full extent of their mission. These apostles still had an incomplete grasp of Who Jesus was and why He came to earth.

Jesus gave the apostles (delegated) *authority*. He said, "As the Father has sent me, so send I you (plural)." The first level of *authority* in the church began with the apostle. Jesus continuously taught them about real life and real situations. He demonstrated *authority* to them so that they could become the vehicle to bring forth the Message of the Kingdom (Mat. 10). And He taught them how to lead with *authority* by serving them ("But I've taken my place among you as the One who serves" Lk. 22:24).

Jesus delegated His *authority* to the apostles while on the earth. Then, He modeled how to use it. He prayed that the glory the Father gave to Him would be given to them – and that the actions of the apostles would further bring Him glory (Jn. 17).

* "And Jesus came and spoke to them, saying, 'ALL AUTHORITY (not some or just a portion) has been given to Me in heaven and on earth'" (Mat. 28:18, NKJV).

* "So Jesus said to them, 'Assuredly I say to you... you who have followed Me will also sit on twelve thrones, judging the twelve tribes of Israel'" (Mat. 9:28, NKJV).

* "...(God) delivered us out of the authority (*exousia*) of darkness, and translated us into the Kingdom of the Son of his love." (The AUTHORITY in Jesus' name legitimates (makes lawful or valid) the POWER to change from darkness to light (Col. 1:13)!

* Even the Holy Spirit does not use His own authority. "However, when He, the Spirit of truth, has come, He will guide you into all truth; for He will NOT SPEAK OF HIS OWN AUTHORITY, but whatever He hears He will speak; and He will tell you things to come" (Jn. 16:13-15).

Authority, "exousia" is
demonstrated
and confirmed
by POWER
(*dunamis* – miracles).

He gave them AUTHORITY to drive out demons and cure diseases. He sent them out to preach the Kingdom of God and to heal the sick (Lk. 9:1-2, NIV). They went from village to village, preaching the gospel and being a demonstration of Kingdom RULE. They were given authority to drive out evil spirits and to heal every disease and sickness (Mat. 10:1) and over all the *exousia* (authority) of the enemy! The authority of Jesus operated through them.

Jesus summed up the apostle's authority when He said, "He that receives you receives Me" (Mt. 10:40).Apostles are gifted and commissioned with the *authority* to establish foundational government that sets things in order and brings believers into maturity.

APOSTLES WERE GIVEN:

Apostles labored and studied in Word and doctrine alongside Jesus.

* The authority to bind and loose in Heaven and Earth (Mat. 18:18).
* *Authority* over all the power of the enemy.
* *Authority* over evil spirits.
* *Authority* to raise the dead and execute judgment (which the seventy did not have).
* *Authority* and responsibility to identify and establish the foundations of Church government, procedure, and doctrine.
* The *authority* to maintain accountability.

Until Apostles fully function and mature leaders, the Kingdom has a shaky foundation (paraphrase of Eph. 4:11-13).

Righteous authority exists when believers respect and honor a minister who manifests the goodness and POWER of God.

Jesus told them this analogy about authority: "For the Son of Man is as a man taking a far journey (He left earth for awhile), who left His house, and gave *authority* to his servants (that's us), and to every man his work (we each have an assignment), and commanded the porter (the Holy Spirit) to watch" (Mk. 13:34).

To have authority means one is given the right to accomplish a goal, to enforce laws, exact compliance, command, determine, or judge. One can have authority to accomplish administrative assignments in a specified field.

The force of authority is "influence and pursuasion."

* Having authority means one becomes an accepted source or an expert in a certain field.
* Those in authority have the ability to give a conclusive statement or make a decision that could be used as a precedent or guide.

CHURCH AUTHORITY

"Living in reality is living within God's perspective a
Dennis Peacock

GOVERNMENT can be defined as the exercise of God's dele
AUTHORITY within an organization or institution that brings a
lished system of direction, rule, and management. Governmenta
authority structure helps bind believers around what is considered
sacred, inspirational, and moral. Leaders in authority put structure to
the sacred, communicate the inspirational, and interpret and establish
the moral. These proper activities of government create cohesion,
stability, and meaning in our civilization. Without spiritual authority,
society fragments and declines.

- Governmental authority takes us to the objective – which is building the KINGDOM of the Lord Jesus.
- Spiritual government activates and enables each individual according to how he/she is gifted.

"Apostles do not exist to govern, but govern what they cause to exist."
Paula Price

Leaders should rule over cities and nations – not just teach about sitting
on clouds playing harps and polishing halos. It's not enough to belong to
an invisible and mystical Body. They must make a difference.

The *authority* of a minister is the imparted right to bring the power of
God into operation. That means we change the way we have been going.
We affect all arenas of life: the local church and the global church
should impact the systems of the WORLD (*cosmos*).

There is a clarion call for the church leaders to migrate into a stronger
place of governmental authority. This new view is a dramatic and
breathtaking new coastline with rugged, undiscovered possibilities for
Kingdom advancement. Today is a rare opportunity to be pioneers of a
new kind who discover uncharted lands.

THE LOCAL CHURCH: Generally, the Local Church should be self-
governing, rather than controlled by a denomination. The local church
should be autonomous, but accountable relationship and protected by
mature apostolic authority that gives advice and counsel.

> Much of the present church chaos is due to believers NOT
> recognizing spiritual authority in their lives.

Local church is a group comprised of individual people who belong to a
certain local visible church (Acts 1:15, 2:41, 47; Lk. 9:1-2; 10:1-2)
governed by elders. There, they are trained, equipped, nurtured, and
released. In a local assembly, God's *authority* should be exercised co-
equally by the Governing Elders (executive presbytery) who are led by a

t leader is the vision bearer and holds the final
naintaining the vision and mission before the people.

hree are gathered together in My name, I am there IN
THE MIDST of them" (Mat. 18:16-10).

JRCH (Mat. 16:18) incorporates all believers and the
around the earth.

G (mentioned 2,000 times in the Bible) rules THE
)M! God is a God of ORDER and authority (1 Cor.

one refers to the absolute authority of God that issues
is throne. His throne is established upon His authority
His righteousness (Prov. 16:12).

"The church does not produce the Kingdom; the Kingdom produces the church which is the model for Kingdom in culture" (paraphrased from article by Tim Early).

MIGRATING TO KINGDOM OF AUTHORITY

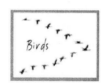

HOW DO BIRDS MIGRATE? Not all birds fly. Ostriches walk, penguins swim. Whatever your talent and ability is – that's the way you will migrate! We are all given unique inborn giftings. We are equal before God, but we are not naturally talented in the same ways. What works for one person may not always work for another. Noah built an ark. Elisha smote a river with a cloak. Gideon won with a small army. How will you migrate? How will you discover your full authority? Your next step to migration is knowing how you will get there.

CHURCH MIGRATION demands that we leave (go away FROM) the old before too much winter sets in. Synonyms: we abandon, depart, egress, escape, exit from what is frozen in time and not working. We move on to the next. We do away with, we separate from, we set forth in a new direction toward the place that God has prepared. We cross over, we explore, we embark on an excursion, march, pass through, we press, we survey that which may be the best routes. We traverse, trek, take a voyage towards. We set things in motion, put into action, advance, change, displace, fly, operate, pass, progress, shift gears, transit, and be transplanted into new dimensions.

The fundamental governmental concerns of an apostle are in the areas of STRUCTURE, FUNCTION, and DOCTRINE.

STRUCTURE: The plan. What is the direction? How will it work? What is needed? How will the parts be held, arranged, or put together in a

God's laws.

gated
estab-

We obtain vision as to where to go.

particular way to form a whole. The interrelation or arrangement of the parts of a complex entity.

FUNCTION: Apostolic leaders instruct believers on how to *function* in their individual authority as the BODY in order to demonstrate the Kingdom on earth.

DOCTRINE: Apostles define doctrine. Doctrine determines a person's belief system which is the basis for their behavior.

Apostles establish a standard new order of accuracy.

FOUNDATIONAL APOSTOLIC DOCTRINE includes: 1) Defining the essential truths and revelations that will build the corporate Church (local and universal) and establish the Kingdom. **2)** Establishing the truths that enable believers to mature and fully function in their destiny.

* Apostolic doctrine has revelatory insight and wisdom of Scriptures (Gal. 1:12; Eph. 3:5; 1 Cor. 14:26; Mat. 16:13-18). Truth is made known through doctrine. It corrects heresy and establishes a new STANDARDS.
* "And they (believers) continued steadfastly in the apostles' (plural possessive) doctrine and fellowship" (Acts 2:42).
* Apostles make decisions on doctrinal issues (Acts 15).
* Doctrine confronts wrong, "And they teach customs which are not lawful for us to receive or observe" (Acts 16:21).

TRUTH is the hinge upon that which all else should be attached.

* True apostles define and authenticate Truth as opposed to imitation or falsehood.
* Divine government demands that every decision is based upon Biblical Truth. Someone's reality is not necessarily Truth.

INDICATORS OF READINESS FOR CHURCH MIGRATION:

* A realization that spiritual authority is about spiritual GOVERNMENT. Our philosophy of government creates our environment.The heart of government rests in its view of authority.
* Kingdom values are integrated into the everyday life (Acts 19:17-20).

* Mature believers recognize their responsibility to yield to leadership and to volunteer (Ps. 110:3)
* Social structure is impacted (2 Chron. 19:10).
* Economic conditions improve in the Body (2 Chron. 17:3-5).
* Increased acceleration of the Kingdom culture rather than World culture.
* Seeing the world through the eyes of the Lord. Mind-sets broadened to global vision.

AUTHORITY over SATAN

God's Authority is missing because

We give the devil has more authority than he really has

Authority is the centerpiece of the dispute that caused Lucifer's fall from Grace. He wanted God's throne (that's the place of authority, Is. 14:12-14). Five times in Isaiah, Lucifer said, "I will be like the Most High."

Lucifer rebelled and left his proper placement (Jude 5) all because he wanted more authority!

Adam forfeited his authority over the world to Satan. That is why it is called "the Fall!" Humanity lost the ability to comprehend their authority in God, therefore, they lost their true identity. The loss of authority caused humans to not be able to fulfill God's INTENTION.

Later, we see the devil offering Jesus *authority* over the world. Jesus did not dispute the assertion that it was Satan's authority to give. Let's read about it: "Then the devil, taking Him up on a high mountain, showed Him all the kingdoms of the world in a moment of time. And the devil said to Him, 'All this AUTHORITY (this is *exousia*, wrongly translated in several renditions as power) I will give You, and their glory; for this has been delivered to me, and I give it to whomever I wish.'" (Lk. 4:5-7).

The devil has authority over the kingdoms of the world.

- Satan walks this world "according to the *authority* of the air" (Eph. 2:2).
- "When I was daily with you in the temple, ye stretched forth no hands against me: but this is your hour, and the *authority* (*exousia*) of darkness" (Lk. 22:53).

The devil has the power (*kratos*) over death (Heb. 2:16).

- All that Satan has to offer leads to death. All these will he give, if a person will follow his ways and forsake God. Satan does "understand the THINGS...THAT BE OF MEN" (Mt. 16:23).
- That through death He (Jesus) might destroy him who had the power (*kratos, volcanic energy*) of death, that is, the devil" (Heb. 2:14). Jesus took that authority and power away from the devil.

The *authority* of satan can entangle humans into a different spirit of success and influence. The power of the enemy seems to greatly influence ministries in the arenas of merchandising, marketing, and finances.[1] Note the words – *authority* of SATAN, *authority* of DARKNESS,

1. See my book on "Revelation" for explanation of this issue.

THE PRINCE OF THE *AUTHORITY* OF THE AIR (Eph. 2:2) who has THE POWER (*kratos*) OF DEATH.

THE ANTICHRIST RECEIVES *AUTHORITY* from the DEVIL. Satan (the dragon) gives his power, his seat and his great *authority* to the beast (Rev. 13:2).

JESUS HAS TOTAL AUTHORITY OVER SATAN.

Jesus possessed ALL true AUTHORITY; He guarded Himself from desiring FALSE AUTHORITY. Satan has only limited authority (*exousia*) over this world's systems. For the believer, his only *authority* is what we concede to him (by willful sin in our lives and bad confession). If we don't give it to him, then he has no *authority* to release his power.

Believers have delegated authority over the devil.

At the cross, JESUS took away the devil's "authority."

* We are exchanged) and from the *authority* of satan unto God, that we may receive forgiveness of sins... (Acts 26:18).
* Jesus delivered us from the "*authority* of darkness and translated us into His Kingdom of light" (Col. 1:13).
* Jesus provided the way for all humanity the honor and privilege to use His *authority* in this world.

JESUS GAVE BELIEVERS AUTHORITY OVER SATAN

"Then I heard a loud voice saying in heaven, 'Now salvation, and strength, and the kingdom of our God, and the authority (exousia) of His Christ have come'" (Rev. 12:10).

Luke tells the story about how the seventy returned with joy exclaiming, "Lord, even the demons submit to us in Your name" (Lk. 10:17-20, NIV). They were excited and wanted to brag about their spiritual success!

Jesus explained WHY the demons submitted in His name... "I SAW Satan fall like lightning from heaven."

Ask yourself, "Do I see that?" Can you see like Jesus?

The ability to SEE that Satan has no seat of *authority* is why the demons submit. This perception (SEEING) is why Jesus continued with this phenomenal statement:

"I HAVE GIVEN YOU *AUTHORITY* (*exousia*, the capability, liberty, right to act, right to decide) to trample (*pateo*, put under foot or subdue) on snakes (can also be translated as a malicious person with sharp vision) and scorpions (something that stings – from the meaning septic), and to overcome all the power (*dunamis*, the ability TO DO something) of the enemy!" (Lk. 10:17)

Then Jesus said, "NOTHING WILL HARM YOU." The apostles were given *AUTHORITY* so that no harm (injustice or injury) could come! Like them, we have HIS *AUTHORITY*! But carefully notice that we are not to rejoice over it. That *authority* is not ours. We rejoice for what God has done *for* us. Jesus gave us "*AUTHORITY* (*exousia*) over all the POWER (*dunamis*) of the enemy" (Lk. 10:17).

- "For this purpose was the Son of God manifest. That he might destroy the works of the evil one (1 Jn. 3:8). Did Jesus fulfil His purpose? Did He accomplish HIs mission or does He need to come back and do it?
- Evil spirits are also subject to God's *authority* (Eph 6:11-12).
- "Then the end will come, when He hands over the kingdom to God the Father after He has destroyed all dominion, *authority* and power" (1 Cor. 15:24, NIV).[1]

Paul said that they received AUTHORITY (*exousia*, which is delegated authority) over all the power (inherent ability) of the devil. Then he said, "You have been given fullness in Christ, who is the head over every power and authority" (Col. 2:10-11). It was no longer a matter of needing to ask God to fight the devil for them – because they already had AUTHORITY OVER the POWER of the devil.

The weakness of most believers and ministries is their overestimation of the authority and influence of the devil.

> If we use our God-given AUTHORITY, the enemy has no POWER – and nothing can hurt us!

There is no need to be fearful and apprehensive about the devil. While we acknowledge that the devil and his forces have power, the disciples have ALL *exousia* over the devil. In Matthew 10:1, God gave *His authority* (*exousia*) to the seventy-two. Jesus tells us to understand His teachings as "little children."

God promises "nothing shall injure us" (Lk. 10:19); therefore, we must commit to the *authority* (which is given for the cause of Christ) and not yield to fear.

"For He [Jesus] delivered us [rescued us] from the *domain* (*exousia*, the *authority*, the right and the might of darkness) and transferred us to the Kingdom of His beloved Son." God has *authority* over us now. We are "bought with a price" – and the devil has NO authority (exousia) or power (*dunamis*) over us anymore! (Col. 1:13). Although, the devil still has authority over "this world."

1. See my book "Connecting" and various articles on "The Demise of the Devil" for full explanation of the full *authority* of the cross over the devil.

If we use our delegated authority from God, we can defeat the enemy... every time!

"And having disarmed the powers and *authorities*, He made a public spectacle of them, triumphing over them by the cross" (Col. 2:15, NIV). Paul's point is that Christ's work includes the defeat of the evil spirits who formerly ruled this age. Evil no longer has the same access to believers. The enemy is so completely conquered that God has put him on public display – leading him in triumphal procession.

Know this -- the devil and evil spirits must obey the Christ in you!

Paul connects Christ's work of having canceled the written code against us (Col. 2:13b -14) with the disarming (*apekduomai* means literally "to take off the clothes") of the enemy.

YES. Having *authority* means we don't have to endlessly fight the devil (we give him no ground – Adam meaning "ruddy ground") – nor do we need to plead with God and angels to overcome the devil. Our *authority* is greater than that of Satan and his demons. Jesus' name is above all names (Phil. 2:9–10). Our declarations of faith establish the Kingdom.

SUMMARY:

The word "*authority*" in Greek can be further defined as, "to beget, project, and stand forth with power and dignity." Many of us go through life without ever knowing about the authority that God has already given us through Jesus Christ. Somehow, we fail to realize that God never blesses us *because* of us, but He blesses *in spite* of us. A lack of perception hinders us from receiving. God never changed His mind about humans learning to subdue, conquer, guard, defend, and take dominion over the enemy.

 The *last sacrifice*, the cross, not only covers but also cleanses us from that sin. Only God's blood restores us to the pre-fall image of God-likeness. When we come into Christ, He comes INTO us. The Savior's perfect atonement permanently returns all lost authority (Col. 2:13-17).

Jesus explained that all *authority* in heaven and on earth was given to Him (Matt. 28:18-20). He gave that same authority to His disciples (Luke 9:1). Now He leaves it up to us to activate that dominion where we live.

Our authority comes from obediently using His name – not from ourselves.

Every believer has authority and dominion.

Men and women are given Grace gifts of authority to lead.

Leaders must be firmly aware of what Christ has ALREADY accomplished for all humankind.

SECTION 3

False & Real Leaders

Elders

False Authority

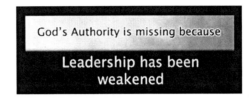

"*When you make your peace with authority, you become authority.*"
Jim Morrison (Lead singer of the Doors)

The challenge against authority can be seen in all arenas of life. Our governmental rulers are being challenged and our values of morality are being questioned.

The only true authority that exists is that to which he or she chooses to submits – not by constraint but by conviction.

The question of accepting church leaders and allowing them to have *authority* is a fundamental issue facing every believer. Its significance cannot be underestimated.

We remember that *authority* was first lost at the downfall of humanity (Gen. 1-3) when they sought independence from external *authority* and established self-determination as the final *authority* in their lives. There are many reasons given for people not wanting to cooperate with spiritual leaders.

* Independent self will. Individualism.
* Hurt and disappointment.
* One of the strongest is the fear of false authority.
* The thought that everyone is equal and should be EQUALLY in charge.
* Misuse of leadership in the past.
* Hierarchy.
* Doctrinal maturity and changing ideas.

FEAR OF FALSE AUTHORITY: In this book, we will discuss these positions above. Many of these reasons stem from a fear of false authority.

The Book of Judges tells us about a particular period when the leaders of Israel lost their ability to influence. "In those days there was no king in Israel and every man did that which was right in his own eyes" (Jdg. 21:25, 17:6). A king is one who has *authority and rule.* In much of the church today, a vast majority of believers do whatever seems right in their own eyes.

> *"I know your works, your labor, your patience, and that you cannot bear those who are evil. And you have TESTED THOSE WHO SAY THEY ARE APOSTLES AND ARE NOT, and have found them liars"*
> (Rev. 2:2-3, NKJV).

Scriptures warn against false apostles (2 Cor. 10:12 - 11:20, 12:11; Rev. 2:2). The Message Bible says in Rev. 2:2, "I know you can't stomach evil, that you weed out apostolic pretenders." These days, lots of people claim to be apostles – we must wonder what they do with the verse above!

False teaching and wrong usages of *authority* had already begun in New Testament times, and soon became more prevalent. There are times when unjust or controlling leadership violates individual freedom and should be disobeyed (Acts 4:15-20).

> It's not about "clergy and laity" anymore – but it is about LEADERSHIP.

False authority figures often try to to engender a dependency upon their spiritual gifting and insight. They also try prevent the maturity of the believer. Paul spoke of false apostles who masquerade as righteous. They pretend to be servants of righteousness. Some follow blindly not discerning that "another gospel" is preached. Paul says, "God will deal with them, I ask you to return to me as your father in the faith. I ask you to return to the message that I first preached to you, and submit again to my leadership." Paul gave people the *authority* to choose to follow him. That's what Jesus did when He told His disciples, "Choose voluntarily who you will serve, choose to live today by following me."

Paul adamantly cautioned believers about submitting to false teachers whose motive to use their "*exousia*" AUTHORITY to make themselves "Lords and masters" and build up lofty power positions against the knowledge of God. (2 Cor. 10:3). False *authority* lacks servanthood and kindheartedness. Instead, it's all about ambition and SELF. False *authority* promotes dependence and fosters immaturity. It frustrates believers by restricting their creativity.

- "In fact, why do you even put up with anyone who enslaves you (brings you into bondage) or exploits you (devours you) or takes advantage of you or pushes himself forward or slaps you in the face..." (2 Cor. 11:18-22, NASB).

- "So we say with confidence, '... I will not be afraid. WHAT CAN MAN DO TO ME?' Remember (recollect all) your LEADERS (*hegeomai*" 2333; those who lead and command with official *authority*), who spoke the word (*logos*) of God to you. Consider (look again at) the outcome (what has come from them) of their way of life (their behavior) and imitate their faith" (Heb. 13:6-7, NIV).

- False ministries generally try to use people for their own purposes (whims or wishes). "Mockers are coming in these last days that are natural men NOT HAVING THE SPIRIT" (Rom. 1:2; Tim. 3:1; 2 Pet. 3:3).

- "Remove the wicked from LEADERSHIP and *AUTHORITY* will be credible and God-honoring." (Prov. 25:5 MSG)

- "Among LEADERS who lack insight, abuse abounds, but for one who hates corruption, the future is bright." (Prov. 28:16 MSG)

- "... An exploiting LEADER leaves a trail of waste" (Prov. 29:4 MSG)

Many believers have been abused by past church experiences. Their trust level is low. They have fled the church in droves because of authoritative manipulation and control. Consequently, much of the church has been "standing still" and motionless for some time now.

- Jesus hated the Nicolaitans who apparently tried to conquer and control others with flattery and manipulation.

- Paul warned that the Judaizers, "....eagerly seek you, not commendably, but they wish to shut you out, in order that you may seek them." (Galatians 4:17, NASB). Judaizers tried to make people dependent. Leaders must not become elitist. Spiritual leaders are not demi-gods, little Nero's, or control freaks.

- Abusive systems demand a misplaced sense of extreme loyalty. Godly *authority* never tries to impose control upon another.

It's all about voluntarily cooperating together with a free will.

I've ministered in many churches where the congregation is not supposed to make any major decision without leadership approval. They ask, "What shall I name my store?" "What color of car should I buy?" "What should I name my baby?" Having *authority* doesn't mean that leaders should replace the Holy Spirit when it comes to areas of guidance and direction for a believer's life. We've said it before... the leader's job is to teach believers how to hear and interpret the Holy Spirit accurately for themselves. God alone is their personal Guide. Leaders can trust the Lord to lead His people.

True leaders submit to Truth.

SUMMARY:

We must have leaders, but not arrogant, unapproachable, and posturing leaders. IT'S OKAY to not be dependent. It's OKAY TO ASK QUESTIONS

about what is being taught. Every believer should feel free to ask questions without threat of embarrassment or lack of respect. Believers SHOULD ask questions – that's the best way to learn. In fact, Acts 17:11 tells how the Bereans were commended as being more "noble" than the Thessalonicans because they "searched the scriptures daily" to check up on Paul's teachings. It's okay to examine the teachings and decisions of leaders and to seek clarifications on issues pertaining to your life.

We don't have to agree on doctrinal issues to be ONE in the spirit.

FALSE NAILS

AN ARTICLE: It's odd... how sometimes little things happen, and then the Lord speaks to us through that incident. And this was such a girl thing. Seemingly so irrelevant.

Upon moving to the States, my friend told me that putting on acrylic nails was "the thing to do!" Well, whatever. I didn't want to be a misfit. Never having lived in America - let alone the south before... who would know that women would do such a thing?

So I did it. Had those fake nails put on right away. That in itself was quite an ordeal. This little lady clipped my own nails off – way back, as short as possible. "Hey!" I shouted, "couldn't you warn me first? Why did you do that?" But there was no answer from this determined person who was fixated on making me look acceptable. Then, she attached these enormously long 4" plastic curves right on the end of my fingers. That was a scary sight! Now, I looked like a Freddy Kruger poster.

She finally spoke, "How long do you want them?"

"Hummmmmmm, I dunno' - what's best?" So she sighed and rolled her eyes. Then finally, after much filing, sanding, and polishing, it was over. The fact that I could no longer tie my shoes, or pick up a small pin seemed irrelevant. The expensive upkeep didn't matter much either. Now I looked up to standard.

But after a few months, my beautiful artificial nails got infected underneath – especially on one finger. So, I had to have them all removed. That took a lot of time and soaking in remover. What a mess. And hurt? Wow! Having those permanently affixed nails pried off the tops of my own nails. (Uck!) Now, my own real nails were really *sensitive* and thin.

Everywhere I went, I felt like apologizing for such horrible looking fingers.

One day, I understood this event as pedagogy – a female insight to what had happened so that I could understand a greater truth of what was happening to the HAND – the representation of the Fivefold ministry.

The hand has withered and needs healing (Mk. 3:1-3; Lk. 6:8). The fingernail represents the visible part of the ministry that is presented.

Much of the FIVEFOLD ministry has covered itself with artificial layers. We've sanded down the natural surface. We've lost our natural luster. We've attached a man-made exterior upon our ministry. And we've allowed others to paint us with whatever colors go with the outfit of the day. A façade, if you will to be what others want to see (or hear). If it is successful, wear it, say it, and do it. If it sells - be it! These days it's hard to be real. We just have to put on another layer of plastic, cuz' it's "the thing to do!"

Artificial means: Synthetic. Fake. Mock. Copied. Unreal. Imitation. Man-made. Bogus. Sham. Phony.

Real nails were created to be useful. They're a tool to scratch ourselves, to play an instrument, to do fine work, or to pick up little things. But with acrylic nails, we can't do any of that.

Thank God, there are those who still refuse this fad. And, there are others whose artificial fingernails are not infected yet. But, they probably soon will be. You know how unclean the procedure is these days.

Our thumb (representing the Apostle) has made lots of progress in understanding the new function and position in the latter day church. But some have now acquired this hardened surface - right at the tip of their ministry. It's something that's not natural and not real. I mean, this artificial "COVERING" is impenetrable.

After awhile, our fingers have become accustomed to this artificial top layer. Not only that, but these layers have to be restored (filled) every couple of weeks with another layer of stinky stuff. And that manicurist has to put on a mask – because of the pungent odor of the acrylic. But, the procedure makes us look good – and these days, that's all that matters.

Sometimes our thumb just doesn't "FEEL" like it did before... our sensitivity is reduced. That imitation extension makes it a lot harder to do things that we once did. Now we often want other people to do things for us. Suddenly, our productivity is limited because we can't work as hard. Like I said, those phony nails make it harder to "pick up" (discern) little things these days. And, it's almost impossible to securely "tie" (bind up) anything anymore. But, we can plan to COVER others... by painting them up to look like us.

As the Prophet, the pointer finger, we realize that God has lots more to say than we can apprehend – but we can't fully function with that false attachment. Many have been unable to completely perceive because that dense opaque covering that now defines our office also hinders our perception and our effectiveness. Besides that, those new long nails cause awful hygiene – bacteria grows rapidly under there. We've made ourselves sick trying to look like others – and trying to reproduce someone else's methodology – We'll have to remember that some of us were created to have long fingers; some have strong ones. That's why some of us need to really stick out there, while others need to "stay down in the quick!"

These days most Evangelists want to look just like all the other Evangelists. For a while we didn't allow an extension of ourselves – and our natural nails resisted being covered artificially. But later, we allowed an unknown formula (a synthetic bonding of chemicals) to be applied so that glossy new artificial nail would adhere and not come off. I mean, who would dare to be a down-to-earth minister anymore? Unpolished, and untrimmed? Who would dare to work with their fingers in the dirt? Surely, we can't do that anymore! And, who would dare to be seen as we really are? Without the pretense?

And that little finger, the teacher... wow! It's exciting how the Bible opens more clearly every day – just as Daniel promised. What a job the teacher has to help reveal these new truths. To continue the analogy, let's remember that God made our natural fingernails somewhat porous and able to receive input. But these new coverings have masked over our sensitivity and now we want to say things "just right," in order to fit into the "status quo." We wouldn't want to look differently from the others.

But remember? There was really bad infection in one finger. The ring finger was weeping with ucky stuff all the way back to the cuticle. It throbbed and pulsed with every heartbeat. Oh, pastors. So many of us are hurt and injured, and no one knows. We've tried to look all polished up on the outside – tried to be everything to everyone. But deep inside there is a festering... an infection that no one can see because it's all covered up with an imitation surface. And that infection continues. Where can we turn? Who can we trust? It seems that the pastor is affected the most by artificial pretension. The pastor can't endure it. People need to get too close. Something has to happen.

This infection affects all the fingers and then... the WHOLE BODY. I asked my Doctor what to do about my throbbing fingers? He said the topical medications that I was using wouldn't help – and the prescriptions that he could give me were really bad for the BODY (they cause liver damage – the blood filter). He said the only thing to do was to take the artificial nail off and let the real nail grow out. Oh, vanity! What a price to pay.

Like I said, it really hurts to remove those hardened layers of what others expect to see. It takes time to recover from complying with the fashion statement of the day. It takes a lot of time to grow out the new nail and discover what was there before. That original call must emerge from the tip of the fivefold. We must apprehend the Love that is unpretentious and regain the Fruit that is unassuming. Gifts must be unaffected and natural. Ministry must recapture our once sincere motivation. The reason that we started is what we need to find again. The person that we were created to be is who God wants to use. Image and likeness cannot be manifested or reproduced from artificial methods.

Oh, beloved, why are we so concerned with the exterior? Can we rip it off? Why do we want to look like others? Why should we do things like they do it? Can we separate from the artificial religious system – even though it hurts? Even though we may not be what others want to see?

We come again as the servant of old who looked up into the sky and saw a cloud the size of a man's HAND (1 Kng. 18:45). The vision of a healed hand growing in the heavenlies causes us to outrun the chariots.

And Jesus looked at His nail pierced hands and said, "Those nails were real." Selah!

THE HAND

In Scripture, the hand is often a symbol of authority, power, and strength (Ps. 60:5; Isa. 28:2). The right hand represented the south, and the left the north (Job 23:9; 1 Sam. 23:19). To give the right hand was a pledge of fidelity (2 Kng. 10:15; Ezr. 10:19); the right hand lifted up was an oath (Gen. 14:22, etc.). God's hand symbolizes His power: when His hand is upon us, it denotes favor (Ezr. 7:6,28; Isa. 1:25; Lk. 1:66, etc.) or punishment (Ex 9:3; Judg. 2:15; Acts 13:11, etc.). Sitting at the right hand was regarded as the chief place of status, honor, and power (Ps. 45:9; 80:17; 110:1; Mat. 26:64).

Do We Need Church Leaders?

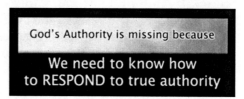

God's Authority is missing because

**We need to know how
to RESPOND to true authority**

"If your actions inspire others to dream more, learn more, do more, and become more, you are a leader." John Quincy Adams

Yes! People need leaders. Sheep need a shepherd. Leaders provide direction and energy to accomplish goals. Leaders unite people around cooperative efforts and focus their efforts. Leaders tend and guard (Gen. 2:15). They send (Rom. 10:15).

Explaining how to lead with Godly authority, Paul wrote: 2 Cor. 10:7-8, "You are looking only on the surface of things... For even if I boast somewhat freely about the *AUTHORITY* the Lord gave us for BUILDING YOU UP rather than PULLING YOU DOWN."

 Notice. Godly leaders have the *authority* to build up the believer! In these precious days, we possess incredible opportunities to manifest our God-given authority – a gift to lead without LORDING over.

Authority is not self-serving. The first apostles didn't use flattering words to cloak intentions, nor did they seek glory from men (1 Thes. 2:5-7). They did not speak from their own AUTHORITY nor seek their own glory (Jn. 7:15-19).

Having accountability to someone else can mean that a person is responsible to another for the performance of tasks assigned. Was it completed on time? Satisfactorily finished?

Correct leadership is vital in this era of the church. God's intention is for us to be diverse parts of the whole, which is greater than the sum of its parts (synergy). WE ARE NOT SUPPOSED TO BE THE SAME. It is the CORPORATE ANOINTING that rests upon the DIVERSITY OF THE NEW MAN – the Body, the Church.

Yet, we still need leadership. Imagine an orchestra insisting upon playing without a conductor. Why, the very word *unity* means symphony! We play the same song at the same time. We sing the same rhythm and syncopate together for the best overall effect. There is a focus on making music together. The goal of the group supersedes our personal agenda. We need to play different instruments with competence. There's no harmony if everyone is on the same note! Someone needs to write the music, compose the chart, and direct it.

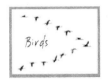

Migrating birds stay within their flock. They don't have to learn why it is best to follow the leader! They don't fly from flock to flock. Birds of a feather do flock together - they belong somewhere. They accept leadership from the one leading.

The Lord sets each one of us into the body "Just as He pleased" (1 Cor. 12:18). There are diversities of gifts that are all manifestations of the same Spirit (12:7). Paul says that the offices of the church function like body parts – demanding that they function in mutual responsibility, mutual dependence, and mutual respect and care (organic unity).

"If we have no peace, it is because we have forgotten that we belong to each other." Mother Teresa

We cooperate with other leaders because it is ordained of God that we profit from their guidance and leadership. Every believer, regardless of how much learning, qualifications, diplomas, or stature, NEEDS to relate to someone else as a leader. Since we have the choice to select which leaders will be involved in our lives... we better do it carefully, because we have a reciprocal obligation:

- Follow their example (Jn. 10:3).
- Appreciate them (1Thes. 5:12).
- Do not despise them for their limitations (1 Tim. 4:12). Don't criticize them or side against them (1 Tim. 5:1; 19-20). See beyond the individual personalities and into God's purposes.
- Esteem (honor, value) them (1 Thes. 5:13; 1 Tim. 5:17-18).
- Yield yourself to their guidance (Heb. 13:17).
- Financially support them (1 Cor. 9:11-14; Gal. 6:6).
- Pray for them (Heb. 13:7; 1 Thes. 5:25; Heb. 13:18-19).

Successful believers allow "sovereignly selected authority" to hold them accountable.

Only through respecting your relational lines of authority will you be brought to your full destiny.

The church needs dedicated leaders – both men and women of all races – who are able to COMMUNICATE quickened insight. Leaders should ready themselves to train their students to exceed what they have accomplished.

TRUE AUTHORITY ALLOWS FOR CORRECTION. The chosen LEADERSHIP should give redirections (corrections – guarding) when a disagreement occurs, and correction when serious repercussions could affect others in the flock. If an incident could

*True
authority
perpetuates
growing life
to all who
embrace it.*

negatively affect the Body, a leader should re-direct the members (with correction, instruction, direction, and advise that will guard the flock).

Each and every decision a LEADER makes may not personally please everyone. But decisions should manifest the expression and formation of Christ and allow a unified congregation to apprehend personal vision and direction for their own lives and interpret it in reference to the prophetic vision of the house. Apostolic *authority* promotes order in society (Lk. 22:26-27).

 The Lord calls us to participate in a local Body in accountable ways. As individual priests and kings, we CHOOSE to allow certain delegated people to have *authority* over the running of the church. Just as we carefully search to find the best dentist, lawyer, and veterinarian, we should search to find true and Godly LEADERS who offer us the chance to be mentored into maturity – and accountability. We must allow our leaders to equip us and enable our spiritual giftings and provide what's necessary for us to become fully functional (Eph.4:11-16).

Finding the right leader and allowing this positional alignment with leadership *authority* will release an even greater freedom to collaborate and work together. The church doesn't need rebels, but a cooperating team.

 A believer's eternal life may depend upon making the correct decision about those who should lead them. Most underestimate the enormity of choosing the right leader.

The way to determine who should become your spiritual leader(s) is to hear from the Lord, analyze the message they bring, and examine the life that they lead.

SOME PEOPLE ARE CALLED TO LEAD THE CHURCH.

Acts 6:2 shows us a distinctive separation: "And the twelve called together the whole community of the disciples and said, 'It is not right that we should neglect the word of God in order to wait (minister) at tables.'" It's not that they wouldn't wait tables – there just were so many things to do, and there needs to be delegation of jobs according to gifting, calling, and experience.

In Acts 13:2 we read about how the Holy Spirit spoke saying, "Set apart for Me Barnabas and Saul for the work that I have called them." There is a "setting apart" that raises leaders to a different standard of accountability. This does not diminish the position of those that follow.

The word RULE (NT:4291 *proistemi*) means to preside (1 Tim 5:17; 1 Thes. 5:12; 1 Tim 3:4, 12), to be a protector or guardian; to give aid... (Rom. 12:8), to care for, give attention to (Titus 3:8, 14).

- Sheep need a shepherd (Mat. 9:36). Shepherds are given the love of God for a specific group of people to whom they are called. God's heart in us empowers us to love.
- Respect which recognizes true character and service of a leader is not the same as deferential partiality shown to persons of position or wealth (rich or poor).

"But MANY (not all) who are first will be last, and MANY who are last will be first (Matt. 19:30, NIV).

> Apostles travel with specific assignments of national importance.

We've all heard it said that the "day of the one-man show is over" – HOWEVER, Jesus is THE "ONE-MAN SHOW." And guess what? Paul was, too! Paul didn't sit around having little home meetings where everyone took turns sharing! Paul actually preached and taught them. Yes. and Paul specifically said that others should imitate him. It's not about everyone having an equal say. It's about each one fulfilling their destiny by operating in their diverse Gifts.

In Paul's epistles, he mentions and favorably acknowledges several of his friends without even pretending to give equal praise to everyone. Didn't he realize how much he was catering to the pride of those he mentioned and causing resentment in those he failed to mention?

Paul recognized believers who led according to their talents.

Scripturally, leaders are given the responsi-bility of leading and guarding the flock.

FITTING TOGETHER

> When we dare to treat others with respect, our own self-respect will increase.

We should desire God's plan to be fully released in us individually and collectively. How SHOULD we FIT together? How can we respect others and value their roles in our lives?

Tim Early explains: "So, while we are all brothers on a horizontal plane, with Jesus Christ as the Head of every man, nevertheless, THERE ARE THOSE AMONG US WHO ARE WORTHY OF DOUBLE HONOR. THEY DESERVE OUR RESPECT for who they are in Christ and in our lives. We are to obey (outward actions) and be submissive (inward attitudes) to them and to their legitimate, delegated spiritual *authority*."

There are leaders in many realms of society. However, there is a difference. Bottom line: There are those who fully serve with authority as ecclesial ministers and there are those who minister in secular positions.

There's an Ecclesial leader (who oversees churches) and a Marketplace leader (who influences the business world). It is the job of Ecumenical leaders to have the *authority* from God to perform, officiate, or administer various religious rites (marriage, funerals, communion, etc.). These two realms should be complimentary and not striving for position. Furthermore, they are **NOT** generally **THE SAME**.

Not everyone is suited for Ecclesial leadership – it demands exceptional patience, kindness, self-sacrifice, and dedication to serve in this capacity. Bishop Joseph Mattera aptly points this out on his blog:

> "A proper understanding of the jurisdictions should help bring clarity in regards to this issue." He explains further that "The ecclesial realm is the lead agent in the kingdom and influences all the other realms... This ecclesial realm equips the saints to fill the earth and take the lead in every jurisdiction of the earth."

> "Marketplace ministers may function as apostles and prophets in their respective realms, but are not necessarily ecclesiastical apostles... Some people have hyphenated callings (are able to function as both, such as Daniel or Nehemiah... However, most people excel in either one or the other (realms)."

> *"An egalitarian idea (such as this) can divide the church, because many marketplace leaders are considering themselves as equal to ecclesial apostles and prophets... Even though a marketplace leader may be apostolic, there is no clear scriptural or historical precedent to give them the TITLE of apostle; thus they function apostolically but are not equal to ecclesiastical apostles in the kingdom mandate to disciple the nations... Although both ecclesial and marketplace ministers serve in distinct jurisdictions, both function together as part of the body of Christ in the multi-jurisdictional kingdom of God."* (Emphasis, parentheses remarks, and phrase selections are mine, printed with permission.) End.

Certainly, we realize that any rights we have to represent the "governmental authority of God here on earth" must be carefully handled. We are still trying to work out how to do that. However, it seems Biblically clear that God allows us to become under-shepherds and to minister WITH Him (the Great Shepherd). He allows us to replicate His ministry.

How Authority Works Through Elders

God's Authority is missing because

We have preferred GIFTS over AUTHORITY

Being "apostolic" implies governing with an apostolic mind-set.

The New Testament shows the plurality of CO-EQUAL Elders; they were called "brothers." However, that doesn't mean they were equal in *authority*! They were, however, equal in OFFICE in that all apostles were ELDERS. When Elders operate under the leading of the Holy Ghost, they complement each other to bring the fullness of the glory of the Lord Jesus Christ into the earth.

Many people have difficulty not swinging to extremes with these two truths. Co-equality of office does not negate having a "presiding elder" or "set-person" in place. There is equality in office (all being fellow-elders) but not necessarily in ability, spirituality, responsibility, metron of influence, or Grace Gifting. There are firsts among equals.

All members of the 5-fold ministry are ELDERS. APOSTLES ARE ELDERS who function with a particular AUTHORITY.

Each elder has a measure of rule (2 Cor. 10:12-18). No one can be the perfect choice for every situation to the exclusion of others. Maturity shows us that understanding our "measure of rule" protects us and brings perfect inter-dependence and order. The Lord has placed others in the Body whom you NEED to bring you further.

All the Five-Fold are ELDERS

All elders "shepherd the flock of God." This assignment doesn't change because of varying offices such as apostles, prophets, evangelists, pastors, and teachers (Acts 20:28, 1 Cor. 12:28). ALL THE 5-FOLD MINISTRY FUNCTIONS OUT OF THE OFFICE OF ELDER.

* In the New Testament, just being proficient in a Spiritual Gift doesn't imply that someone should be an "elder."
* The Lord governs through the chosen and qualified leaders that He selects for the task.

Apostles are elders. Peter called himself an elder (1 Peter 5:1-4). "To the elders (Strong's NT #4245 *presbuteros*) among you, I appeal as a FELLOW ELDER (sun-*presuterosa*) witness of Christ's sufferings and one who also will share in the glory to be revealed." Wow! The apostle Peter called himself a "fellow elder." Read it again! The person who by some is considered a primary leader in the church says that he is "sun-*presbuteros*." That's an amazing statement!

> *"Sun"* is a primary preposition denoting union; with or together by association, companionship, process, resemblance, possession, instrumentality, addition, etc. including completeness.

 ALL 5-FOLD MINISTERS ARE ELDERS. While all 5-fold are elders, their degree of influence may vary. All apostles are elders. However, the position of apostle (or prophet, etc.) does not necessarily describe RANK of IMPORTANCE but EMPHASIS and FUNCTION of Eldership.

BISHOPS ARE ELDERS

It is often taught that Bishops are a higher level of (hierarchical) ministry than elders. However both Peter and Paul mention these offices interchangeably. Peter says (1Pet. 5:2), "Be shepherds (*poimeino*, or FEEDER) of God's flock that is under your care, serving as overseers." (Overseer is *episkopeo* from EPI which means TOWARD OR AMONG and *skopos* meaning a watch (sentry or guard). *Episcopeo* can be defined as one who "looks carefully upon to contemplate." This word translated "bishop" and "overseer" (*episkopeo*) is another word for an elder who watches as a guard among the flock. He TENDS AND GUARDS the sheep!

> NOTE: Various forms of this word for "bishop" are used including *episkopeo, episkopeo,* and *episcopos*).

Peter continues (vs. 3), "Not because you must, but because you are willing, as God wants you to be; not greedy for money, but eager to serve; not Lording (NOT TO SUBJUGATE OR TAKE DOMINION) over those entrusted to you, but being examples [#5179 *tupos* (too'-pos)]; a stamp, a shape, a sampler ("a type") or a model (for imitation) A PATTERN OF GOOD WORKS!" In other words, a bishop (*episkopeo*) should serve as a model to shape character.

Renowned Bible scholar F.F. Bruce explains that the words translated "Bishop" (*episcopas*) and "Elder" (*presbuteros*) are interchangeable. He says, "the bishops were also called elders. The difference is in name only. Generally, the elder had a Jewish background, and the Bishop had a Gentile background."

Historian and Theologian Bishop Lightfoot says, "The fact is generally recognized by theologians... that the office called bishop is also called elder." Around the throne were twenty four *presbuteros*.

Many EArly Church Fathers agreed that there is a synonymous usage of the terms *episkopos* and *presbyteros* as referring to one and the same office (Titus 1:5, 7; Acts 20:17, 28; also see 1 Clemets. 441, 5; Jerome, Letter 59).

Paul also used the terms (elder and bishop) INTERCHANGEABLY. "The reason I left you in Crete was that you might straighten out what was left unfinished and appoint elders (NT #4245 *presbuteros*) in every town, as I directed you." An ELDER (this word *elder* is not in the original, it says "if any") must be blameless, the husband of but one wife (at a time), a man whose children believe and are not open to the charge of being wild... Since an OVERSEER (*episcopos*) is entrusted with God's work, he must be blameless – not overbearing, not quick-tempered, not given to drunkenness, not violent, not pursuing dishonest gain. Rather he must be hospitable, one who loves what is good, who is self-controlled, upright, holy and disciplined" (Titus 1:5-9 NIV).

- Early official Catholic doctrine teaches that after the first apostles died, that office went to those called "Bishops" (this process was called Apostolic Succession). St. Ignatius of Antioch claimed that he obtained his *authority to be a Bishop* "from God through Christ" (Letter to the Philadelphians, i).

"We must strive therefore in common to keep the faith which has come down to us today, through the Apostolic Succession." Pope Celestine [reign A.D. 422-432], To the Council of Ephesus, Epistle 18 (A.D. 431).

- Clement of Rome, in his Letter to the Church of Corinth (about 96 AD), defended the legitimacy of the ministry of bishops saying the first apostles established the next leaders as successors to govern the churches (xlii-xliv).
- By 180 AD we find only one "chief elder" or BISHOP for every church. By the end of the 2nd century, the "Bishop" was regarded as the only legitimate successor of the Apostles. By the third century the title "Archbishop" is used. This is of primary influence to the emergence of hierarchy in the pyramid type of church government.

THE JOB OF ELDERS

> **God's Authority is missing because**
>
> ## We have lacked job definition

There are several words used in the scripture to explain the word elder: *Zagen, siyb, episkopos, epesdopoa, supresbuteros, pressbuteros.* There's no record of the origin of elders, but in Acts this function was clearly understood by all. Their authority was enhanced because:

* Elders are ALWAYS PLURAL in number. Elders help carry the weight of the responsibility of leading God's people.
* Elders have specific function and responsibility that may differ.
* Elders were never elected; they were APPOINTED by the foundational ministries and other elders (Acts 20:28, 14:23).
* There is no reference to the length of an Elder's term in the Scripture.

The job of elders varies according to their individual assignment. The most important area of leadership of elders is that of hearing the voice of God and then correctly communicating what God has spoken to the right people. There is no value to hearing unless it is communicated and understood by the flock.

As examples to the flock, the Elders lead with diverse talents and gifts. Acts 20:28 states that the elders' FIRST CONCERN must be for themselves: "Take heed therefore unto yourselves and to all the flock..." (1 Tim. 4:16). Elders also:

* Ordain elders.
* Assist with the spiritual oversight and spiritual welfare of the church. The main function of the elders is that they RULE (*proistemi*, meaning to stand before, to preside, and to practice – as used in 1 Tim. 3:4,5,12, 5:17; Heb.13:7; I Thes. 5:12). They rule, lead, and manage. They tend and guard.
* Elders have the *authority* from God to LAY HANDS on the sick (Jam. 5:14, 15). (Believers are told to "*PRAY for the sick and they will recover.*") When elders lay hands, there is an impartation of *authority* of their OFFICE released to heal.
* Some of these elders functioned in pastoring (feeding, tending, and guarding the flock).

* Elders build the body. They guard the vision of the house rather than promoting their own personal ministry and agenda.
* They influence the Body by example (1 Pet. 5:3).
* Elders impact communities.
* Elders bring a ministry of reconciliation.
* Elders are ambassadors for Christ – which includes actual participation in Christ's ministry (2 Cor. 5:20).
* They preach the gospel and teach the Word.
* They worship (Rev. 4:10-11).
* They give care to "all the churches" (2 Cor. 11:28).
* They assist in decisions of business and practical concerns.
* Elders maintain respect, dignity and personal holiness.
* They can not be manipulated by others.
* Elders give sacrificial service to others (Lk. 14:25-33).
* An elder is confidential – never making a problem more public than it ought to be. There is a loneliness in keeping a confidence. God often calls leaders to keep confidential information in the best interest of others.
* Elders must be respectful and not degrading to others.
* They maintain a positive and professional attitude.
* They pray for the church and flock.
* They develop leadership and accountability in others. They learn the talents and gifts of the body and help develop them (Jn. 10:14).
* They bear burdens (Ex. 18:22, Gal. 6:5).
* They work hard (Phil. 2:30, 1 Tim. 3:1, 1 Thes. 5:13, 1 Cor. 3:13-15, Eph. 4:12, etc.).
* Elders serve (1 Pet. 5:1-3).
* Elders are loyal (Prov. 17:17), committed, and covenantal.
* They assume duties of correction. Elders should spot potential conflict situations. They can solve issues, disputes, and mediate all controversy for restoration and healing.
* They minister in their gifts and strengths.
* They encourage (Gal. 6:1-2, Phil. 2:25-27, 2 Tim. 1:2-4, etc.) and motivate.
* They listen and are teachable (Prov. 19:20). They give advise, solve problems, bring solutions. Problem solvers don't dwell on fault and blame – they spend energy on finding solutions.
* They promote evangelism.
* They pre-plan and anticipate.
* Elders share the vision of the house and can work in teams.

- They must know how to rule and lead and not "laud over" God's people with dominating tendencies (1 Peter 5:3).
- They have relational contact with the body.
- They provide support to the various functions of the church.
- They oversee all other departments; guiding, integrating and directing human efforts toward accomplishing specified tasks.
- Elders rule with dignity and authentic integrity.
- They are teachable and faithful.
- They lead the way with sacrificial service and liberal giving (2 Cor. 9:1-6).
- Elders don't find fault, murmur or dispute (Phil. 2:14-15). Elders should function as Aaron and Hur, who supported and held up Moses hands during war (Ex. 17:12), and not like Aaron and Miriam who murmured and accused him (Numb. 12:1-10). They should defend and guard the set leader and the corporate vision.

Elders often endure persecution and live as a "witness" (give their life) for the Gospel. Elders address church culture and penetrate the rigid social paradigms that incorrectly hold mind-sets in place.

An elder is worth double *honor* (this word means to be supported, i.e., especially by money, 1 Tim. 5:7); he is not to be rebuked, but to be entreated as a father. No accusation against an elder is to be received without two or three witnesses (1 Tim. 5:19). Otherwise it must not be believed.

ORDAINING LEADERS

MOSES SELECTED JOSHUA: GOD said to Moses, "Take Joshua–the Spirit is in him – and place your hand on him. Stand him before Eleazar the priest in front of the entire congregation and commission him with everyone watching. Pass (IMPART) your MAGISTERIAL *AUTHORITY* over to him so that the whole congregation of the People of Israel will listen obediently to him. He will command the People of Israel... Moses laid his hands on him and commissioned him, following the procedures (PATTERN) GOD had given" (Num. 27:18).

LAYING ON OF HANDS can impart greater authority.

"Encourage [Joshua], for he shall cause Israel to inherit (the land)" (Deut. 1:38). The chief leader provides encouragement that will "CAUSE" others to SUCCEED AND INHERIT THE PROMISES – even the ones we have not received.

"Now Joshua the son of Nun was filled with the spirit of wisdom, for (because) *Moses had laid his hands on him*..." (Deut 34:9). Impartation

of leadership is not from ritualized ceremonies but rather comes from close ASSOCIATION with those who can fully release potential. As Moses laid his hands on Joshua, he imparted God's "spirit of wisdom." Joshua was then able to lead the Israelites, AND it was his leading that caused them to inherit God's promises!

- Paul reminds Timothy of the unique gift of God that he received through the laying on of hands (1 Tim. 4:14, 5:22; 2 Tim. 1:6; Acts 6:6).

SELECTING LEADERS TO ORDAIN

 THE ELDERS OF THE EARLY CHURCH SET APART THE APOSTLES. Acts 6:6 – (the elders) "*prayed (making certain of their decision), they LAID HANDS on them* (apostles)" (NKJV).

 THE APOSTLES ORDAINED THE ELDERS. Some who performed specific responsibilities were not mentioned as being ordained as elders (Acts 6:8, 13:1, 15:30). We are not told that prophets or teachers were ordained; however, they were acknowledged as they fulfilled their positions.

> Ordination confirms what already exists.

As mere humans, we can lay hands on people all day long and sign documents and certificates galore... but unless the Holy Spirit comes, nothing happens. When apostles come into agreement with the will of God, they can set aside those elders who should be ordained through the power of spiritual impartation.

- "*Paul and Barnabas handpicked LEADERS in each church...*"(Acts 13:23, MSG).
- "*And when they (the apostles) had appointed and ordained elders (plural) in every church...*" (Acts 14:23)

Paul said that he was *ordained* a preacher and an apostle of the Gentiles (1 Tim. 2:7). Who ordained Paul? Jesus chose him on the road to Damascus (Acts 9:5). Paul said he was "an apostle of Jesus Christ by the will of God, to the saints" (Eph. 1:1; 1 Cor. 1:1).

 Ordination does not necessarily need to be a fancy formal ceremony – but a specific setting apart.

- The Body does not choose, vote for, or affirm elders. This is an important distinction from other jobs. ELDERS CHOOSE ELDERS. Elder selection must be by unanimity of eldership involved.

Those in recognized authority can give greater impartation.

- The elder's term of office is never restricted by time. This office may be for life or as long as this person is walking in oversight.
- Eldership is a delegated position of trust and should always remain accountable to other foundational and/or peer level apostolic ministries (Eph. 2:20).

"Don't appoint people to church LEADERSHIP positions too hastily. If a person is involved in some serious sins, you don't want to become an unwitting accomplice. In any event, keep a close check on yourself" (1 Tim. 5:22).

Hands should never be laid upon any man suddenly (1 Tim. 5:22).

QUALIFICATIONS FOR SUCCESSFUL APOSTOLIC LEADERS

"This is a true saying, if a person DESIRES the office of a bishop, they must desire a good work" (1 Tim. 3:1).

1. Paul tells us that the most imperative quality of leadership is *desire* (1 Tim. 3:1). Those who are successful in their assignment are motivated by a power of desire. In the Greek, the word *desire* is *"orgidzo"* and means craving, longing, urge, yearning to achieve something. Desire means that no matter what, they will continue with consistency and passion.

One of the greatest frustrations is trying to work with people who have great gifts but live in apathy. Apostolic leaders demonstrate the strong inward desire to lead, the desire to relate, the desire to be effective. Desire motivates action and gives fierce intention to go forward. Desire is responsive, concerned, and active.

2. Leaders must walk in integrity. The root of that word means wholeness and soundness (integer, whole). That means they are AUTHENTIC. Without being overly "religious" or pious, they demonstrate a life of actually being who they say.

Accompanying this God-given desire and integrity are the true values of: Maturity, Sonship, Character, Calling, Competencies, Loyalty, and Giving

3. MATURITY

"When I was a boy of fourteen, my father was so ignorant I could hardly stand to have the old man around. But when I got to be twenty-one, I was astonished at how much the old man had learned in seven years." Mark Twain

Adolescence is a time of rejecting *authority*. It is a SEASON of life where most question all rules and boundaries. Adolescence is when a lot of young people believe that they already know it all and strike out on their own searching for adventure and fulfillment. Their own CHOICE is primary.

As time goes on, there comes a time of realizing the consequences of their own choices. Decisions have to be made concerning the future. As the church emerges into this new DAY, we must decide if we are going to continue disastrously on this same course – or will we change the way we see the direction of the church, our self goals, and our reality of God's intended destiny?

My kids have *authority* in our house because they are part of my family. But, my neighbors' kids have no *authority* to walk around and use our things. When my kids were younger they had fewer freedoms than they do now.

We grow by caring about what God cares about.

Mature leaders maintain a perspective that there is something new to learn. Maturity is a SEASON of life. It is the SEASON of apprehending our inheritance. Paul discussed this connection between maturity and *authority*: "What I am saying is that AS LONG AS THE HEIR IS A CHILD, HE IS NO DIFFERENT FROM A SLAVE, ALTHOUGH HE OWNS THE WHOLE ESTATE" (Gal. 4:1).

Even though we are heirs to full inheritance, we do not have the AUTHORITY to receive it until we are grown. Our carnal programs won't work and we will become frustrated because we have failed to mature the saints (Eph. 4:11-15).

Maturity brings greater authority.

Many in ministry have a dichotomist's view of human nature – putting great value on the spirit and little on the soul. This is a convenient escape for allowing moral latitude. They call it venial "sins of the flesh" rather than the unacceptable "sins of the spirit."

One who desires true spiritual maturity and authority values the whole person (spirit, body, and soul). There is a definitive restraint and balance in the life of one exhibiting TRUE spiritual AUTHORITY.

What could be more exciting than to come to this new time in the era of the church? To realize that we as leaders are the first of a new breed. We have the opportunity to solve the problems of the past adolescent church and bring it to full maturity. We must face the reality of current conditions, see the crisis of our own making and put our differences and imperfections to creative use. We must not give up. We must face our foolish pride, adopt humility, gain a wider perspective, and progress with divine answers.

4. SONSHIP:

"*You received the Spirit of sonship*" (Rom. 8:13-14).

True leaders do not keep their followers dependent upon them for every need but rather mature the flock by teaching them how to Biblically

Maturity comes by exercising our authority over that which we have responsible stewardship.

solve their own problems. Maturity removes the cloak of childhood and enables mature SONS to receive the signet ring of their Father (Lk. 15:13). Grown SONS represent the Lord.

"I became your father through the gospel. Therefore, I urge you to imitate me" **(1 Cor. 4:14-16).**

Right now, at this urgent hour, the TRUE SONS OF GOD must be poised to manifest. Jesus brought many sons to glory (Heb. 2:10). With that in mind, apostles must bring forth the MAN CHILD. And, they must maintain **THE ABILITY TO REPRODUCE GROWN-UP SONS.**

* The apostle Paul spoke of "pressing on" to full maturity in the faith (Phil. 3:12-14), and not remaining as "infants, tossed back and forth" by the waves of life (Eph. 4:14). Because God values all of our parts equally, He gives us leaders so that this kind of growth can and will take place.

* At age seventeen, David killed Goliath, but he wasn't king until he was thirty-eight.

Maturity has to do with making decisions. Maturity deals with relating properly to others – which includes understanding how to honor and respect those in *authority*, civil, parental, employer, or spiritual.

> Maturity is the ability to live peaceably in unresolved conflict.

Maturity is the ability to control anger and settle differences without violence or destruction. Maturity is the patient willingness to pass up immediate pleasure for the long-term goal. Maturity is perseverance in spite of heavy opposition and set-backs. Maturity is the capacity to face unpleasant circumstances without complaint or collapse. It is not angrily impulsive. Maturity can say "I was wrong." And, when right, does not need to say, "I told you so." Mature people make decisions and stand by them. They keep their word. They are dependable and responsible. They do not give excuses. They are covenantal.

 Leading others into maturity and ownership of their responsibilities is the key to success.

"With eyes wide open to the mercies of God, I beg you, my brothers, as an act of intelligent worship, to give him your bodies, as a living sacrifice... let God re-mold your minds from within, so that you may prove in practice that the plan of God for you is good, meets all his demands and moves towards the goal of true MATURITY."
(Rom. 12:1-2 AMP)

5. CHARACTER

The strength of leadership is not gifting but character.

"But there are preconditions: A LEADER must be well-thought-of, committed to his wife, cool and collected, accessible, and hospitable. He must know what he's talking about..." (1 Tim. 3:2, MSG).

The Greek word for character is *charakter* and can be translated as "imagine." It comes from *charasso*, which means a notch, indentation, or writing on stone. Later, it meant to be embossed with a stamp. Character is the impressed mark upon an individual. Their inner and outer thoughts. Their home life and their public life. Their behavior in every situation.

The integrity and authenticity of a person is demonstrated in character.

"Impartation does not come from the Gift but through the character. Character gives credibility to the gifting." Dr. J.A. Tetsola

Character is the inner person and motivation of integrity and God-like characteristics. It is not a job to do but it is the value of life to be lived out. Character is the basic qualification for elders (1 Tim. 3:1-7; Tit. 1:6-9); spiritual gifts were not mentioned as required. Character also involves the quality of their personal lives, hospitality, and the maturity of their doctrine. Their nature is spiritual in love, prayer, and holiness.

6. Our CALLING is to know God's purposes. COMPETENCY means that the leader has the necessary gifts, proficiency, and expertise to lead the flock of God to the achievement of His intentions.

Elders should have exemplary character, cannot be novices, and must have a proven calling in one or more of the five-fold ministries.

 If a leader is not trained to walk in the spirit, it cannot be expected that those who follow will do it either.

The change needed in the church can easily be discerned. The New Testament emphasizes the character (fruit) of someone – rather than just their GIFT. The church-universe no longer rotates around the "GIFT" or a great personality! (1 Cor. 14:8)

Leaders must have maturity, responsibility, and integrity BEFORE selecting them as an elder.

"The time is always right to do what is right." – Martin Luther King, Jr.

Gifts must never be elevated above offices.

"If I take care of my character, my reputation will take care of itself." D. L. Moody

Paul says that the genuineness of the apostle must hold up to the inspection of the consciences of others. An apostle should deal with continual character examination (2 Cor. 4:2).

1 Timothy 3:2-3 and Titus 1:7, 3:8 tell us about an integrity "above reproach." The Amplified translation says there "is not ground for accusation." Leaders are of good reputation. They are temperate, free from extreme ideas, fair, respectable, hospitable, and not self-willed. Not quick-tempered or contentious. Capable of governing themselves. Not contentious. Peaceable. Gentle. Free from the love of money. They rule (manage) their house well. Love good. Promote virtue. Just. Devout. Not a novice. Not double tongued (1 Tim. 3:8).

Apostles do not tolerate deceiving actions of independence that disrespect God's righteous expectations.

True apostles give up on the hidden dishonesty and things that could disgrace the gospel or other apostles. They aren't crafty. They don't change or alter the Word of God to cause it to say what they want it to say – or to cause it to bring base gain. But, they manifest truth in accuracy and uprightness in their lives; they present themselves to every man's conscience before the sight of God (2 Cor. 4:2)

Elders must exhibit transformed lives. Gifts are given (the seed is in us when we are born) but fruit of character grows over time. Growth takes time. Many people have great abilities but no fruit (Mat. 7:21-23).

Apostolic leaders are clothed with humility. They are not given to self-glorification or desire pre-eminence (1 Cor. 4:9; Jn. 5:44; 3 Jn. 9, 10). Peter Wagner points out that Apostles exemplify extraordinary character (1 Tim. 3:1-7), Humility (1 Cor. 12:28), leadership *authority*, integrity (1 Tim. 3:2), wisdom, and a disciplined and effective prayer life (Acts 6:4).

"Reputation is what the world thinks a man is; character is what he really is." Anonymous

God places more emphasis on character and integrity than personality. No degree of education makes a person effective without character. The character qualifications of I Timothy 3:2 and Titus 1:6 are to be acquired by those in leadership.

Elders are to be held to the highest standard of accountability and receive greater judgment for failure to properly execute their responsibilities (Jms. 3:1; Heb. 13:7).

"It's important that a church LEADER, responsible for the affairs in God's house, be looked up to–not pushy, not short-tempered, not a drunk, not a bully, not money-hungry" (Tit. 1:7, MSG).

"An intemperate LEADER wreaks havoc in lives; you're smart to stay clear of someone like that" (Prov. 16:14, MSG).

"Mean-tempered LEADERS are like mad dogs..." (Prov. 19:12a, MSG). They are personified by patient endurance (2 Cor. 12:12).

"Quick-tempered LEADERS are like mad dogs– cross them and they bite your head off" (Prov. 20:2, MSG).

"Good-tempered LEADERS invigorate lives; they're like spring rain and sunshine" (Prov. 16:15, MSG).

"The good-natured are like fresh morning dew" (Prov. 19b, MSG).

 Stability, faithfulness, loyalty, integrity, servanthood, and availability are all far more important than ability.

CALLING

6. CALLING: Paul describes his calling here in Galatians 1:13-16, "For you have heard of my former conduct in Judaism, how I persecuted the church of God beyond measure and [tried to] destroy it.... But it pleased God, who SEPARATED ME from my mother's womb and CALLED [ME] through His grace, to REVEAL HIS SON IN ME, THAT I MIGHT PREACH HIM among the Gentiles... "

EVERYONE IS CALLED to serve God with their whole mind and heart. Notice in the above verse that it does "please God" to separate *some* and truly call them to preach. That particular calling doesn't make anyone better than anyone else. The Lord works with everyone. However, as in the above example of Paul, there is a separating out of SOME people who are particularly assigned to specific tasks.

The call isn't necessarily to the naturally strong, intelligent, nice, rich, or handsome. Generally, it is to those who appear least likely (1 Cor. 1:26).

COMPETENCY

7. COMPETENCY: In spite of our individual faults, the Holy Spirit made distinctions concerning the gifting that we hold. We are given Gifts depending upon the Sovereign will of God. The fullness of that Gift depends upon our cooperation with being "LIKE CHRIST." Our competency depends on experience by being trained and mentored until skill is developed.

 One does not have authority if there is no ability in that area. Ability and competency can be part of a determination for function!

LOYALTY

8. LOYALTY: Paul instructed Timothy to disciple faithful men. That means, we take our time and prayerfully look for faithfulness beyond giftedness. To be faithful means to be dependable, loyal, and stable.

THE LOYALTY OF AMASAI: David didn't recruit people, but, there were many who gathered around him. He always knew to check their motives. He asked, "Why are you here?" AMASAI answered, "We are yours, we want to serve you because the Lord is with you" (1 Chron. 12:16-18). Those desiring to team up with a leader should recognize the spiritual *connection* and together they should both make a joint *decision* for commitment.

Set-leaders should not have to keep affirming, "God is with me – so be faithful to me!" Loyalty and commitment should be the automatic response of the team to the set person.

 Set-leaders must develop a spiritual strategy to determine the true motives of those who serve on a team with them.

Set-leaders should have LOYAL leaders in their INNER CIRCLE.

1. These are the ones who really "know" their leader.

2. These are the ones the set-leader can trust with confidential information.

3. The inner circle are the closest SONS – not just associates.

Loyalty is faithfulness to a cause. It is displayed by personal sacrificial commitment to a relationship and/or the vision, not just longevity of service. Jesus described loyalty when he said, "No one can serve two masters. Either he will hate the one and love the other... (Mat. 6:24). Trying to serve two masters (or visions) is "double-mindedness" (Jms. 4:8), which will undermine the cause of loyalty.

Ministry must be more than just a job. To gain loyalty, experience with you must be a rewarding life where people are naturally motivated and inspired. They need to be encouraged to view necessary but more tedious assignments of their job in the context of the bigger picture.

> Sincere encouragement impacts!

Know them and treat them as individuals. Connect with them personally. Relate to them beyond the surface. Connect for the long term.

Grow SONS in-house. Build time for deep instruction. Have a meaningful open door policy with them.

Allow them to communicate their ideas for team success – and promote team unity. Be genuinely open to their new ideas.

Make appraisals meaningful. Cause their failures to become a wonderful learning experience. Learn what to do better.

Build trust. Merge your expectations with reality – tell them you care.

Leadership teams need to be involved and empowered to do good. Develop and communicate your visionary philosophies. Then offer teams a challenge of opportunities where they can participate and be recognized in those efforts. Invest in their developmental training. **The more they understand, the more improved their performance becomes.**

Pay them as well as possible. You can't buy loyalty – but if you don't pay them what they are worth, you can destroy loyalty ties. Also be verbal in giving appreciative praise.

GIVING

9. GIVING: Any leader should lead in their financial commitment to the principles of giving. Financial accountability is an obedience of grace. There is a place of generosity and abundance where believers are destined to live.

We look to ordain servant people who are dependable, courageous, genuine, truthful, walk in favor, hard working, and committed to the long haul.

SUMMARY:

Leaders exist to serve the people; they do not exist for themselves.

Godly leadership
MODELS a
lifestyle
that should be
reproduced.

True leaders have a passion to assemble the Bride into that living, breathing organism with members connected to function as collaborative enterprise.

Recognizing the Priesthood of ALL believers allows the chosen "leader" to make competent decisions that bring release to those who agree to be led.

Scriptures distinctly differentiate between the essential need for ecclesiastical governmental *authority* and the unnecessary need for compliance to unjust tradition. It's time to grab hold of your promised freedom-in-Christ; but, it's a liberty not rooted in the expense of order and discipline. Godly freedom maintains synchronization with Bible facts. Jesus already paid the highest ransom for your freedom. No one should accept the bondage of CONTROL from another person.

Leadership
is
still in!

It's not the saints that are supposed to take over the *running* of the church. Saints are supposed to take over the world! The leadership of the church stays in tact with the 5-fold "UNTIL" (Eph. 4:11). That *until* hasn't happened yet. We haven't yet come to maturity of the faith or the stature of the perfect man.

True leadership leads people to spiritual adulthood.

There are 24 "elders" around the throne mentioned in the Book of Revelation. Remember, leadership remains until the end!

The necessity of leadership authority exists in order to help groups successfully move forward and accomplish greatness. Jeremiah 10:23 says that the "way of man is not in himself." We're fallible. Our thoughts are not His thoughts (Is. 55:8). The wise man reminded, "There is a way that seems right unto a man; But the end thereof are the ways of death" (Prov. 14:12). Personal opinions often vary too much to give us strong direction. Modern day apostles and prophets are supposed to build up the Lord's house and establish it upon a proper foundation of Present Truth (2 Pet. 1:12).

"The function of leadership is to produce more leaders, not more followers." – Ralph Nader

Each of us is a uniquely created facet of God's image. None of us are the same. That's why we merge together – for mutual benefit.

1. Each function and talent differs from another (Eph. 4:7, 13, 16). Therefore, each leader is supposed to differ in abilities and gifts.

2. Diversity of gifts allows ministers to impact the whole Body.

3. Differences allow us to form a corporate infrastructure and genuine need for one another rather than superiority. Differences create an interconnection and interdependence reflecting ONE intention.

4. Some people are chosen to lead in the Ecclesia.

5. Respect is to be shown to Christian leaders (1 Thes. 5:12). God is no respecter of persons AND He tells us to respect our leaders.

"I have a special concern for you church LEADERS. I know what it's like to be a leader, in on Christ's sufferings as well as the coming glory" (1 Pet. 5:1, MSG).

 Each individual has something valuably important to offer (Eph. 5:19-20) and true leaders search for ways to include them.

 Great leaders maintain healthy relationships with those they lead. They must perceive the abilities and potential of others while also recognizing their limitations.

Church isn't supposed to be just a place or a meeting packed with superficial and cliché-bound phrases of a spitting, shouting preacher. Nor is it a place where believers go to live their vicarious lives through a great speaker.

Real church is a life lived *together* (the called out ones) with the Lord.

There are called out leaders who are chosen to motivate, give direction, and encourage.

Certainly there should be many meetings centering on worship and small group involvement. But, that's not all! There needs to be general vision and a leader to train believers to "do the work" of the ministry.

SECTION 4

Teams and The Principle Of Migration.

How Elders Operate in Teams.

Set Leaders

Why Birds Migrate Together

God's Authority is missing because

We need to FORM stronger TEAMS

"Cranes (storks) know when it's time to move south for winter. And... when it's time to come back again. But my people? My people know nothing, not the first thing of GOD and his rule." (Jer. 8:7, MSG)

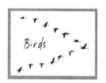

We are looking at birds to learn more about progressing together as a leadership team. It is fascinating to discover HOW HIGH BIRDS FLY! Pilots have reported seeing birds as high as 26,000 feet! That's over five miles high! Some species can fly higher than Mt. Everest. Some geese have been recorded flying across the Himalayas at 29,000 feet. The swan has been seen above 20,000 feet.

Moving toward destiny takes us to HIGHER heights and awareness in the Spirit. And, it includes everyone in our company who has aligned with us. A group that moves together discovers a momentum that causes acceleration of everyone from level to level, from glory to glory. When we come into flight order, rightful cooperation with God's ordered position for our lives, our altitude and distance of flight increases.

There is a pressing need for restructuring and reordering which can only be accomplished by the migration of the church mind-set into this new *kairos* time. In order for the church to migrate, we must know why and when. The primary advantage of migration is energetic. The main reasons for bird migration are: 1. To reproduce, 2. Need of food, 3. Weather, 4. Space. LEADERS NEED TO MIGRATE FOR THE SAME REASONS:

TO REPRODUCE:

"There is no more noble occupation in the world than to assist another human being and help them succeed." Alan Loy McGinnis

Birds build nests and lay eggs. Then the tedious time of incubation begins. Each egg must be turned regularly, allowing every part of the egg's surface to contact the parent's bare skin (called the 'brood patch') that contains the warm blood vessels. The hatched chick demands warmth and continuous feeding.

We must reproduce ourselves and bring SONS into leadership abilities. Only then, can we impact nations.

We must reproduce SONS! The most important thing apostolic leaders can do is to reproduce themselves and nourish their spiritual children. It's interesting that the first migrating bird mentioned by our text scripture is THE STORK: The sighting of storks has long been linked in legends about REPRODUCTION.

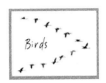

The legend that the stork brings babies probably originated in northern Europe, perhaps because storks arrive on their breeding grounds in Poland and Germany nine months after midsummer. One of the first legends began as a famous Urkish folktale which told about a huge stone a few miles from their shore. This stone was called the *"Ommelebommelestien"* (Ommel Bommel Stone). It was from there that the stork obtained the babies.

For centuries, storks have migrated in a direct path over the Holy Land. There have always been many stories about flying stork carrying a little "bundle of joy" to new parents. Storks were considered "good luck" and encouraged to nest on people's housetops in the hope that they would bring fertility and prosperity. The stork was a widespread symbol of expecting children.

> Migrators are pioneers of change.

Storks are *altricial* (which means that the children require that the parents care for them). Both stork parents busily fly back and forth to feed them food. They can eat up to 60 percent of their own body weight per day to feed their young.

Leaders need to reproduce SONS. Apostolic leaders raise GROWN-UP SONS.

TO FIND FOOD: Pioneering leaders must migrate to places with fresh and abundant food and nourishment. We must have fresh revelation beyond the rigid definement of the past. There's nourishment available in the new pasture lands of God's provision. Leaders need to feed their SONS the optimum food.

"(God) *teaches more to us than to the beasts of the earth, and makes us wiser than the birds of the air.*" (Elihu, Job 35:11)

TO FIND GOOD WEATHER: Birds migrate BEFORE winter looking for good weather and lots of food. As days shorten, food becomes more scarce and birds move to warmer regions and available food supplies. We must keep ourselves in the most conducive climates to reproduce ourselves.

Leaders must prepare the best environment for their SONS. TO HAVE MORE SPACE: Birds journey to find space and FREEDOM.

"*I will take refuge under the shadow of Your wings*" (Is. 34:15; Ps. 63:7, 61:4, 57:1, 17:8, 36:7; Ruth 2:2; Mat. 23:37; Lk. 13:34).

"Let birds fly above the earth and across the expanse of sky. So the Lord God created... every winged bird according to its kind. And God saw that it was good (Gen. 1:20, 21).

BIRDS OF A FEATHER FLOCK TOGETHER

"TWO ARE BETTER THAN ONE... a threefold cord is not quickly broken" (Ecc. 4:9-12).

From the beginning, God set out to authorize His decreed eternal plan for Kingdom co-regency on this earth. We (the body corporate) are a Kingdom of priests (1 Peter 2:4-5). Together we are a company of royal priests moving as one. We can function together without jealousy and contention because we are assured of our position with God as a unanimous priesthood of royal believers.

70% easier

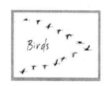

The benefit of teams can be seen by observing how each beat of that bird's wings downward, forces air off the wing tip making the flight of those behind 70% easier. Each forward bird consecutively adds to the lift that assists the weaker birds in the center.

The "V" migration flight pattern resembles the strategy used in a bicycle race: one bird rotates back into the formation, and another more aggressive bird flies to the point position. It is a FORM-ation.

LEAD BIRDS CHANGE position often, not because of social orders, but because of fatigue from leading. The changing position distributes the effort and demand of leading.

A bird flying by itself has to work a lot harder than in a flock. Likewise, a one-person ministry is limited. A team (formation) creates a FORCE of unity and oneness that accomplishes a goal together.

ONENESS in Scripture

Leaders should inspire teams to work together as ONE NEW MAN (Eph. 2:15). The Scriptures often refer to a multiple oneness. Genesis 1:26-27 shows us this unified singularity, "Let US make man in OUR image, after OUR likeness." Elohim (God's title) speaks to the plurality of the Trinity which exists as ONE.

* "The Hebrew nouns "image" and "likeness" are singular displaying what we might call a unity-in-plurality.
* God refers to Himself (PLURAL) in the personal singular pronouns "My."
* The Body is the Many-membered Bride, the Manchild, and the "Sons of God."

The corporate anointing of apostolic TEAMS accomplishes much.

To better understand teams and corporate unity, let's look at the principle of *echad*. *Echad* is a compound-unity Hebrew noun which demonstrates oneness or unity while containing several entities at the same time. The plural ONE (*echad*) demonstrates plurality within oneness. This is KINGDOM UNITY.

Genesis 1:5 speaks of the first day as *echad*. The one-day, both light and darkness – evening and day. ONE DAY has two PARTS.

> Genesis 2:24 uses the word *echad* and we translate it as "one flesh." One man plus one woman equals ONE FLESH.

> Ezra 2:64 refers to the "whole congregation" as *echad*.

> Jeremiah 32:38 calls the entire nation of Israelites into "one heart" (*echad*). That's ONE congregation of 42,360 Israelites.

> Numbers 13:23 describes ONE (*echad*) in a cluster of grapes (pl).

> The leadership we need arises from within the FORM-ation of the corporate MAN (Eph. 2:15) – within the team.

This multiplicity in oneness is common in our thinking. One family. One church. It is "OUR Father who art in heaven," not just mine. It is Christ in "you" (pl., collectively) that is the hope of Glory.

No one needs just "yes" people around them.

Wise leaders surround themselves with other strong leaders who are not afraid to fully respond in Godly strength and speak Truth together. A plurality of elders can work as one. The interdependence of five-fold ministries brings credibility and safety.

ELDERS SHOULD OPERATE IN TEAMS

Re-FORM-ation brings us into precise alignment of the rule and reign of Christ. When the early church was formed, the only offices mentioned were the ELDERS and the DEACONS. Elders were appointed by apostles and were given responsibility of churches.

Each Elder had their area of responsibility as it related to the overall purpose. The diagram may help us see that relational sense of the function of plurality in the

91

local church. With this PATTERN, there is no reason for jealousy or vying for position. We each have our distinctive purposes focusing on the centrality of the Lord and, by that focus on the Lord, we form a cohesive unit together.

The New Testament PATTERN generally shows that multiple elders lead the churches. (Not a single pastor as is common today.)

Not all modern-day local church elders are necessarily a five-fold gifting. Some local elders may be administrative, helps, etc. But, all the five-fold ministries are by definition elders.

Right relationship of the five-fold ministry team is the KEY in leading.

This plurality does not necessarily mean that all function at the same level of responsibility or influence, or are due the same honor (I Tim. 5:17).

For co-equality and set-leadership to work inside plurality there must be proper relationship and distinctive function established by the set-person.

- ELDERS are given a measure of RULE in and toward the Body of Christ. Of course, some elder/leaders are given more authority than others.
- Multiple eldership leading a church affords the opportunity and gives *authority* (to each one) to speak into the other.
- A Divine Grace is given to multiple eldership which allows them to symbiotically function together. (A symbiotic relationship is when two separate organisms or people "work together," each benefiting from the relationship.)
- Each elder must have a personal spiritual relationship with the Lord and be secure in their own destiny. Competitiveness must yield to loyalty and commitment.
- Each elder must have and maintain intimate fellowship and unity with one other (Ps. 133).
- They must accept the safety of being in the (*echad*) cluster (Is. 65:8) and be joined in the Spirit (Num. 18).
- They must be submissive to one another (1 Pet. 5:1-3).
- They do not try to draw believers after themselves (Acts 20:28-36).

The PLURALITY ELDERS is Scriptural government form. Biblical history shows that early churches were under the direction of multiple leadership (plurality or presbytery), and never just one person.

- In Lystra, Iconium and Antioch "Paul and Barnabus... ordained elders (plural) in EVERY church" (Acts 14:23).

- Acts 17 shows a plurality of ELDERS leading after the apostles leave.
- During the famine in Antioch, the Judean church sent a letter addressed "to the ELDERS" (plural) (Acts 11:30).
- A plurality of elders served in the Ephesian church where Paul labored for three years. "He sent to Ephesus and called the elders of the church" (Acts 20:17).
- In Crete, the church had a plurality of elders (Titus 1:5), "For this cause I left you (Timothy) in Crete, that thou should set in order the things that are wanting, and ordain elders in every city as I had appointed you."
- Philippians 1:1 refers to multiple leaders – not just one.
- The rulers of the Hebrew church are multiple, "... Salute ALL THEM THAT HAVE RULE over you" (Heb. 13:24 NIV).
- 1 Peter 5:1, "The elders (plural) among you I exhort."

AUTHORITY OF TEAMS

No individual can fulfill Kingdom vision by himself.

Authority is released as the Set-person delegates elders and leaders to projects. This is a moveable "situational" management that can quickly change leaders and styles as changing situations demand. This multiple leadership style helps to develop SONS by introducing them to varying projects.

The set-leader remains in overall charge of direction and vision. The decentralization of singular leadership must not dilute the vision of the house.

In order to operate in *authority*, TEAMS must develop a positive and professional overall group style:

1. Strength of character interacting together.
2. Stability of mind and emotions.
3. Knowledge of Scripture.
4. Clarity of individual and TEAM vision.
5. Grace to accept and bear with the faults of others without pro-longed discouragement or rejection.
6. Urgency to build trust, cooperation, and understanding.
7. Vision to teach "plurality" as opposed to independence.
8. Ability to observe God mercifully operate in and through other imperfect vessels.

TEAM elders don't preach just to bring another message, but speak in unison with the mind of God bringing life and freedom to accomplish purpose and vision.

ESPRIT DE CORPS. Teams must be characterized by a connectivity that believes in one another. Even though they may not always agree, they respect one another and never allow themselves to become so familiar with the individual's humanity that could cause a loss of respect for one another (2 Cor. 5:16, Jn. 7:5, Mark 6:2-3). TEAMS should offset and cover one another's week spots and not discuss them with the non-TEAM members or the congregation. They should defend one another. Those that come to advance their own personal ambitions and promote themselves should be dismissed.

A leader may have done well in a previous position, but performance alone does not qualify him for a new responsibility in the TEAM.

When elders in a TEAM maintain and strengthen relationships, they are more able to "speak the truth in love." However, we must remember that HOW we say things is as important as WHAT we say. People are what we are about.

 LEADERS should represent, protect, and secure the vision of the house. They should defend the vision of the house and their TEAM TO THE CONGREGATION.

Their job is NOT to represent or defend the murmuring congregation to the leadership.

MULTIPLE ELDERSHIP

- A team of peers allows us to build the v-formation which spreads out the influence and vision of leadership. Leadership can see farther when spread out.
- Horizontal positioning allows more gift ministry to the Body.
- Horizontal eldership provides the capacity to stand with others of like mindedness.
- Ministry must be relational and based on function and not based on position. The power of institutionalism, traditions, and denominationalism must be broken and the Church must become relational.
- The danger of vertical elders is the tendency to be autocratic and hierarchical.
- Peer level elders should never be involved in a competitive posture. For integrity of the unit to be maintained, there should be no comparisons.
- A plurality of Elders hears from God the best. Believers can "defer" to them because they hear and defer to one another.
- Plurality demands that elders cooperate with others. There is no Lone ranger without Tonto. Batman still needs Robin. We need each other. I appeal to you, brothers... that all of you agree with one another so that there may be no divisions

among you and that you may be perfectly united in mind and thought (1 Cor. 1:10-11 NIV).

Leadership brings the efficiency necessary to accomplish a plan.

Although there is freedom within this group to disagree, there must ALWAYS be a united front presented before the congregation. Though differing opinion is encouraged, argumentativeness is discouraged. Disloyalty is betrayal. Decisions are made for the benefit of others according to the will of the Lord.

MULTIPLE ELDERSHIP TEAMS STRIVE TO preserve the unity of Spirit, one mind, one purpose, one voice and one judgment. They also:

* Develop intimate relationships with each other.
* Understand that safety is in one another.
* Know one another after the Spirit and be joined together.
* Maintain honesty, transparency and open communication.
* Develop a servant spirit.
* To edify one another rather than compete.
* Continue being loyal to one another and committed to God's vision.
* Are taught, reproved, corrected and trained by the Word.
* Are examples to one another.
* Have control of their tongues and words, they take heed to themselves in order to have the mind of Christ.

"Appreciate your pastoral LEADERS who gave you the Word of God. Take a good look at the way they live, and let their faithfulness instruct you, as well as their truthfulness. There should be a consistency that runs through us all" (Heb. 13:7, MSG).

TEAM & BIRD FORM-ATION

"I know all the birds of the air, and the creatures of the field are mine" (Ps. 50:11).

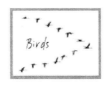

The V-formation of flight is an example of SITUATIONAL LEADERSHIP. Any bird following the leader bird experiences a 70% energy-savings from the slip-stream lift of their wake. Also, the leader bird experiences a lift from those directly at the apex of the V behind.

Saves 70% energy

A lazy bird who tries to tuck inside the V to save energy does nothing to enhance the flight efficiency of the flock. Migrating birds won't stand for malingerers delaying the flock – if they don't do their part, they won't be allowed to fly along.

We have seen through the study of migration, how the strongest bird rotates the lead. Leadership changes from time-to-time according to circumstances. We call this type of leadership "situational leadership." The set-leader determines who will lead a task at any given time.

Birds help us understand how Church government can be brought into proper formation – not a pyramid but a wedge moving forward. Differing teams in the church represent part of a whole.

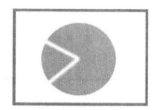

The grounding nature of the apostolic ministry is the ability to identify and release those who are qualified to lead in alternating positions.

Allows rest!

When the lead bird gets tired, it returns back inside the flock and allows another to take the lead. The problems that people have is generally we never want to back off and let someone else do something.

 All ministry gift offices (Eph. 4:11) should function so that the "work of the ministry" is not totally dependant on any one person.

We learn from birds ways to correctly align in FORM-ation and continuous re-FORM-ation. Leading isn't static. From observing this strategy of nature, we find that bird migration always happens in a rotating flock. In this FORM-ation, the bird who can do the best job at that time is given the leadership. That allows each individual bird to retain strength.

> You don't lose any authority by allowing others to lead along side. In fact, it makes you stronger.

Likewise No one person can do everything. Apostolic *leadership* determines who can lead effectively in certain areas.

"Anointing comes through impartation, and impartation through association." Pastor Frank O. Appiah

To have formation, we must have a reformation!

REFORMATION: What is it that we notice about the word "Reformation?" It is first, "re" or do again the "form" or the configuration of something. Re-FORM-ation realigns things into Divine Kingdom PATTERNS of order. Apostolic leaders forcefully move forward taking dominion of territories and false principalities. This is accomplished by dispossessing and dislodging that which opposes God's intentions.

Apostolic alignment into correct re-FORM-ation is one of the most powerful concepts we can gain. Correct alignment allows us to travel farther than ever before.

Some people lead some areas better than others. It does not threaten authority to allow others to take part in leading.

SITUATIONAL LEADERSHIP allows for others to come forward to solve certain problems. Some leaders are more effective in one situation but not in others. A co- divided management team allows for more equal division of work load – and much less burnout.

Situational leadership assumes that variable conditions require unique abilities that don't exist in a single leader. This re-FORM-ational model demands that leaders are skilled in a variety of ways.

EXAMPLE: Suppose this problem is given to a strong team of leaders: There's a lion loose downtown. Fortunately, we have a team of three very strong leaders. Daniel is on our team, and he says, "I'll have the Lord shut his mouth... then we'll have no more problems with that lion!"

Samson says, "I'll grab the jawbone of a donkey and whop on it!"

King David says, "I've killed many a lion and still have my slingshot. In fact, I never miss. And I can kill this lion too."

Now, which leader is right? Their purpose is the same – contain the lion! Each viewpoint is very valid and tried. Teams allow us to use individuality to capture this lion. We can pool our resources and decide which solution to choose: to have the Lord shut that lion's mouth, beat it with the jawbone, or kill it with the sling shot. Team leadership can access member's giftings and RELEASE PEOPLE IN THEIR UNIQUENESS in activities that maximize their gifts.

"It's all right to have butterflies in your stomach. Just get them to fly in formation." Dr. Rob Gilbert

Some examples of plural leadership might be:

1. VISIONARY LEADERS (motivators and vision casters). The set-leader is the main vision holder who communicates the vision to the other leaders so that everyone moves toward the same goal. Visionaries must consider situational variables – such as understanding the expectations of this particular "flock of birds" or people.

2. STRATEGIC LEADERS develop how to implement those communicated plans from the set-leader. This could be the methodology for a project.

For example, setting the objectives on how to arrive at the predetermined vision – like deciding on which "flyway" or best migration route this group needs to get to their destination. Considerations of how

> God's intention was never sigular leadership, "Let THEM rule over..." (Gen. 1:26) always was the plan.

Teamwork makes the yearly task of migration much easier.

97

to negotiate the impending difficulties (environment, weather, and/or culture in which task is to occur, etc.). These leaders could also determine the "followership" or measure how well that project is attended or supported.

3. **TEAM MOTIVATORS** are those who build the morale and encourage team activities. This could include the rallying together of those who were going on this particular flight (discipleship training, evangelism, team building, and etc.).

4. **ADMINISTRATIVE LEADERS** organize proper protocol to operate and administrate the church. For example they could detail the nature of the task and anticipate a measurable response from the followers.

- Tasks can be rotated depending on the capabilities of the diverse team leaders.
- Teamwork makes the task of migration much easier.
- Team leadership expects excellent character and performance not only of the set-leader but also of one other.

"Apostolic authority occurs when the behavior or conditions of an individual or group is favorably influenced." Daniel Simpson

Successful teamwork motivates, adapts, builds curiosity, encourages imaginative intuitiveness, and enables the ability to co-exist together. The ones who succeed are teachable and quickly adaptable.

WHY BIRDS FLY IN FLOCKS

"Can two walk together, unless they are agreed?" (Amos 3:3).

"WATCH THE BIRDS!" (Jesus, Mat. 6:26)

If migratory birds don't fly together, they will die.

Birds

Jesus told us to be bird-watchers! In Matthew 6:26, He said to behold them and observe them. The Greek verb used here means to fix your eyes on and watch their behavior intently. Watch them in the sky; they don't sow or reap or store food in barns. Yet, the Lord feeds them. Don't you know that you are worth more than the birds?... How small your faith is! (Mat. 6:26-30).

- Birds cooperate because it is in their best interest to do so. Teamwork works when the team has a common goal, incentive to work towards that common goal, and is "rewarded" for reaching these common goals.
- Migratory birds are NOT instructed on how to work together as a team; they instinctively function this way. Birds flying in formation take more efficient routes home than those flying alone.

Greater efficiency!

*Broader
perspective!*

- Flying with others in a V-formation provides a WIDER VIEW of difficulties that face the flock.
- Birds show deference. When one gets tired, there's another to help. If a goose is injured and unable to fly, two will go back and wait with the injured bird.

It is vital to have the lead bird fly in the "right direction."

MIGRATION requires less sleep: A newly published study by a University of Wisconsin research team studied how birds migrate every year on very little sleep. During times when these birds were not migrating, however, sleep deprivation impaired their performance. During "migrating" times, birds sleep about 1/3 as much as normal – and move more quickly into REM sleep (rapid eye movements).[1]

More alert!

When birds migrate, they have an IMPROVED ABILITY TO LEARN – on less sleep. Researchers do not know why migration works this way. So, my fellow traveler, WAKE UP! It's time to move! Feel the energy and anticipation of speeding together to a new destination! Migrations bring greater alertness and doesn't allow for apathy.

"The mark of a good LEADER (king, monarch, ruler) is loyal followers; leadership is nothing without a following" (Prov. 14:28).

EASE OF FLIGHT IS A MAJOR REASON WHY BIRDS KEEP IN A FLOCK. Ease-ability encourages the formation of one flock and allows a group of birds with differing abilities to fly together at a constant speed with a common endurance.

WHY DO WE CREATE A FLOCK or TRIBE?

Why do people come to church? What do they want? The answer is simple. The number one reason why people go to church is that they dream of a place to be ACCEPTED and BELONG.

> If we stay in formation and head the same direction, we will get where we're going! >

The significance of self is a universal need. People desire to be affirmed and recognized. They want to contribute into that belonging. Relationship is the number one reason that they come at all. Now hold on!... It's not because of your great preaching... it really isn't. People need to be validated.

1.http://www.sciencedaily.com/releases/2004/07/040714090317

True apostles have meaningful relationships. Paul loved people and longed to see them. "They all wept as they embraced him (Paul) and kissed him" knowing they would "never see his face again" (Acts 20:37-38). "Night and day we pray most earnestly that we may see you again and supply what is needed for your faith" (1 Thess. 3:10).

> Belonging matters!

We MUST learn what people want and need so that we impact them.

Believers want relationships, individualized placement, and identity within the community. They need purpose, love, and answers. They search for acceptance, hope, forgiveness, guidance, and encouragement. They need to be maximized, equipped, and developed in spiritual maturity. To function in *authority*, they need to belong to healthy FLOCKS.

"The Bible knows nothing of solitary religion. Christianity is a religion of fellowship." John Wesley

The main reason why people go to church is to belong and to HAVE VALUE. People MUST "feel" that they belong and that they are important to you and your vision. Flocks need leaders who give value, activate their potential, teach the truth, establish proper goals to develop them, know the Scriptures, have answers, and give LIFE.

"Do what you say you're going to do – what you say to others, and what you say to yourself. Offer value. Cultivate relationships. Do it especially when you don't want anything in return." Jeffrey Gitomer

People stay in FLOCKS at church for much the same reasons as birds stay in flocks - belonging. Ease of travel. When straggler birds break out of the V pattern, they immediately encounter increased air friction which demands increasing energy to sustain speed than it does when flying in the flock.

70% further!

The V system is self-stabilizing and enables the whole flock to fly 70% farther than an individual bird flying alone – using the SAME AMOUNT OF ENERGY. Even the strongest young birds know these advantages.

70% faster!

Flying together not only causes their flight to be 70% easier and faster, but extends the whole flock's flying range an additional 70%. That's why birds move into formations and take advantage of lifting power!

Individuals perform at optimum best in teams. Team output far exceeds the sum of its parts.

Why are birds able to know how to migrate and we don't? That was what Jeremiah wanted to know! The answer begins with teams

leading – that's THE RIGHT WAY TO DO THINGS. Mu'
causes us to be able to go farther and faster.

Acronym for T.E.A.M. = Together Everyone Accom

Effective apostles know how to work in a T.E.A.M.

T = TRAINING

E = EXCELLENT

A = ANOINTED

M = MINISTERS

An apostolic team jointly subordinates his or her individual interests and opinions in order to harmonize with the unity and efficiency of the team as a whole.

Communication through concentric circles of relationship.

Apostles support, coach, direct, develop, and supervise teams of leaders with whom they relate.

Relationship driven organization should provide communication so that everyone maintains a sense of ownership.

Ministry is about people and not just property, buildings, and things. People come to church for relationships, development, and the validation of belonging. Good leaders must lean how to add value to their participation.

Apostolic teams with various talents working together causes significant synergism and forward momentum.

The Set Leader

The Scriptural PATTERN for leading a church is multiple elders working together as a mutually submissive TEAM with a "set person" (Num. 27:15-23) whom God recognizes and has appointed as the chief leader or visionary of a multiple-eldership.

The set person may be chosen to be a spokesman or representative of the collaborative group of elders. The set person should be affirmed as such – the "chief (or first) among equals." The other elders AGREE to submit to this leadership as peers. Often the final decision would belong to that set person – as it did to James.

The LEAD-BIRD sets the direction for the rest of the flock. This leader is always in a gigantic learning mode that requires a keen awareness of the environment as his/her's wing-tips constantly gauge the air currents, thermals, etc. The lead bird at the tip of the FORMATION even benefits from the wind currents produced by the birds directly behind it.

Clearly, James (who was the presiding elder at the Jerusalem Council, Acts 15) made binding decisions when a consensus could not be reached. Both Paul and Peter deferred to James (Acts 12:17, 21:18, 15:19;1 Cor. 15:7; Gal. 2:12). All translations clearly agree that James personally made final decisions that were binding.

> "*Let the Lord, the God of the spirits of all flesh, SET A MAN OVER THE CONGREGATION*" (Num. 27:16).

> "*I will establish ONE SHEPHERED over them, and he shall feed them...* (Ez. 24:23).

Remember... someone needs to be the Chief of Police and the Chief Fireman. Someone needs to be the chief engineer on a train. Somebody needs to be the judge in a jury trial. Final decisions for direction must belong to someone, otherwise there is confusion, lack of decisive direction, and frustration.

> The authority
> to lead
> is manifested
> by the ability
> to be relevant.

- There were "chief musicians" in the Tabernacle of David (1 Chron. 15:22; Ps. 4,5,6).
- Paul and Barnabas were called "chief men among the brethren" (Acts 15:22; 14:12) who commanded with official *authority*.
- There were "chief priests" (Lk. 9:22, 20:1).

- There were chief Apostles (2 Cor. 11:5, 12:11).
- Michael is called the "Chief Archangel" (Dan. 10:13).

Functionally, the set leader should demonstrate inspiration. The set person must be esteemed by the other elders as a "chief among equals." "*Authority*" is inherently limited to the particular (territorial) sphere where God has established a particular set-person. In that realm of *authority* (geographic region), they operate as a guide and mentor.[1] Their sphere of influence either can be territorial or issue-defined. Their sphere of *authority* can unlock revelation relevant to their expertise.

 REMEMBER: The Set Leader does not rule the eldership team by control. Everyone works together in unity of purpose as a TEAM.

- Genuine authority is always revelational.
- Genuine authority is always relational.
- Authority in true apostolic leaders should transcend the walls of the local church.

The corporate vision is always more important than the individual.

Governmental *authority* and management of the local church is not an issue of BESTING, but of functional servanthood. Together, the five-fold should evangelize and mature believers in order to release them into effectiveness.

Generally speaking, relationships with other apostles may be vertical in terms of seniority and respectfully horizontal in relationship. All Five-fold apostles function differently with individualized gifts. All five-fold ministers guide, teach, and govern – no matter what their gifting.

- From monopoly and competition to network partnership.
- From just gaining numbers to discipleship and maturity.
- From endless word searches and unending information – to relevant substance and content.
- From superficially emotional preaching to enabling activation.
- From giving money in vague hope of receiving to stewardship giving with purposeful intent.

JOBS OF THE SET-LEADERS:

I. *Regularly Share the Corporate Vision and Direction of the Church.* The set-leader needs to share the vision and new ideas with the team elders FIRST – allow them a chance to process ideas before others hear about it. Processing new ideas with leaders can be a great way to build unity and develop a spirit of proprietorship among the eldership team.

---

1. See my book "Connecting" for further discussion on "spheres of *authority*."

2. *Bring the Team to Maturity Through Grace.* God gives set-leaders a firm decisiveness and "grace" that challenges and helps establish order in the lives of people to become whole and fully established (Acts 4:33; 1 Cor. 3:10, 15:10).

3. *Allow Their Gifting and Ministry to Be Released.* One of the most imperative responsibilities of the set-leader is to discern, release, and send the elders into their greatest giftedness and destiny!

4. *Consistently Pray WITH and FOR the team so God Can Speak Corporately.* It is important for teams to spend quality corporate time together in prayer regarding a particular direction the church was moving toward.

5. *Give Honest and Regular Assessments.* It is vital for teams not to evade issues of difficulty such as personal failures and shortcomings. Most appreciate an honest assessment.

6. *Attempt to Operate With a Consensus of Opinion When Dealing With Major Issues.* With much counsel we should make war and in the multitude of counselors there is safety (Prov. 11:14, also 15:22, 24:6).

Although the Lord generally operates by giving major direction and vision FIRST to the set leader (Ex. 18:19), the methodology and application of how that vision could be implemented generally should result from a consensus of the eldership team. (Of course, the set-leader has the final say, as in Acts 15:13 and Titus 2:15).

> Biblical examples of NOT needing a consensus (idea above):

- 1) When God gave Moses the plan for the tabernacle; and
- 2) When God gave Solomon the plan for the Temple.

7. *Relate into Their Lives as a Mentor and Spiritual Parent.* Don't just address co-workers in the context of their roles in the church. Make your relationship personal and value them as spiritual children. Spend time deepening friendships and building covenant. It is very difficult to love someone you don't know. Set-leaders must take time to build transparent relationships in the teams. Apostolic leaders must care for others.

8. *Guard against holding your team members back.* Allow members of the team to demonstrate strong leadership. Don't override their ideas with rigidly strong opinions. Don't become emotionally frustrated with their performance. Be able to admit your limitations.

8. *Expose The Team to Other Ministers and Ministries to Expand Their Thinking and Vision.* Regularly bring other fivefold ministers (Ephesians 4:11) into their presence so that they can have a perspective on how other anointing function.

9. *Develop the Ability to Work in Diverse Assignments.* Leaders need to be flexible regarding their giftings, knowing that sometimes they may

have to function in a ministry they aren't particularly passionate about until a replacement is developed for that job.

GUIDELINES for SET-LEADERS to CONNECT TO TEAM LEADERS

Be personable. Be friendly. Be real. Tell the truth. True friendliness breeds trust. Leaders are looking for someone to trust.

Seek and keep genuine lifetime covenantal connections. Really care about others and be there without always having an agenda.

Look people in the eye when you talk to them and demonstrate respect.

Provide value to them as often as possible. Dare to risk vulnerability. Be interested in them before asking them to be interested in you.

Be an excellent communicator. Be prepared. Make your messages engaging and compelling enough to active the hearer.

Know your vision and your material. Tell stories about them. Tell how. Provide productive information that need to know and replicate. Information that helps them build their lives and/or increase productivity.

Be courageous. Courage gains momentum every time. Your passion, values, and attitude are the fundamentals of what it takes to connect.

Be positive. Stay enthusiastic. Be respectful. Be helpful and encouraging. Pray with them and for them.

Ministry brings the Kingdom toward the people.

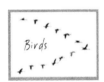

Birds WORK in teams even though they are not capable of setting deliberate goals. They busily sustain their lives with instinctual and continual momentum.

SECTION 5

Apostles

Description & Function

Who Are Apostles?

s

The Greek *word apostolos* means sent one or "MESSENGER" with a particular purpose or goal. According to "Vines Dictionary" the word "Apostle" *apostello* means "to send forth," and "to dispatch."

Apostolos (apostle) is a messenger or delegate who is entrusted and sent with a mission (not always a foreign mission).

Apostles are sent forth to bring new culture. Apostolic colonization brings heaven to earth.

In the word *apostle*, the prefix "apo" means "away from" or a sharp separation or severing.

Various expositors add, "as a delegate, messenger sent forth with orders" (Thayer). An agent, bearer of a commission (Analytical Greek Lexicon). Delegate, envoy, messenger, missionary (Arndt and Gingrich).

The Classic Encyclopedia Britanica defines apostle (*airovroXos*, as "one sent forth on a mission, an ENVOY of Jesus, a primary witness and preacher of the Kingdom."

This word *apostle* does was a common secular word used in society at the time Jesus was alive. "Apostle" was a term that Jesus specifically applied to His certain leaders under the New Covenant. Jesus formally appointed twelve to a determined office with connected *authority* and responsibility. The term appears 79 times in the New Testament.

Actually, Jesus (who spoke an Aramaic dialect), called His apostles the Aramaic title *selliah.* This was a word commonly used by the Jews of that day to denote "those who were dispatched from the mother city by the rulers of a foreign mission, especially such as were charged with collecting the tribute paid to the temple service."

The apostolic mentality plants, pioneers, launches, and raises up believers to accomplish their destiny. The focus is mainly on future expansion (not just the past or present).

Jesus said, "I must preach the Kingdom of God to other cities also; for therefore am I sent" (*apostello*, Lk. 4:43). The apostles (the twelve) were

Apostles don't come to "fit in," they are born to change nations and cultures.

"sent forth" with the commandment to not go in certain places and to go specifically to the lost of Israel (Mat 10:5).

The basic definition of an "apostle" is the person who is "sent." This sending has a mission which is often to establish a church or a work. The apostle is often the parent to the churches that he/she established. When starting a church work, the role of the apostle is to teach and train and to begin to form a local leadership. With the strong direction and leadership of an apostle, the church grows up. The aim of the apostle is to train and ordain SONS (elders) who model after his/her own example.

- The Hebrew noun *aspostolos* is found once in the Old Testament (1 Kings 14:6) when Ahijah is sent by Jeroboam's wife.
- Rabbis used the term *shalack* to send someone as an authorized person of god. Isaiah was "sent" (Is. 6:8).

GENERALS and ADMIRALS

Gifford's Dictionary defines *apostoulos* as a naval term that denotes the admiral over a fleet that sails to conquer and colonize. Admirals oversee the NAVIGATATION of naval fleets that lead into new frontiers beyond past borders and boundaries with a specific objective and mission. They establish and colonize. Admirals are always faithful to represent and reflect the wishes of the sender. Therefore, a primary attribute of a true apostle is to faithfully represent the Lord.

Some apostles have a "General-ship" type of rule – meaning they are "in charge." They can turn conflict into opportunity, de-escalate emotional confrontation, inspire people to follow, and express correction without hostility.

Apostles who are the General type (also know as Admiral type) have a gift of the Divine GLOBAL Kingdom strategy and leading. These strong leaders are born to solve problems, embrace confrontation, and take dominion. They take cities and nations. They are gifted to SEE IN THE FUTURE (anticipate). They are empowered for warfare. Generals create (cause) war not just fight.

It is natural for these kinds of apostles to live in conflict and battle for DOMINION every day. Mobilization is their gift. Initiation, confrontation, declaration is what they are all about.

Apostle John Kelly explains that the word "apostle" was always a confrontational word that had a very negative meaning to the Jew. They knew about the Mesopotamians and Syrophenicians who led groups of war ships into battle. The group of ships created fleets called "armadas." This title of apostle is the equivalent to "Admiral." Therefore, when the Jews heard the word "apostle," it communicated a dangerous person who "had an army."

General type apostles are "strategists" (a word derived from "*strateria*" which comes from a root word that means "Military service), who serve in a military campaign, to execute the apostolate (regions, territories, cities, nations) with arduous duties and functions... like a soldier" They launch and release Kingdom dimensions upon the earth. Apostles move with strategic weapons and tactics.

- Similarly, the related word "*stratiotes*" means warrior. Stratologeo" means to gather as a warrior or to enlist in an army." *Stratopedarches*" means to rule an army, and "*stratopedon*" means to storm the camping-ground of the troops. Apostolic strategy involves seizing and acquiring land, territory, and possessions for the Kingdom.

- The word "church" (*ecclesia*) was a familiar institutional word used for centuries before Jesus. *Ecclesia* referred to the assembly that ruled over civic affairs. Originally, *ecclesia* was a confrontational political word meaning "called out for revolution." It was a group with a drastically relevant message to "take over." The early believers were able to turn the world upside down (Acts 17:6). Jesus called His Body *ecclesia* and He intended for us to have *authority* in world affairs.

AUTHORITY brings heaven to earth.

When Caesar of Centuria heard of the coming "apostles," he assumed they were a counter-culture group of revolutionaries and he prepared armed men ready for battle against them.

Apostles are often called to a specific location(s). Apostles BUILD bridges towards interaction with nations, governments, the social community, the market place, and the financial realms in order to broaden the platform of church effectiveness.

THE BASIC QUALIFICATIONS FOR BEING AN APOSTLE

A modern-day apostle must significantly encounter Jesus.

FIRSTLY, the original apostles were a witness to the Resurrection. Paul's claim to the apostolic was that Jesus appeared to him. The true mark of an apostle today is not just that he/she knows about Jesus, but knows Jesus as an actual living Presence and Person.

SECONDLY, the qualification for an apostle is that every aspect of their life should clearly reflect a close relationship with the Lord.

THIRDLY, the essence and motivation of all *authority* must be to serve the Kingdom of God and the welfare of others. The Antioch Church flourished during persecution, famine, poverty, and victimization (Acts 11:20). It was marked by compassionate and benevolent caring.

Apostles emphasize walking in the "purpose of the heart" toward the Lord (Acts 11:23). This PUPRPOSE driven emphasis emphasized concern over the Kingdom reality rather than just material convenience. They also emphasized group goals over individual goals.

FOURTHLY, through delegated apostolic *authority* the assignment was/ is to UNLOCK and release the power of God, to apprehend and preach the Mystery, and to obtain and release God's promised inheritance for His people.

FIFTHLY, they positioned themselves in heavenly places and ministered out of that realm. Their message was, "The Kingdom of heaven is at hand (available now).

 The signs of an apostle (the authenticity of their AUTHORITY) are signs and wonders and works of God's power (*dunamis*) miracles (2 Cor. 12:12).

AMBASSADOR

God does not always call those who are qualified – He qualifies those He calls.

Paul said the apostles were "ambassadors." This word is the from same root as elder – *presbeuo*. "Now then, we are AMBASSADORS for Christ, as though God were pleading through us: we implore you on Christ's behalf, be reconciled to God" (2 Cor. 5:20, NKJV). The Bible is clear. Earth was not their home. Ambassadors RE-PRESENT the KING and His Kingdom.

Strongs Dictionary also defines *ambassadors* as "commissioners of Christ with miraculous powers. One who is delegated on a mission assignment from GOD to MAN. One who is sent in the interest of the sending country."

- Every ambassador is sent to establish an embassy (the Kingdom in that area).
- An ambassador is one sent with a burden to be the voice of the one who sent them – and given the right to rule and reign in their place.
- An ambassador presents the wishes and interests of the nation that sent him. The ambassador is fully backed by the *authority* and the credentials of the sending nation.
- Diplomatic relations with an ambassador is equivalent to having diplomatic relations with the country itself.
- Ambassadors have teams or emissaries who can function as observers, spies, and secret agents.
- There is a oneness of purpose with the ambassador and the one who sent him or her.

Zerubbabel, the governor of Judah was given an AMBASSADORIAL assignment, "I will make you as a SIGNET; for I have chosen you, says the Lord of hosts" (Hag. 2:21-23). Zerubbabel is called to be a "signet" (The King's signature was embedded in hot wax from a special signet ring used only by an authorized person.) Zerubbabel is given the *Divine Authority* to use the awesome Name of God and to carry out distinct responsibilities of building the new temple (4:6-7). Clearly, this authorization to use God's NAME is for us as well.

This Scripture shows us a type of emerging high ranking national leader who lives in the AUTHORITY OF THE NAME OF GOD. For "His hand will complete" the temple (which is the BODY of Christ).

NOTICE THE SEQUENCE:

> Acts 2-8 shows that apostles (1) go forth, (2) take the lead, (3) set up churches, and (4) teach others.

> Acts 11-16 often shows APOSTLES ordaining elders and then training and leading together with those ELDERS they have installed.

> Acts 17- 28 shows that the apostle establishes the church with a plurality of local eldership, and the apostle continues to travel.

> Violent persecution continued as believers scattered worldwide

JESUS CHOSE TWELVE

Authority was the ground of our Lord's commissions to His apostles (Mk. 6:6-7). TRUE *AUTHORITY* belongs only to HIm. He permitted them (and us) to use His. It's never ours. God's *authority* is unconditional and "absolute" (Ps. 29:10; Isa. 40:1), making Him supreme over all things. Because Jesus was and is God, His *authority* was and is intrinsic. His power knows no limitations (Mat. 28:18).

There is an established order of *AUTHORITY* by which God's church operates. The appointing and validation of eldership is a sacred trust and must never be given to those not ready.

Jesus prayed all night before choosing the twelve apostles (Lk. 6:13). His objective in selecting these leaders is summarized in Mark: "He appointed twelve, designating them apostles, that they might be 1) WITH Him and that e might 2) send them out to preach and 3) to have *authority* to drive out demons (Mk. 3:14-15). This profound Scripture distills the purpose of WHY Jesus nurtured His leaders.

> *"He appointed TWELVE... designating them apostles... that they might be with Him and that He might send them out to preach and to have authority to drive out demons"* (Mk. 3:14-15).

1. *"That they might be with Him."* Relationship is foremost in the selection consideration.

2. *"That He might send them out."* Being sent is central to their commissioning. Apostles are sent out *from* the presence and relationship *with* God.

3. *"To have authority."* Spiritual authority is the clear evidence of apostolic grace. True apostles impart authority, set in order, bring fruitfulness, govern and protect the church, and pull down principalities.

Jesus set Himself aside and prayed for revelation concerning who to train. He didn't use a church building. He taught his apostles on the hillside, in the streets, and during His travels. They watched as He healed the sick and cast out devils... and through it all, He taught and released them to be fully equipped (Acts 1:8-10). This doesn't mean that they were "independent" ministries just running around doing whatever they wanted. It meant that they could *activate* what they were taught.

This Divine invitation included personal direct mentoring of Jesus. He included His apostles in a spiritual relationship that gave instruction and example by which they developed their abilities and character. Through personal relationship and first-hand experience, these men were transformed and developed. The apostles were enabled because they were allowed to experience the Divine Presence of God and were given strategic assignments and opportunities to function.

Jesus spoke of the Kingdom being fully available (as it is now). He used the term "apostle" to specifically position twelve men to be particularly trained by Him. They did not understand many of the concepts that He taught – about the day that was upon them. They didn't fully realize Who He was!

- He taught them specific principles while He taught the masses generalities.
- He instructed them individually and in small groups. The subject of these meetings was more intense and more advanced than teaching the multitudes. The individual training was specific to their need.
- He had them practice what He taught them. He had them report on what happened when they practiced what had been taught. Accountability sessions were actually practiced.
- His last command was for them to "make disciples" (Mat. 28:19-20).

Who Were The Twelve?

The NAS translation speaks of the "Twelve" (1 Cor. 15:5) as the "most eminent apostles" with a marginal notation saying, "the super apostles." The American Version calls them "the chiefest apostles." (See also 2 Cor. 11:5; 12:11).

The name (*dodeka* the twelve) initially denoted the twelve apostles together. After the death of Jesus, they were called the *hendeka*, the eleven.

- The assignment for apostles was to the Jew first" (Rom. 1:16; 2:9). Later in the Gospel narratives the Twelve Apostles were commissioned to preach *the* Gospel to both Jew and Gentile.
- These twelve are to rule on twelve thrones over the twelve tribes of Israel (Mat. 19:28).
- The twelve were not Levitical Priests.
- Although the Apostles are thought to have been Galilean Jews, ten of their names are Aramaic, the other four names are Greek derivatives. These twelve were the distinctively JEWISH twelve. All of them were Jews born in Judea or Galilee. They were all descendents of the House of Judah.

WHO WERE THEY? According to the list occurring in each of the Synoptic Gospels (Mk. 3:13-19, Mat. 10:1-4; Luke 6:12-16), the Twelve whom Jesus chose and *named Apostles*, were:

- Simon called Peter (*petros* meaning rock) also called Simon bar Jonah and Simon bar Jochanan. Paul called him Cephas. Peter was a fisherman from Galilee (Jn. 1:44,12:21).
- Andrew was Peter's brother, also a fisherman and a disciple of John the Baptist. Andrew was the first one called Apostle.
- James ("the Great") was a son of Zebedee and Salome. This James was the brother of John the Evangelist. Mark says that Jesus called James and John "*Boanerges*," an Aramaic name explained in Mk. 3:17 as meaning the "Sons of Thunder" (3:17). Acts 12:1-2 records that King Herod had James executed by sword (Ac.12:1-2) AD 44.
- John (also called a son of Zebedee) is thought to be the author of the Gospel of John, 1st, 2nd, and 3rd John, and Revelation. He wrote of himself as the disciple that Jesus "loved." He stayed at the foot of the cross, ran first to the tomb with Peter. Jesus asked John to care for His mother Mary. Strong tradition and historical evidence says that he took Mary to Ephesus and cared for her there.
- Philip from Bethesda (Jn. 1:44, 12:21). Philip is said to come from Bethsaida, as did Andrew and Peter (Jn. 1:43–44). Philip introduced Nathaniel to Jesus (John 1:45–47).
- Bartholomew (Aramaic "bar-Talema") from Ptolemais. Most identify this person as also being called Nathaniel.
- Thomas (aka *Judas Thomas Didymus* - his Aramaic name *T'oma'* means "twin," and Greek *Didymous* means "twin").

- James ("the Less"), son of Alphaeus (probably not the same person as James the Just). This James was the brother of the Apostle Matthew (Levi).
- Matthew the tax collector (aka Levi son of Alphaeus).
- Simon the Canaanite (called in Luke and Acts "Simon the Zealot" (or Zealous) and also thought to be Simeon of Jerusalem.
- Judas (Greek for Judah) Iscariot (may refer to the Judean towns in Kerioth); he was the first to die.
- The identity of the twelfth apostle is traditionally named as Jude, but this name varies in the Gospels and also in the ancient manuscripts. Mark calls him Thaddeus. Matthew names him as *Lebbaeus (and or* Judas the Zealot), Luke names him as Judas, "son of James" or "brother of James" (Lk. 6:16).
- The Gospel of John names the twelfth apostle as *Judas (not Iscariot,* 14:22) Also known as "Jude" who is honored by the Armenian Apostolic church as their patron saint. He is thought to be the brother of James the Less.
- Second century documents list Simon Magus as being the twelfth (who was also Simeon of Jerusalem, who became the second leader of the Jerusalem church, after James).
- After Judas died, cast lots chose Matthias as one of the "Twelve." Matthias is mentioned: Before Pentecost (Acts 1:26). At Pentecost (Acts 2:14). After Pentecost (Acts 6:2); And by Paul himself (1 Cor. 15:5). All but Matthias were appointment by Jesus before He died.

> **Jesus only appointed APOSTLES. No prophets, evangelists, teachers, or pastors were chosen until after His Resurrection. This is a distinct change in order from the Old Testament.**

We don't know why and Titus and Mark were not "called" Apostles; it seems their jobs warranted the name. Remember, the Scriptures DID NOT document every detail.

Other APOSTLES were NAMED in the Bible AFTER the ASCENSION of CHRIST. These were apostles who did not actually walk with Jesus and were not of the original twelve: Paul (Acts 14:14; 22:21), Barnabas (Acts 4:36; 11:22-30; 14:1, 4. 14), Silas (Silvanus, 1 Thes. 1:1, 2:6), Erastus (Acts 19:22), Apollos and Sosthenes (1 Cor. 4:6-9), Tychius (2 Tim. 4:12), Epaphroditus (called *apostolos,* "messenger" or apostle, Phil. 2:25; Titus 2 Cor. 8:23), Judas (Acts 15:23; 1 Thes. 2:6), Junia (Rom. 16:7, probably female), the two unnamed apostles who were chosen for the collection in Corinth (2 Cor. 8:23), Andronicus,

(Rom.16:7), Silas (aka Silvanus, Acts 15:23), Timothy (*aka* Timotheus, Acts 19:22), Matthias (Acts 1:26), James (the Lord's brother, Acts 1:14; 1 Cor. 15:7; Gal. 1:10; 2:9), Titus was also called *apostolos* but not listed as one of the twelve (2 Cor. 8:23).

James the Just, the brother of Jesus, is not called an apostle in the Gospel list of the original twelve. However, he was described by Paul as a "pillar" (Gal 2:9 NIV). Acts tells that James sas the leader of the apostles at the Jerusalem Church. He is called an apostle in Gal. 1:19. James was murdered in 62 AD. Jerome supported the identification of James as being the actual blood brother of Jesus. Orthodox tradition said he was the first of the Seventy (Luke 10:1-20).

- Many scholars assert that the Seventy were also apostles because the Greek text uses the verb form *apostello* in sending the seventy away – and the rest of the text strongly implies that they functioned as apostles.
- A second Simon (not Zealot) was another brother of Jesus who became the second bishop of Jerusalem after James the Just.

There were many others who claimed apostleship: Some disciples of John, Polycarp, Ignatius, Irenaeus, and Eusebius (who is know as the Father of Church History), and the African Apostle Tertullian, etc.

TWELVE

Twelve (*dodeka*) is the governmental number of apostolic foundations. Twelve is the number of the Church and government. This number is prominent in the history of Israel. Some examples follow:

- 12 sons of Jacob (Gen. 48-49) the 12 tribes of Israel
- 12 wells of water (Ex. 15:27)
- 12 pillars at Mt. Sinai (Ex. 24)
- 12 princes (Numb. 7)
- The High priest wore a breastplate with 12 stones with 12 names of 12 tribes
- 12 loaves of shewbread (Ex. 25:23-50) and twelve golden dishes for the dedication of the alter
- 12 lions on Solomon's throne (1 Kng. 10:20), 12 oxen holding the molten sea (1 Kng. 7:25, 44), 12 porters at gates of Jerusalem (1 Chron. 26:13-19)
- Jesus was 12 when he went to the temple
- Jarius' daughter was 12. The woman with the issue of blood was sick for 12 years. (Mt. 9:20; Mk. 5:25; Lk. 8:43-44)
- The city of God has 12 gates, 12 names on 12 foundations, 12 kinds of fruits, 12 pearly gates

- There are 12 apostles of the Lamb (Rev. 21:14)
- 12 baskets with fragments (Jn. 6:13)
- The 12 stars on the woman's head
- Twice 12 is the number of the heavenly elders
- The tree of life bears 12 manner of fruit (Rev. 22:2)
- 12 months of the year.
- 12 half steps in an octave

WOMEN APOSTLES

According to several extra-Biblical manuscripts, twelve women in the early church were said to be commissioned to operate in significant positions of apostolic leadership.

Susanna (the daughter of the former *chazan* of the Nazareth synagogue) was elected chief leader of the women. Suzanna is widely mentioned in historical documents and there are many pictures of her in the catacombs.

Next there was Joanna (the wife of Chuza, the steward of Herod Antipas) who was elected treasurer); Elizabeth (the daughter of a wealthy Jew of Tiberias and Sepphoris); Martha (the older sister of Andrew and Peter); Rachel (the sister-in-law of Jude, the brother of Jesus); Nasanta (the daughter of Elman, the Syrian physician); Milcha (a cousin of the Apostle Thomas); Ruth (Matthew's oldest daughter); Celta (the daughter of the Roman centurion); Agaman (a widow of Damascus), and Rebecca (the daughter of Joseph of Arimathea).

It is said that Jesus authorized these women to preach, teach, build, and direct others.[1] Judas was instructed to provide funds for their equipment and necessary animal transportation. It is documented that after the initial offerings, they earned their own monetary support.

The Gnostic Gospels name Mary Magdalene the "apostle to all apostles" or "the favorite apostle." Also as potential apostles were: Lydia, Phoebe (called *diakonos* or "fellow worker," Rom. 16.1-2), The Elect Lady, Priscilla, Junia (whom Paul called his compatriot who was prominent among the apostles), Euodia, and Syntyche and maybe many more.

BATALIA: I visited the catacombs in Naples where Batilia is pictured as a leader of an entire city. Her fresco covers the entire entrance and behind it are the rest of the burials. In her hands are two books that say, "Matthew, Mark, Luke, and John." She is a tremendous testimony to the

1. See "From Enmity to Equality."

power of women moving apostolically in the early church. (See her picture in my book, "*Understanding Headship.*")

One of my favorites was the apostle named Thecla (pictured here). Though not mentioned in Scripture, much historical narrative evidence considers Thecla to have been an apostle and associate of Paul. "The Acts of Paul" contains her first century accounts, which were probably greatly embellished as time went on.

I visited her still existing gigantic complex that included a huge church, a monastery, convent, and hospital that SHE BUILT near Selleucia. Amazingly, these remains still stand today.

In 1902, Germans excavated Thecla's center, which apparently remained in active use for over 1,000 years under strong female apostleship and oversight.

CONSIDERATIONS ON HOW GOD WORKS WITH APOSTLES

"If this matter of authority remains unsolved, nothing can be solved"
Watchman Nee (SA, p.23)

Many denominations teach that the ministry of an apostle ended at the Book of Acts. It was thought that the death of the apostle John completed the New Testament Scriptures. However, the book of Ephesians distinctly says that after His ascension, Jesus gave gifts to men, and "He gave some apostles." This ministry was given for the time period of "UNTIL." Until what? Until unity and maturity develop in the believers. Obviously, the church is still in desperate need of the apostolic ministry today.

PROTON: 1 Corinthians 12:28 says, "...FIRST (*proton*) apostles, second prophets, third teachers, after that miracles, then gifts of healings, helps, administrations, varieties of tongues."

Apostles are the "*PROTON*" and that means they are the "first one in" with an idea, concept, or ministry. Apostles are the "first" because of their relationship and responsibility to the other 5-fold ministry gifts. The first in the foundation – not the top and not the most important. Apostles are "first" in establishing function and releasing the specific metron (reach, territorial sphere of influence) of the *authority* for the rest of the Offices. Apostles are "first" in receiving major world changing revelation that will unveil the Kingdom and assemble the Bride for the Son (Mat. 28:18-20).

- Protons are voices of authority to the lawless. They contribute to civic and social awareness. They engage within the culture to turn it to Kingdom mindedness.
- In physics a proton is the stable positively charged particle that makes up part of the nucleus (CENTER) of an atom.
- Jesus mentions "Whoever wants to be first" must serve (Mat. 20:25-28).

THE APOSTOLIC FOUNDATION

"...But you are of God's household, having been built upon the foundation of the apostles and prophets, Christ Jesus Himself being the corner stone" (Eph. 2:19, 20).

If the foundation is not build correctly, it will cause irreparable structural problems. Apostles must not build a shabby structure but must build the Body for the generational ages to come. Apostolic foundation should be immovable, fixed, solid, and steadily anchored.

The foundation (apostles/prophets) is the under-layment of the building. That means it is UNDERNEATH to hold up! Apostles enable. They support. They strengthen. And, from that position of being underneath, the Apostles (as foundational ministers) can rightfully help set things in order, correct doctrine, recognize incorrect behavior, and call for answer-ability. The government is on our shoulder.

 The FOUNDATION is SUPPORT underneath – not "covering" on top.

True *AUTHORITY* (exousia) comes from being the foundation (not the tip of the top). The foundation brings instruction – not insis-tence. That's being a greater servant – not the big wheel! It's all a matter of ATTITUDE. *Authority* must become the position of strength and support to others – to sustain, to be there, to undergird, to reinforce, to collaborate. That's why apostles are SENT in first (proton) – to confirm, to supply, nurture, and adjust the rest.

In building a structure, everything must be planned *BEFORE* the FOUNDATION is put into place. Where is the plumbing supposed to be? How high is the building? What is needed? The foundation holds the iron rebar for strengthening. All plans are in place before the foundation is laid.

- The Thesaurus defines a FOUNDATION as "the act of founding or establishing: constitution, creation, establishment, institution, organization, origination, start-up. The lowest or

supporting part or structure: base, bedrock, footing, fundamental, groundwork, substratum, and underpinning."
- The City of God has TWELVE foundations.

Notice this list of what happened BEFORE the FOUNDATION of the world the Kingdom was prepared for us (Mt. 25:34); the Father loved Jesus and gave Him Glory (Jn. 17:24); God chose us in Christ (Eph. 1:4); the works were finished from before the foundation (Heb. 4:3); Jesus was foreordained (1 Pet. 1:20); The Lamb was slain (Rev. 13:8); our names were written in the Book of Life (Rev. 17:8).

The future success of the church revolves around HOW well apostolic revelation becomes functional and established. The "house" can only be as strong as its FOUNDATION (infastructure, Eph.2:19-21; 1 Cor.12:28). Apostles and prophets are the foundation upon which all is built, and Jesus is the chief corner stone (that upon which all else stands, Eph. 2:20).

> God "set" (*etheto*) the FOUNDATION of the church with apostles and prophets (Eph. 2:20).

- The Tabernacle of Moses was built upon the foundation of the silver sockets (of redemption, Ex. 26:19, 21, 25).
- The Tabernacle of David was pitched on the rock of Mt. Zion (1 Chron. 17).
- Temple of Solomon was built on the foundation of Mt. Moriah (also the sacrifice of Isaac, the threshing floor, etc. (Sam. 12:4, Gen. 22:1; 1 Chron. 1-7; 2 Chron. 3:1-2).
- Paul laid the only foundation that could be laid which is Christ (1 Cor. 3:9-15) and didn't want to build on another man's foundations (Rom. 15:20).
- The grace of God causes apostles to be wise architects (master builders). Apostles lay a foundation that others can take heed and knowingly build upon (1 Cor 3:10).
- The wise person builds on the SURE foundation and not upon shifting, sinking sands.

Here's exactly why the Pyramid formation is not the correct model! Being first doesn't mean on top. To be a FOUNDATION means it is put in first and it means being BELOW not on TOP.

PAUL

Paul said he was "born out of due season" (1 Cor. 15:5-8). He wasn't one of the original twelve, but came on the scene as a foundational apostle to write most of the New Testament. Paul accounts how he was discipled in the Arabic desert of aloneness (Gal.1:11, 18-20; 2:1-2).

Paul mentored disciples, but no leader nurtured him.

"Then after three years (after the Damascus Road experience), I went up to Jerusalem TO GET ACQUAINTED (not to be instructed) with Peter and stayed with him fifteen days. I saw none of the other apostles - only James the Lord's brother."

Uninvitedly, Paul boldly stepped onto the stage of the First Century Church to assume the position of a full-fledged apostle.

Many scholars wonder if Paul had really been the Lord's choice to replace Judas as one of the Twelve because Matthias was chosen by lot and Paul by direct encounter.

Fourteen years of desert later, Paul returned to Jerusalem with Barnabas and Titus. He needed to "Clarify with them what had been revealed" to him. Paul PRIVATELY told the LEADERS EXACTLY what he was preaching to the non-Jews. His concern was to NOT cause a controversial public debate about ethnic tension. He said he didn't wish to expose his "years of work to denigration and endangering my present ministry." ("I wanted to make sure they did not disagree, or my ministry would have been useless," Gal. 2:1). Peter accepted Paul as an apostle (Gal. 2:17-19).

 Paul understood how to be accountable and submitted to leaders.

We see here how Paul submitted his revelation to other apostles, BUT NOT HIS CALLING NOR HIS POSITION OF APOSTOLIC *AUTHORITY*. Accountability and clarification was important to him - but he did not waiver in *authority*. This is the way of some great apostles – they have personal revelation that God gives only to them. Their regulation and supervision is from God – yet they desire to be open with those of like calling. Their message is always contemporary. Apostles look at the future differently. They are concerned about taking nations – they aren't looking for a place to hide.

- Paul was directly commissioned especially to the Gentiles and the uncircumcised (Gal. 2:7-8; Acts 9:15, 26:15-18; Rom. 11:13, 15:15-20; Gal. 1:15-17; 1 Tim. 2:7). He was the primary apostle for Crete, Corinth, Ephesus, Galatia, Philippi, Colossae, and Thessalonica. Paul was centered at the Church at Antioch. (Peter was the apostle of the circumcision and centered at the Church in Jerusalem.)
- Paul insisted that he was not one wit behind the chiefest of apostles (2 Cor. 11:15, 12:11-12).
- Paul said that by the authority of the Lord Jesus, he gave INSTRUCTIONS ON HOW TO LIVE "in order to please God" (1 Thes. 4:1-2).

Paul was respectful of others in *authority*, but was never intimidated or overridden by the position of others. He corrected Peter publicly (Gal. 2:11) – clearly never attacking Peter's *authority* because just three verses earlier (2: 9) Paul calls Peter the Aramaic name "*Cephas*" (Matt. 16:18) and tells us that he is the "Pillar" of the church.

- David was told to "touch not the Lord's anointed" (1 Sam. 26). It is important to realize that Saul was the anointed King – in a class by himself. David was told to not KILL SAUL.
- However, David continuously spoke against the wrong things that Saul did. That command did not mean that believers cannot verbalize a truth that is contrary to what leadership teaches.

Paul modeled how we should confront *authority* on the basis of the truth. He confronts Peter directly (who was clearly the senior apostle at that time) and tells him that he needs to change his behavior. It's okay to disagree with a leader if you go to them first privately.

Authority reveals revelation.

Paul wrote his epistles in all the *authority* of his ordained position, "Paul, an apostle, sent not from men nor by man, but by Jesus Christ and God...." Paul knew who he was in the natural and who he was in the spirit. He consistently commanded recognition of his function and the title he bore (1 Cor. 15:9; Rom. 1:1; 2 Cor. 1:1, etc.).

Paul used his *authority* for edification (2 Cor. 1:24, 10:8). He used his authority because of his care and concern for all the churches (2 Cor. 11:28). But, he exercised greater *authority* over the churches he founded. These Churches were the "seal of his apostleship" (1 Cor. 9:1-2, 7:17, 11:34; 2 Thes. 3:14).

Paul was "free from all to be servant of all" (1 Cor. 12:26-29), but he periodically reported to the Church in Antioch (Acts 13-14).

Paul "MAGNIFIED" his *diakonia* (official service and ability as a minister) (Rom. 11:13). That's the flavor we're after. That's Apostolic talking – and it has a certain "ring" to it. This magnification is part of the commission! However, it may well provoke others to jealousy if they walk in the flesh (vs. 14).

Paul discusses the issue of *authority* with the Corinthians, "For even if I should boast somewhat more about our *authority*, which the Lord GAVE US FOR EDIFICATION (the purpose) and not for your destruction, I shall not be ashamed" (1:24). Some had obviously complained that his letters were too "weighty and powerful, but his bodily presence is weak, and his speech contemptible." (Apparently, bodily stature and the ability to give a great oration is not particularly relevant to having *authority*!) But, Paul maintained that the way he wrote was an accurate representation of who he was. (Apostles don't need to look like someone special, or walk around with an arrogant demeanor, or say what others expect.)

Paul demonstrated an *authority* that was not based on personality, looks, human wisdom, or personal competence. Instead, his position of authority resulted because of God's sovereign choice. At the same time, the allegiance of his followers was very much *personal* and also because of his authority.

> AUTHORITY is the presence of the Holy Spirit that enables a person to operate in POWER and cause a significant effect.

PAUL SUBMITTED TO DIVERSE ELDERS

The Jerusalem Church was multi-lingual and multi-ethnic but was not trans-cultural because they never reached out beyond the Jew and Judaism. On the other hand, the Antioch church was started by Peter in AD 34. In Antioch, diverse nationalities and economic groups lived separately and were divided by walls within that city. The congregation crossed social and cultural divisions and boundaries to assemble together. The Antioch leadership and congregation were a multi-ethnic and trans-cultural group (Acts 13).

During this time in Antioch, prophets and teachers led the church. This core leadership of the church in Antioch prayed for a full year. This group was a multicultural task force. "In the church at Antioch there were prophets and teachers: Barnabas, Simeon called Niger, Lucius of Cyrene, Manaen [who had been brought up with Herod the Tetrarch (as probably a foster-brother) and served in his court] and Saul. While they were worshiping the Lord and fasting, the Holy Spirit said, "Set apart for me Barnabas and Saul for the work to which I have called them. So after they had fasted and prayed, they placed their hands on them and sent them off" (Acts 13:1-3).

Of the five mentioned, two were black (40%) – there was Simeon called Niger (black—maybe the same person as Simeon Cyrene). And there was Lucius of Cyrene. Cyrene was an African city that is now known as "Tripoli." For the most part, the Cyreneans objected to the Gospel.

These five Antioch leaders were vocationally diverse (Acts 13). It seems that Barnabas was interested in real estate (Acts 2 and 4); Paul was a religious leader who built tents on the side; and Manaen was involved in politics. We see from this group how it requires a diversity of leadership ability to transform a culture or nation (see Esther, Nehemiah, Ezra, Daniel, etc.). An Antiochian leadership model demonstrates how business and political, leaders can work together within the religious leadership team.

Manaen was raised in the wealthy environment of the house of Herod the Tetrarch in Rome. He may have been a disciple of Jesus along with "Joanna, the wife of Chusa, Herod's steward" (Lk. 8:3).

This think tank decided to SEND Paul and Barnabas with the Gospel to Europe.

It is vital to notice that it was this group that decided where Paul was to go. Apostles, prophets, and teachers WORKED TOGETHER. First they fasted and prayed. Then they laid hands and sent them off. NOTICE that Paul did not consider himself "over" these others, but was submissive to their overall decision of the group.

 Submission is vitally demonstrated and defined here – Paul didn't leave until the elders all received confirmation from the Holy Spirit.

 Generally, Paul was decisive over doctrine and submissive over assignments.

PAUL WAS ABLE TO RECONCILE PAST DIFFERENCES.
Another time we find that John Mark (the nephew of Barnabas) had a disagreement and split from Paul (Acts 15:36-40). Paul later reconciled to John Mark (2 Tim. 4:11). "Only Luke is with me. Get Mark and bring him with you, because he is helpful to me in my ministry." Paul and Barnabas took John Mark to Patmos to find a sorcerer.

- The Assyrian church believes that this is the Mark who wrote the Gospel of Mark. Peter calls Mark "my son" and Assyrians generally concur that Mark was actually Peter's son.
- If that's true, then Mary (John Mark's mother) was Peter's wife. Peter goes to Mary's house after he was released from prison (Acts 12:12). It is likely that Barnabas was the brother of Peter's wife and John Mark's uncle. Perhaps this is how John Mark becomes Paul's companion and was able to write the gospel information that we have today. John Mark was not mentioned as an apostle.

GRACE OFFICE GIFT

Paul talked a lot about grace. GRACE (*charis*) is said to be the divine influence upon the heart and its reflection in the life, benefit, favour, gift, etc. Being an apostle is a GRACE Gift. Apostles receive GRACE to fulfill their office (Rom. 1:5). The apostolic function exists strictly out of God's GRACE. God gave Paul "grace" for the people (Eph. 3:1-2). The apostolic set-leader has the grace to act as a conduit to connect others to the Lord.

Apostles receive an outward grace gift for powerful ministry and also an inner grace to passionately continue what must be accomplished.

> Leaders are "real people" who are given God's GRACE to be able to function in a God-given OFFICE.

Paul said, "By the GRACE of God, I am what I am" (1 Cor. 15:10). This grace to be an apostle is given as a seed to which God gives a body. The seed grows by faith in God's *authority* to give us our office.

Doing what you are supposed to do releases your GRACE GIFT. Grace is the favor and power of God extending on your behalf. Paul spoke of the GRACE GIFT OFFICE (potential function) when he beseeched (begged) the believers to come into a metamorphosis or renewal of their mind and to be changed completely by a special GRACE to become who God intended them to be (Rom. 12:1-7).

* "I became a servant of this gospel by the GIFT of God's GRACE given me through the working of His power" (Eph. 3:7, NIV).
* "And I thank Christ Jesus our Lord, who has enabled me (given me a measure of GRACE), and that He counted me faithful, putting me into the ministry..." (1 Tim. 1:12-14).
* Paul said that we (like him) through the GRACE (the known will of God for him to be an apostle) must learn to not think more highly of ourselves than we should (Rom. 12:3). (See also 1 Cor. 3:10, 15:10).

Certain believers are anointed by an equipping GRACE to lead other believers.

The authority to hold a grace office is sovereignly given by the choice of the Holy Spirit. We choose to activate that GIFT by faith.

When we use the term "Gift Office," it means "official function" (*praxis*, Rom. 12:4) of leadership. An "office" requires a person to meet certain qualifications, recognized by other spiritual authorities (1Tim. 3:1-13; Titus 1:5; Acts 14:23).

"But, be sober when considering that through your FAITH you will be transformed into your function! Even though we are ONE (interdependent, intermingled, part of the whole), we don't have the same function (office). OUR GIFTS DIFFER (that's because of the energy of our office) because of grace (function) according to the portion (measure of apprehending) of our faith (that which grows the seed). He who leads – needs diligence" (Rom. 12:3-6, literal paraphrase).

The apostle is GRACE gifted to prepare the Bride for Christ.

The Measure of Apostolic Authority

 Paul knew his measure of authority and who it included. Paul said that he would "not boast beyond measure (*metron*), but within the LIMITS of the SPHERE which God appointed" (2 Cor. 10:13).

It was a sphere which especially included those to whom he wrote. He said that as their faith is increased, "We shall be greatly enlarged by you IN OUR SPHERE (measure, reach, or portion), to preach the gospel in the regions beyond you, and not to boast in another man's sphere of accomplishment. But "he who glories, let him glory in the LORD" (2 Cor. 10:8-17, NKJV).

Greater *authority* to lead is derived from operating IN the correct OFFICE. For example, when a person stands in the OFFICE of an apostle there is greater *authority* than when years ago that same person functioned as an elder who taught Sunday School.

 There is little tangible AUTHORITY when the person is NOT divinely positioned in the correct OFFICE.

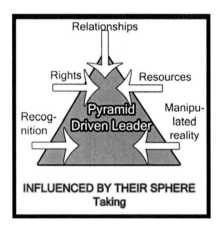

In the past, the constant misuse of authority is demonstrated by limited pyramid-type leaders who always demand from others. Their success is generally defined by how well their surroundings give back into them. They TAKE and TAKE.

Congregations tied to leaders in pyramid styles of demand are always tied to obligation, limitations, and duties. Believers out of position are like a flock of caged birds. Much of their struggle is resistance to an incorrect model and a desire to become free to migrate to where they belong (to find their flock, locate their tribe, and get into position).

Proper governmental leaders center around the LORD who imparts to them MEASURES of influence. God gives righteous leaders jurisdictional authority on earth where they can have optimum influence. Each believer must position and align themselves within their measure of destiny.

 When we find the right connections with the right leaders, we activate the metron (measure) of our lives.

 Our metron is connected to a location and to a people. Commitment to this location and people (spiritual or physical realms) is where you find the release of blessing, favor, fruit, provision, protection, destiny, and promotion.

There are several New Testament models describing how the early apostles actually held a universality of jurisdiction. The apostles preached and traveled as if they were not bound by territorial limits. Their known world was turned upside down.

"... God has allotted to each a MEASURE (*metron*, a degree, a limited portion) of faith... and since we have gifts that differ according to the grace given to us, let each exercise them accordingly... "(Rom. 12:3-6). Our metron of authority is a RELEASE from the center or SOURCE of the God in us. (The center is the centrality of Christ.)

Each ministry and gift of God uniquely contains a specific measure of Christ's GRACE given.

Focus on developing the metron of leadership that you have been given.

Not every apostle is on an equal plane of maturity, gifting, measure of rule, or scope of reach. All Apostles are unique among themselves and differ one from another because of the "measure" or reach of their portion of Christ's Grace (Eph. 4:7, 13, 16). Therefore, every church and ministry is to be unique for several reasons. It is God's great pleasure to create us in the distinctive way that He wants us to function, such as:

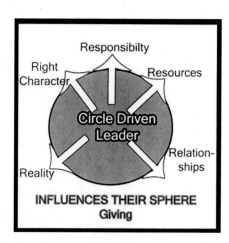

1. The design of the Lord is for us together to impact and permeate the locale as a whole. Because of our divergent gifts and differing functions, each of us has a region or "sphere" (2 Cor. 10:8-16).

- Paul had a "measure" of *authority* to work with the Gentiles – and Peter worked with the Jews, etc.

- Both John and Paul had "spheres" in Ephesus. Both Paul had *authority* in Corinth (1 Cor.1:10-13; 12:12-31, 10:13).
- Early apostles operated together in supportive and cooperative association and deliberate co-laboring within the districts they occupied.

2. The interaction between the local and trans-local ministries must be interconnected by relationships (ministry to ministry).

3. Differing gifts allow the overall apostolic influence to extend (reach, measure) locally, trans-regionally, nationally, and globally.

 The greatest anointing happens when we minister within our *metron* (scope of authority, scope of influence). Leaders must learn to minister to those with whom they have authority and keep within the established order of the Lord.

 The Lord gives us the ability to manage that which is within our metron. He gives us the authority to have the ability to accomplish that task.

Authority, Gifts of the Spirit, direction, and influence come to those positioned within their assignment. Confidence flows from within as we yield to our assignment and stay within the scope of our metron.

Walking in the metron of our GRACE GIFT-OFFICE causes greater authority.

Walking in the fullness of our delegated *authority* is glorious, holy, mighty, and noble. It is courageous and valiant. *True authority* has the force and ability to cause mobilization. Apostolic leaders INFLUENCE the world around them. They GIVE out. Sometimes these leaders seem confrontive, corrective, and even sometimes non-conforming. But Godly *authority* is never arrogant, untouchable, brash, presumptive, or overbearing. Leaders in *authority* have the right to expect a response from those they lead because of RELATIONSHIP LINKING.

1. There is no authority without relationship. Institutional Christianity no longer works. If you don't have relationship, you do not have full authority.

2. Relationship gives permission for authority to be released. If people refuse to cooperate with you, you have no influence with them.

3. There is no genuine authority without a sense of responsibility for how it affects the lives of people.

Alexander the Great became king of Macedonia when he was nineteen. In the next eleven years, he conquered most of the known world. His armies followed him because he led by example of real relationships

d complete confidence. Because of his leadership, no earthly force
ld stop them.

SIDER: How, who, and where do you have influence? It is fulfilling
scope of influence that determines your success. Allow wisdom to
to you. Discover what is preventing your access to greater
rity. What is the measure of the realm of the Spirit God has given
for you in ministry? What is your permitted realm of *authority*?
FOCUS on what needs to be released from you. You have Divine
permission to know, ask, and explore your potential sphere of ministry.

WHAT APOSTLES HAVE THE AUTHORITY TO DO

The way it goes with apostolic leaders determines the Church. Generally
speaking, apostles move in Kingdom *Authority* and Power (1 Cor. 2:4-5,
4:20) as follows:

Paul says that apostles are not just random self-appointed peddlers
of God's *authority* but are actually commissioned by God Himself (2
Cor. 2:17). Certain people are qualified by God to be ministers of a
New Covenant (2 Cor. 3:6).

They establish Christ's presence (Eph. 3:9-12).

They have encountered Jesus on a personal level.

They are commissioned and "sent forth" by God (Rom. 10:13-15,
Acts 13:2-4, Lk. 4:18-19).

They communicate God's Garden INTENTION.

Apostles reintroduce the intention of the Cross - concerning what
the Lord died for us to receive, what He really taught, what He
intended to communicate, and how He wanted us to apply these
Truths.

Apostles have specific authority over all principalities in Jesus
Name (Mk. 3:15).

The anointing to rule is upon an apostle.

They have "authority in heaven and on earth" (Mt. 28:18-20).

Apostles look beyond their limitations.

Apostles think objectively and are not reactive (they are not always
fire fighting). They are proactive.

They are strategists (2 Cor. 10:3-6).

They are wise (2 Pet. 3:15, 16; 1 Cor. 1:2-3).

They are visionaries always looking forward. Vision does not make someone an apostle, but all apostles have vision.

Apostles impart and activate gifts, blessings, success, and increase.

Apostles target the success and vision of others. They look outward, and not on themselves. Their ego is not threatened by the strength of others.

Apostles have authority over finances (Acts 4:34-37). They were trusted with finances, they directed and they dispersed the resources of the Church.

They start and win wars (2 Cor. 9:3-6, Eph. 6:10-18). They are catalysts and motivators. They provoke confrontation (Acts 7). Apostles like Stephen "stir up trouble" in many cities (Acts 16:20-21) in order to bring the plan of the ages into this earth (Acts 17:6, Jn. 8:58-59, Lk. 24:5).

Apostles are risk-takers and innovators.

They know how to connect into the presence of God. They bring a God encounter!

They seek the new sounds from heaven in worship (Acts 16:25).

They have learned how live and to co-exist on earth as it is in heaven.

They are concerned about what is actually being lived – rather than just learned.

They have suffered persecution, learned to overcome, and use this experience for the benefit of others.

Their gifting is observable to others.

They maintain a specific and relevant functionality in a given metron (sphere, scope of reach) of *authority*. They use their influence to affect their sphere of *authority*.

They persuade with life-changing reformational concepts that declare the total redemption of Christ Jesus.

They convert the world into the Kingdom.

They know how to refine others to become a positive contributor.

Apostles SEE believers as the New Creation. They apprehend the promises of God in the NOW and press beyond past limits. They activate the Body with a sense of mission. They birth, re-birth, and re-build into a spiritual dimension. They bless.

APOSTLES ARE WILLING TO MINISTER IN OTHER 5-fold OFFICES

Paul was an apostle/teacher (2 Tim. 1:11).

Paul and Barnabas were accounted among the prophets/teachers in Antioch (Acts 13:1).

Peter also operated as a pastor/apostle (Jn. 21:15-17).

Timothy was an evangelist/prophet (2 Tim. 4:5).

APOSTLES OFTEN PLANT NEW WORKS

They establish and build new works (churches, ministries, outreach – 1 Cor. 3:10-11; Is. 58:12, 61:1-7). Not all were involved in establishing new churches or pioneering them, but all were involved in establishing them.

They lead powerfully and others follow.

They build teams (Acts 21:8, Mat. 10:5-8, Lk. 10:1-2).

They commission, release, and "send" others (Acts 13:2-4).

THEY OPERATE IN GIFTS OF THE SPIRIT

They are involved in the baptism of the Holy Spirit (Acts 8:14-18, 10:1-16, 19:1-6). They usually move in several diverse Power Gifts, and activate miracles, signs, and wonders (2 Cor. 12:12).

Use breakthrough anointing (Micah 2:13, Is. 45:1-4, 2 Sam. 5:20).

They specialize in causing the heavenlies to manifest on earth.

They hear what God is saying TODAY (present truth).

They minister in powerful distinctiveness – with fresh revelation that transmits illuminated vision and purpose.

They walk in wisdom and understanding.

They have the mentality and wisdom to KNOW how to advance the Kingdom of God according to the nature of Christ.

THEY DEMONSTRATE THE FRUIT OF THE SPIRIT. IRREPROACHABLE, GODLY CHARACTER AND INTEGRITY SHOULD BE THE HALLMARKS OF A TRUE APOSTLE.

APOSTLES ARE GOVERNMENTAL AND RIGHTLY UNDERSTAND HOW TO USE THEIR AUTHORITY. They can potentially do the following:

Enforce forward momentum – proper direction for the whole church.

Set up foundational governments (1 Cor. 12:28, Is. 9:6-7).

Keep the church from drifting off-course into seeker sensitivity, fads, and cultural relevancy.

Know the next step. CROSS OVER.

FINISH their assignments (Heb. 12:1-4, 2 Tim. 4:7-8).

Avoid undue and excessive structure.

APOSTLES ENABLE ACCOUNTABILITY.

Build the Body of Christ into the Habitation for God.

Teach functioning and bring believers into DESTINY (Eph.4:11-16).

Equip, mentor, bless, and release leadership into right function, accountability, and understanding of etiquette (Acts 4:33, 16:4-5; Eph. 1:11-16). Teach by experiences and example.

Facilitate connections and networking with like-minded people.

APOSTLES HAVE THE AUTHORITY TO DISCIPLINE and MAINTAIN ORDER.

Apostles bring forceful discipline (Acts 5:1-11; 1 Cor. 5:1-5). Biblical discipline and correction are the God-ordained assignments of apostolic ministers. The apostle gives other elders and local shepherds instructions concerning discipline to hold others in relational answerability. This *authority* is given in order to protect the flock and keep them safe.

- They bring order and discipline (I.E. Sapphira and Ananias, Acts 5:1-11; Elymas, Acts 13:11; the Corinthian fornicator, 1 Cor. 4:21; 5:1; 2 Cor. 2:6-11; 13:2, 10).
- Discipline to Diotrephes, 3 Jn. 9, 10; because of false doctrine and speaking maliciously about others (1 Tim. 1:20) and to divisionaries (Rom. 16:17).
- They correct and reprimand when necessary (Acts 5:8:9-24).
- Paul instructed Timothy to turn Hymenaeus and Alexander over to Satan so they would learn not to blaspheme (1 Tim. 1:18-20). Elders have the *authority* to excommunicate/anathemize (also spelled anathematize -- "to deliver to satan") (also see 1 Cor. 5:3-5, 16:22; Gal 1:8; Matt. 18:17).
- Paul told Timothy that he had the *authority* to make binding decisions (1 Cor. 5:1-5). He told him to "Rebuke with all *authority*" (Tit. 2:15).
- Paul showed that he had the *authority* to give instruction concerning the company that believers should not engage (2 Thes. 3:6-14; 1 Cor. 5:11-13; 2 Thes. 3:6; Rom. 16:17).
- Paul said that he wrote this letter while he was absent, so that he wouldn't have to be "Harsh" in his "use of authority" (2 Cor. 13:10). That authority was to build up and not tear down.

"Setting boundaries, (essentially saying 'no' to someone) is a bit of an art form, which requires detachment from the situation. It is like disci-

Apostles bring a strong message of the restoration of spiritual truths.

plining your children -- never do it when you are angry, and never go grocery shopping when you are hungry." Apostle Stan DeKoven, Ph.D.

APOSTLES BRING ACCURATE REFORMATIONAL INSIGHT AND CONCEPTS

They establish, define, and continue steadfastly with DOCTRINE. Much doctrine that is taught in today's Church must be corrected.

They establish and maintain Biblical PROCEDURES for implementing government within the churches.

They defend the faith (Phil. 1:17, Jude 3, 1 Pet. 3:15).

They avoid competitive mind-sets.

They expose heresy.

They bring revolution!

 These leaders are the ARROWHEAD of the Spirit. They are the thrust of reform "called out" to soar into unfamiliar terrain and unexplored expressions of "becoming the Church."

They are innovative and inventive new thinkers, pioneers, trail blazers, revolutionists, ground breakers, re-calibrators, re-formers, re-freshers, re-vivalists, re-configurers, re-captivators, re-producers, re-locaters, re-establishers, re-concilers, re-generators, re-newalists, re-structurers, re-aligners, re-joicers, and world-shattering men and women who affect the world.

They move with God's wisdom and not empirical understanding.

They are multicultural and multinational. They enable men and women of all races, cultures, classes, and ethnic backgrounds (Micah 4:11-12; Is. 2:1-4; Acts 1:8, 17:26).

They work transgenerationally (1 Cor. 4:15-17, Prov. 13:22).

They de-emphasize cultural forms of power, status and influence.

THEY FACILITATE TRUE PROSPERITY IN THE SPIRIT, SOUL, AND BODY.

The *authority* of God only flows through humans operating in proper function. God's anointing flows greater through a foundational minister of Jesus. Apostles operate on the cutting edge and are directly truthful.

- Apostles ALWAYS have a CAUSE and RELEVANT DIRECTION for SUCCESS.
- They teach a stewardship that funds the mission of the Church (2 Cor. 8, 9).

No one chooses to be an apostle for themselves. God selects and sends (1 Cor. 1:1). God Himself appoints "some to be apostles" (Eph. 4:11). The Father, who raised Jesus from the dead, calls forth apostles (Gal. 1:1).

Apostles always obey God rather than men (Acts 5:29). Apostles cannot be men-pleasers.

Apostles function with the full identification of God's *power* in proportion to how much he/she operates in the *authority* of God.

> Apostles are not called by men – they are only recognized by them.

Jesus taught them that apostles live every moment by and through the Father who sends them (John 6:57). The objective of the life of an apostle is to carry out the works of the Father. Jesus taught apostles that their life mission is to continuously live out of God – just as a tree must live out of its roots (Jn. 8:42). The apostle has utter dependency upon their connection to the Father.

An apostle is raised up by Jesus as a bond slave having true humility.

The apostle of Jesus Christ lives by the commandments of God and proclaims His commandments (1 Tim. 1:1).

If someone receives an apostle, they give welcome to the Lord (Mat. 10:40). Those who despise apostles, despise Jesus (Luke 10:16).

The apostle's work originates in God. Apostles are given a greater witness than that of John (John 5:36). The Father gives apostles work to complete. These works bear witness of Him.

Apostles don't abandon their assignments to serve tables (Acts 6:2).

The apostle's work is to continually (steadfastly and without pause) pray and minister the word (Acts 6:4).

Apostles facilitate. They recognize the flow of the Holy Spirit and can direct meetings to go that way. They know who to call upon to participate in that endeavor. They recognize who has a prophetic word, who should be next, etc.

Paul increased in "strength" (*dunamis*, which confounded the Damascus Jews) and proved the presence of God (Acts 9:22). Being strengthened is a constant responsibility of the apostle. Those that oppose apostles are confounded by the apostle's increasing strength.

Apostles speak with the mind of God. Those who hear apostles are not able to resist the wisdom and spirit of their words (Acts 6:10).

Apostles move with great power and grace (Acts 4:33). They are to witness the REALITY of the resurrection of Jesus.

The apostle does not hold his life dear or precious (Acts 20:24).

Apostles live to execute what the Lord wants. They are task focused.

Apostles receive their office as a Gift – and with it, they receive mercy. That means they don't faint and they don't get discouraged. God will take care of them so they don't lose heart (2 Cor. 4:1).

Apostolic *AUTHORITY* MUST SHOW A SPIRIT OF EXCELLENCE.

NOTE: When apostolic authority is lacking, the body is disunited, infantile, and unsteady (Eph. 4:15-16).

THE MESSAGE OF AN APOSTLE

"What is the riches of the glory of this MYSTERY among the Gentiles? The unsearchable riches of Christ. The MYSTERY is CHRIST IN US the hope of glory" (Col. 1:27).

The apostle Paul called himself a "STEWARD of the *MYSTERY*" (1 Cor. 4:1). A Steward is one who is actively concerned with the directions of the affairs of an organization. One who superintends for another, to have the charge and oversight of; to care for with *authority*. This is someone who TENDS and GUARDS. He/she is a servant by heart function.

> Authority is the abilitly to impart the wisdom and mystery of particular revelation.

The Message Bible translates this responsibility of apostles like this: "We (LEADERS) are servants of Christ, not his masters. We are GUIDES INTO GOD'S MOST SUBLIME SECRETS, not security guards posted to protect them. The requirements for a good guide are reliability and accurate knowledge. It matters very little to me what you think of me, even less where I rank in popular opinion... I'm not aware of anything that would disqualify me from being a good guide for you..." (1 Cor. 4:1-4, MSG).

The elders are stewards of God's sacred truth and are charged with the responsibility of teaching and preserving the pure Word. They are to teach sound doctrine (2 Tim. 4:1, 3; Tit. 2:1-8). The apostle must preach the *mystery* of the revealed Personhood of Christ:

Paul said that "GRACE was given" to him (even though he was less than all saints) to know the mystery. **APOSTLES HAVE A MEASURE OF GRACE TO KNOW THE MYSTERY.**

The primary apostolic message concerned the release of a basic message - the MYSTERY. Paul requested prayer from the church to be given utterance to boldly make known the MYSTERY of the Gospel (Eph. 6:19). The mystery is hidden from the prideful, from reason, and from aspiring humans. This huge subject can only be generalized here.

- Paul certified that the gospel which he preached was not after man, but that he received it by revelation (Gal. 1:11-12).
- Christ is God's great *mystery*. "All the richest treasures of wisdom and knowledge are embedded in that *mystery* and nowhere else. And we've been shown the *mystery*" (Col. 2:2-3, MSG).
- The resurrection of the body is a *mystery* (1 Cor. 15:42, MSG).
- The *mystery* is that all believers stand on the same equal ground before God (Eph. 3:4, 6).
- The *mystery* is one flesh (Eph. 5:32). Racial and gender prejudice dissolves.The *mystery* is for the church to become "one flesh" (Eph. 5:23). One New Man.

The New Creation is not denominational. It is a new ethnic group – being One Body (1 Cor. 12:13).

- "The *mystery* in a nutshell is just this: Christ is in you, therefore you can look forward to sharing in God's glory. It's that simple. That is the substance of our Message" (Col. 1:27, MSG).
- An apostle cannot be discerned by physical appearance but by the measure of GRACE God gives to this office to make known the *MYSTERY* of the gospel and the revelation of Christ (Gal. 1:11-12). God gives us revelation of the *mystery* of Christ that can only come through GRACE.
- Paul said he had a dispensation (measure) of grace of God given to him and by "revelation He made known unto me (Paul) the *MYSTERY*..." (Eph. 3:2-3). This *mystery* transforms culture as we know it.
- Paul's ministry was "To make all men see (understand) what is the fellowship (*koininea*) of the MYSTERY, which from the beginning of the world has been had in God..." (Eph. 3:9).
- The "revelation" of "the *mystery* of Christ IN US" was given to His apostles in order to release the "vision" for what Christ wanted them to build (Eph. 3:4-5; Mt. 16:18; 1Cor. 2:16).
- Paul emphasizes the revelation of these riches which are "IN THE SAINTS" (CHRIST IN US). The church then builds upon this foundation, which allows the individuals to fulfill the "hope of

the calling." The greater the apostle and prophet reveals the revelation of the Lord, the greater will be the manifestation of the riches of the Lord.

- God MADE KNOWN to the apostles the *MYSTERY* OF HIS WILL, according to His good pleasure which He has purposed in Himself (Eph. 1:9).

"All of our praise rises to ...Jesus Christ, precisely as REVEALED IN THE MYSTERY KEPT SECRET FOR SO LONG but now an open book through the prophetic Scriptures" (Rom. 16:25-26, MSG).

- This Christian life is a great *mystery* (1 Tim. 3:15-16).
- When the 7th angel is about to sound his trumpet, the *MYSTERY* of God will be accomplished (completed, accomplished, finished, Rev. 10:7).

The New Creation is totally already IN CHRIST.

The mystery was the equality of personhood – that the Gentiles were to be fellow heirs of the same body (Eph. 3:1-6) receiving the fullness of blessing. This was a new dispensation. The "wall of partition" was broken down (Eph. 2:12-22). This unveiling continues today.

The Great Commission concerns the Gospel to every creature (Mat. 28:19; Mk. 16:15, 20; Acts 1:8). The Jew and Gentile, bond and free, male and female are the *Mystery* Body of Christ (Eph. 3:1-9). It is the UNION of all believers by spiritual birth.

The apostle and the prophet are divinely anointed ministers appointed to reveal to the church how these riches OF and IN CHRIST are available NOW (Eph. 1:18). After the apostle delivers the revelation of these riches, he or she then mentors the believer as to how to participate in this truth.

The MYSTERY:

The FELLOWSHIP (*koininea*, communion) of the *MYSTERY*, that was hidden IN the creator God from the beginning (Eph. 3:0). Christ in you (plural), THE HOPE OF GLORY (Eph. 3:8-9, Col. 1:27). Apostles speak the concerning the *MYSTERY* and the hidden wisdom (will of God) which was God's intention before the foundation of the world (1 Cor. 2:7).

- Warning every man (exhorting, admonishing and warning).
- And teaching everybody in all wisdom.
- So that everyone will become mature (in the likeness of Christ's character) (Col. 1:28).

THE DESTINY of APOSTLES

Full restoration means that the Church receives those who are SENT! -- Don Atkin

God expected apostles to be exhibited (as in a theatre) as a spectacle to the world, to the angels, and to be the last in receiving honor and the recognition of men (1 Cor. 4:9).

Apostles were sentenced and *doomed to die* (1 Cor. 4:9). They put trust only in the God who raises the DEAD (2 Cor. 1:9). They were often martyrs, though in many times it was not a physical death, but rather a total loss of reputation. They were defamed as the offscouring (food scraps on a dirty plate) of the world (1 Cor. 4:13).

The highly esteemed of men are an abomination to God (Lk. 16:15).

Apostles willingly become fools (literally "morons") to the world, but wise in Christ. Honorable but despised (without respect, Cor. 4:10).

In order that others can partake of God's power, apostles sacrifice (1 Cor. 9:12). Sometimes they are hungry, thirsty, naked (without good clothes), and beaten. Often, they have no home of their own. They can work with their hands. They patiently endure persecution and bless their abusers (1 Cor. 4:11-12). No matter how bad it gets, their behavior exhibits the ways of the Lord (2 Cor. 5:13).

THE AUTHORITY OF APOSTOLIC LEADERS

APOSTLES HAVE THE AUTHORITY TO FORGIVE SIN. "... If you forgive anyone his sins, they are forgiven; if you don't forgive, they are not forgiven" (Jn. 20:23).

God gives authority to His apostles (2 Cor. 10:8). Apostles have the *authority* to *correct* others (1 Cor. 1 MSG) because of their *authority* IN Christ (1 Cor. 5:4-5). Apostles speak, exhort, and *rebuke* with ALL *AUTHORITY* (Titus 2:15). They *admonish* (1 Thes. 5:12).

Apostles can *ask others to FOLLOW them:* "... I have begotten you through the gospel. Wherefore I beseech you, be ye followers of me" (1 Cor. 4:15-16, 11:1, 16:15-16; 2 Thes. 3:7; Phil. 3:17).

They are *sent to know your faith* (1 Thes. 3:5-6). Apostles know *whether you are obedient in all things* (2 Cor. 2:9). If people don't obey them, apostles have the *authority* to tell others to have nothing to do with them (2 Thes. 3:14).

Apostles have *authority* from God to try to *perfect that which is lacking in your faith* (1 Thes. 3:10).

The apostle *decrees* and it is established (Job 22:28).

They are to be *helpers of your joy* (2 Cor. 1:24).

They are to *feed you with knowledge and understanding* (Jer. 3:15).

Apostles are *bold against some* who think that they live by the standards of this world (2 Cor. 10:2, NIV).

They can boldly *order* others to do things. "*In Christ I could be (very) bold and order you to do what you ought to do*" (Phil. 1:8, Literal).

SECTION 6

Correct Patterns

The Correct Pattern

God's Authority is missing because

We need the RIGHT PATTERN

The Lord moves with those who choose to align with Him in accuracy.

What we see is that the pattern for Church government was never supposed to be a pyramid – iT can be expressed as a CIRCLE. We see this Divine pattern revealed everywhere in Scripture and also

nature. Within that circle we find sections (churches) in a V formation, like a cut pie. That means the V formations all need to be connected (relationally) within that circle.

God is NOT ecumenical. He does not just "go along" with everything that everyone says. God demands that we do things ACCORDING TO HIS PATTERN.

CIRCULAR STRUCTURE IS the NEXT "REVOLUTION" in CHURCH GOVERNMENT.

rev-o-lu-tion *noun* - a turning around, exchange.

1. *An Overthrow* or replacement of an established government or political system by the people governed.

2. *Sociology* – a radical and pervasive change in society and the social structure, often made suddenly and often accompanied by violence.

3. A sudden or marked change such as the present revolution in church government. Succession of one thing to another. An alteration from one state to another essence. Creative variation.

4. *Mechanics* – a single turn of this kind.
   a. a turning round or rotating, as on an axis.
   b. a moving in a circular course, as about a central point.

5. *Astronomy* – the orbiting of one heavenly body around another. A single course. A cycle of events in time or a recurring event.

MOSES

Moses crossed the Red Sea with the mass of millions of Israelites. On the other side, they came out as identifiable **TRIBES IN ORDER** and governmental rank. They were given Divine provision and they camped in tents circling **AROUND** the **TABERNACLE**. Each tribe had its own appointed and ordered location assignment to camp.

12 Tribes Encirling the Arc at their banner

Ephriam — Dan, Asher, Naphtali — Judah

Manasseh Benjamin — Ruben, Simon, Gad — Issachar Zebulon

Tabernacle of Moses

Four living creatures Exk. 1:4-10
Four beasts Rev. 4:6-7

Here, in the wilderness, the Lord said: "Then have them make a sanctuary for me, and I will dwell among them. **MAKE THIS TABERNACLE AND ALL ITS FURNISHINGS EXACTLY LIKE THE PATTERN**" (Ex. 25:8-9).

Seventeen times Moses was instructed to build everything and complete it "according to pattern." There were to be no alterations, no shortcuts, and no human ideas added. It took them nine months to complete the task and then the Shekinah Glory filled the Tabernacle.

NOTICE the eagle, the lion, the bull, and the man were the flags or standards placed **AROUND** the Tabernacle. These ensigns or flags were held high in the air to show the various tribes where to camp – and they did so encircling the tabernacling presence of God. These same images are used in several types of our circle pattern. They represent the multiple leaders who operate more near the center with the tribes gathered near. The tribes were divided into four main groups under four flags. This circular theme radiates outward.

JERUSALEM: The city of Jerusalem was built by David **AROUND** the temple and then exteriorly surrounded by a circular wall. We sing about Jerusalem, the city in heaven, being foursquare – but we find on the ancient maps that it was a **CIRCLE**. In fact, all fortified cities were in a circle. Jericho being a famous example of circular cities.

GILGAL: Joshua conquered Gilgal (literally **CIRCLE OF STANDING STONES**). Elisha and Elijah were there. Samuel annually circled back to Gilgal.

"And the LORD said unto Joshua, 'This day have I ROLLED away the reproach of Egypt from off you.' Wherefore the name of the place is called GILGAL unto this day" (Josh. 5:9).

The root word of Gilgal (*gal-gal*, circle) is *galah* (# H1540) and is translated as uncovered, returning back again, discovered, opened, or revealed (as in Is. 53:1).

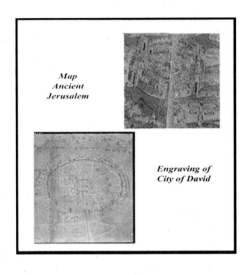

Map Ancient Jerusalem

Engraving of City of David

Galah is the Hebrew *root of the word Revelation* - the revealing of circles that governs the overall geometric structure of Scripture!

The Greek name of the place of the Lord's crucifixion is *Golgotha*. The center of this word is *galah* and has the two letters, the Aleph on the front and the Tav on the end (from A-Z, beginning to end, the essence of all things). These are the first and last letters of the Hebrew alphabet. This gives us the picture of the cross within God's Wheel – the cross being the axis around which the wheel rotates.

The cross is the central event of history and the center of time as can be measured.

Gilgal (galgal) point directly and inevitably to its central event at Golgotha, the crucifixion of the Lord Jesus Christ, where the reproach of our sin was forever rolled away. Glory to God in the highest!

The Septuagint translates *galah* with the Greek verb *apocalupto*, the name of the final New Testament Book, the Apocalypse of Jesus. Jesus used *galah* when He said, "there is nothing covered, that shall not be revealed; neither hid, that shall not be known" (Luke 12:2).

Galgal is a common Hebrew word for "wheel." Galgal appears twelve times in the Old Testament, such as the "wheels (*galgal*) like a whirlwind (circular storm)" (Isa. 5:28), the "take fire from between the wheels" (Ezk. 10:6), and below the throne of God, the "wheels were all ablaze." Daniel said that the Ancient of Days had hair like the pure wool: his throne was like the fiery flame, and his wheels (*galgalim*) as burning fire (Dan. 7:9).

GALILEE: The name means to come back AROUND again.

The Lord God chose the circle upon which to hang His everlasting Word. The circle is unique among all objects in that it alone is infinitely symmetric. A Circle can be drawn from ONE LINE and it can be rotated at any angle and have no variation in form.

DAVID'S TABERNACLE

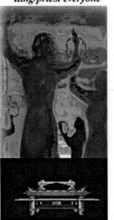

King/priest everyone

The Apostle James says that the Tabernacle of David is rebuilt, "that the rest of mankind may seek the Lord" (Acts 15:16-17). People came from every direction to the top (center). They gathered without a veil to worship the Lord (see Is. 2:2-4; Micah 4:1-5). God's people shall go UP to the mountain of the Lord. This tabernacle is all about government!

How can the rest of mankind seek the Lord because of this Tabernacle? We've been singing and dancing for a while now. What's missing? The PRESENCE gives us a vantage of RULE! Concerning this Tabernacle, God said, "I will rebuild and I will restore it." Notice again that the presence of God is on TOP of the mountain!

SOLOMON'S TEMPLE

Solomon built a circular structure built ACCORDING TO THE PATTERN that David received (1 Chron. 28:12-13, 19). This Temple was built for one reason – to house the GLORY. The musicians centered around the presence of the Lord (in the center). And no one could stand (2 Chron. 5:12-14). Notice the leaders surrounding the near center.

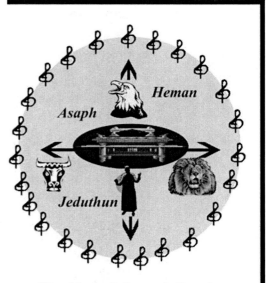

Worship in Solomon's Temple

Acts 3:21   The CIRCLE of God

Jesus waits

The Garden intention.
That which He purchased to be realized.
Until the resoration of all things.
That which was lost to be regained.
For us to be like Him!

We need to come FULL CIRCLE back to what God intended! He waits for us to "get it!" He is the place where it all revolves... the One who is the CENTER of all.

The circle is known to symbolize infinity, completeness, and wholeness, the circle of life and eternity.

EZEKIEL'S WHEEL

Ezekiel 43:10, "Thou son of man... let them measure the pattern." Ezekiel beheld the pattern of the WHEEL (*galgal*, a circle within a circle).[1] Ezekiel also saw FOUR LIVING CREATURES not turning as they moved. Notice that the presence of God is in the center. Where are the leaders? Yes. Around the presence. The center is the dwelling place of God. Much of what we think we know explodes as we consider new concepts of Church government.

HEAVENLY TEMPLE

Twenty-four elders dressed in white (a symbol or type of righteousness) gather around the Lamb of God (Rev. 4:4, 4:10, 5:14, 11:16). This revelation fully shows us the circular PATTERN for worship and assembly around the LORD.

The leaders are closer inside the circle than the rest. These elders (*presbuteros*) have crowns (symbolic of their *authority*).

Where's the presence of God? In the center – as the Lamb.

THE CIRCULAR RAINBOW

John saw the circular rainbow (Rev. 4:2-3), "...Immediately I was in the Spirit; and behold, a throne (seat of governmental power) was standing (literally outstretched) in heaven... and there was a RAINBOW AROUND (circled as a ring around) the throne, like an EMERALD in appearance." RAINBOWS are emblematic of the implementation of God's absolute sovereign *authority* and never ending promises of faithfulness. He remembers His covenant concerning His creation.

---

1. See my book, "Connecting," for a deeper study on Ezekiel's wheel.

- Ezekiel also saw a rainbow (1:27-28). "Like the appearance of a RAINBOW in a cloud on a rainy day, so was the appearance of the brightness all around it. This was the appearance of the likeness of the glory of the LORD..." (NKJV). It was within this arching vision, that Ezekiel received his mandate for ministry.

- Interestingly, the New Testament word for rainbow is "iris" (from NT:2036) which is identical in meaning with #1482 which presents the idea of pouring forth in speech. To SAY. And it is in this way that the Lord SPEAKS from within a rainbow the familiar mandate that ushers in the manifested expansion of His dimensional presence upon the earth.[1]

"Our life is an apprenticeship to the truth that around every circle another can be drawn; that there is no end in nature, but every end is a beginning, and under every deep a lower deep opens."
Ralph Waldo Emerson

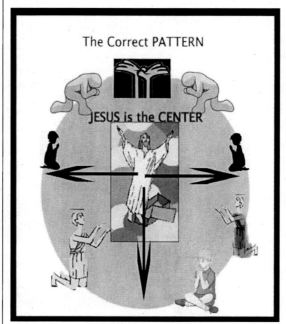

JESUS

When we build around the SON, we have correct structure and lines of accountability. The leaders are situated near the center – as we see in all the patterns. Great changes come as the world sees the Church take her place in the proper PATTERN.

The ONLY pattern for effective Church government is when the LORD is the center of all. Only the infallible Divine Son can effectively govern and direct the Church. He uses us as we connect to Him. He alone is our SOURCE.

Government should be built around the presence of the Lord. He is center.

---

1. Excerpt from my "Wisdom" book.

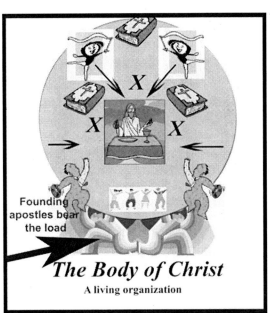

The Body of Christ

A living organization

Founding apostles bear the load

Apostles are the FOUNDATION. They undergird and support. They are NOT the top of the structure but below. They are the PROTON or first in to serve and position the church.

The *Circle Pattern with elder/leaders near the center* provides interactions among all dimensions. The leaders can quickly see the whole story and gain insights into the creative strengths of those nearby.

LAMPSTAND REVELATION

On Patmos, John saw twenty-four Elders CIRCLED around the throne with harps in their hands and He heard them sing a new song (Rev. 5:9-10).

The LORD is IN THE MIDST of the churches that surround Him (Rev. 1:10-20, 4:6-7). Christ appears "in the midst" of the seven golden lamp stands which represent the seven Asian Churches.

> "*Where two or three are gathered together in My Name, there I AM IN THE MIDST of them*" (Mat. 18:15-20).

In the MIDST of the 7 golden lampstands I saw One like the son of God...

We look to the "Heavenly Jerusa.lem" (Heb. 12:22-23) where Jesus is the omnipotent Apostle of the Church.

He alone can meet the needs of His people. Jesus personally addressed each "angel" or MESSENGER (a definition of an apostle) of each local Church (Rev. 1:10-20). He spoke to each representative personally (notice that each church was locally governed – no "head church"). No one had "control" over them but they were connected relationally. within the circle, the Lord can interact with every participant. The whole circle (strengths and weakness, balance and imbalance, internal operating system, and external interaction) is immediately apparent.

 Reformation is accomplished by FOLLOWING GOD'S PATTERN. A good example is Josiah. At age 8, he became king over Israel. Obviously, this reformer had little previous training or personal maturity. Josiah's advisors were under old patterns of idolatry. Josiah went back to study the last established pattern that had worked. He studied what David said. As he established the proper pattern, God's blessings came upon an entire nation.

Circles help us visualize the RELATIONSHIP that should exist between the Lord, His selected leaders and their teams, and believers. There is one SOURCE, but many members in the Body. All members are equal as members, each having unique assignments.

Church government must be brought into proper formation – not a pyramid anymore. Individual ministries within that church could be seen as a wedge moving forward. Being in formation is coming into proper ALIGNMENT with others and then going together with them.

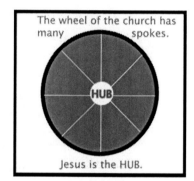

The wheel of the church has many spokes.

HUB

Jesus is the HUB.

A church is like a circle with Jesus as the HUB. The spokes represent the different leaders reaching from the HUB to the expanding RIM. All spokes (separate ministries working together) rotate the ever expanding circle and rim of their own geographical locations.

BODY OF CHIRST

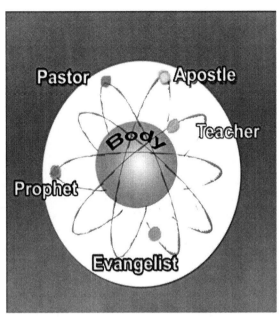

There is great value and advantage to plural leadership within a circular structure. There can be no jealousy, no striving or jockeying for position when we are situated correctly around the throne.

In the Book of Acts, there was no real "Central Church Headquarters."The apostles in Jerusalem didn't try to dominate every local Church. Jerusalem was NOT the governing body OVER Antioch or Corinth. Greater authority comes as we align more closely with God's PATTERN.

The unveiling of what God has made, shows the tendency to return to Him. The whole course of history is like a mighty circle bringing us back to garden intention. Circles are found in DNA unwinding the double helix, planets and their orbits, water dropping into a still lake, babies in the womb, galaxies, and solar systems, planets.

We can gradate color on the color wheel and music on the circle of fifths – to name only a few.

RIGHT PATTERNS = DIVINE SPIRITUAL ORDER.

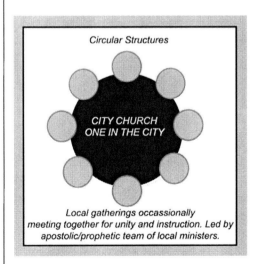

DIVINE SPIRITUAL ORDER = DIVINE PRESENCE. This concept (in diagram) shows circles joining together into the bigger one. This can occur when city Elders are established as overseers of a city.

The New Testament Church is identified as ALL THE BELIEVERS IN A CITY – never individual groups (study Corinth and Ephesus). The *ecclesia* is the assembly of intermingled covenant communities, embodied with God's passion and presence. This concept returns us FULL CIRCLE back to the Lord's original commissioning charge of having dominion rule to change this world.

"He has described a CIRCLE upon the face of the waters at the boundary between light and darkness" (Job 26:10, Is. 40:22).

We find that the Great Divine Architect carved the universe in circles. Galileo wrote that if one is to understand the Bible and the universe, one must understand the language in which it is written. That language is the mathematics of concentric geometrical figures.

"I was there when He set a CIRCLE upon the face of the deep" (Prov. 8:27).

Circular geometricals depicted in this enhanced Icon show Jesus as The Word (circle halo) the Alpha and Omega.

Please note that all the illustrations for this portion are available as overheads on www.kluane.org website.

A Different Spirit

MUTUALLY BEARING THE LOAD

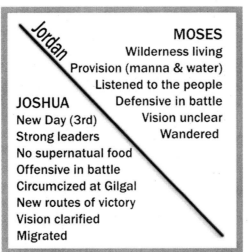

MOSES
Wilderness living
Provision (manna & water)
Listened to the people
Defensive in battle
Vision unclear
Wandered

JOSHUA
New Day (3rd)
Strong leaders
No supernatual food
Offensive in battle
Circumcized at Gilgal
New routes of victory
Vision clarified
Migrated

We talked earlier about how Moses couldn't lead the Israelites INTO the Promise Land. He tried to divide the groups into teams with leaders – but that didn't work. Then, he selected seventy with talents and giftings. But, they all perished in the wilderness.

Forty YEARS later A BRAND NEW TYPE OF PEOPLE emerged. Joshua and Caleb were God's intended representative for a different direction for the people.

Joshua and Caleb were leaders with a "different spirit" who were able to LEAD PEOPLE into the Promise Land. This concept marks a transition in the spirit of leadership. A new breed. Joshua was eighty years old (625 B.C.) when he took charge (Josh. 1:2) and began to cross the Jordan.

- Like Joshua and Caleb, we have been appointed as leaders toward this awesome migration of His Church.
- For us, this new crossing over will break through and press beyond religious mind-sets, customs, and traditions of the past.

They had "NEVER BEEN THIS WAY BEFORE!" (We must move past the present revelations and not camp at a comfortable place.) "Consecrate and SEPARATE yourselves, for tomorrow (the 3rd Day) the LORD will do amazing WONDERS among you." Every generation must cross into a new revelation of His will.

Joshua defined a new era – he was a strong LEADER – a person with insight and discernment. Because the presence of God (upon the ark)

and the governmental *authority* (twelve) *equally* rested on the shoulders of the priests, the river Jordan parted. It was then that the octogenarian shouted out with determination, "We're CROSSING OVER!"

When the Jordan parted, every priest had to LIFT UP, GET UNDER, and CROSS OVER for himself. They had to pass individually, as a unit.

How did they do that? Submission to *authority*. Someone had to be the set-person to lead and tell them when and where to CROSS OVER – then they had to join their individual destinies into the greater collective mission.

> ## Apostolic leaders are FOUNDATIONAL. They get under and LIFT UP. That's submission!

True leaders become the platform to serve and release the corporate and individual destiny of others.

Here is a perfect PICTURE of true SUBMISSION: "GETTING UNDER AND GIVING SUPPORT." It is a voluntary yielding of your preferences for the sake of the greater mandate – it is agreement with a common purpose. In this hour there must be submission to the one who declares the order of steps.

The Jordan had to be crossed. (The word "Jordan" means a place of sudden descent). We must have a revelation to set aside our individual preferences in order to lead others to "cross over" (migrate). It's the only way to take the cities on the other side.

The presence of GOD WENT FIRST (Josh. 3:11) on the shoulders of the priests and made the way through that flooding river. JOSHUA WENT LAST. He waited until everyone else "crossed over" before he could cross. The visionary made sure everyone crossed over before crossing himself.

Joshua's success came early because he had leaders work together and "share the load" – each priest took hold and lifted the weight of God's presence (that was in that arc) onto their shoulder – and only then did they step together into the river Jordan.

> ## Leaders must SUBMIT (GET UNDER AND LIFT UP) to the presence of God in order to move.

The Lord looks for those who understand that the ark of God cannot move with just one person. No one holds all the anointing or strength to carry the presence of God. We must mutually bear the load.

The twelve (the number of government – the team of *authority*) priests bore the glory and went before the others. They walked with the weight of the GLORY on their shoulders. No one walked out of order.

Walking together means that competitive insecurity ends. We're all priests and together we can lift His presence and move toward the promise.

The set-leader commands the ministers to get UNDER that ark together. Those in ministry positions (the team of elders) are not supposed to be self-ruling. They're just supposed to put their foot in the water with someone else and get under and lift up the presence of God. Be joined together under the ark and CROSS OVER.

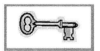 True submission means, "Getting under and giving support." Submission is always voluntarily yielding your preferences for the sake of a greater mandate. It is agreement with a common purpose.

* TOGETHER means we don't look for someone else to carry all the load of the presence of God.
* Notice that when priests cross over together (in a team) they enter into prophetic vision and purpose.

LIFTING UP

"Be RESPONSIVE to your pastoral LEADERS. Listen to their counsel. They are alert to the condition of your lives and work under the strict supervision of God. Contribute to the joy of their leadership, not its drudgery. Why... make things harder for them?" (Heb. 13:17, MSG)

Leaders "get under" and support believers.

Believers "get under" and support leaders.

As mentioned above, Hebrews 13:17-19 gives us a command. The King James says, "Obey!" (The word actually means to believe, yield, respond, trust, have confidence in, yield to, support from *"hupo"* to get UNDER. See also Rom. 2:8; Gal. 5:7; Heb. 13:17; James 3:3).

"Obey" does not mean unflinching obedience.

Support and trust your leaders." Why? "Because "they keep watch (stay awake) over you (your mind and soul – *psuche*) as men who must give an account (#3056 *logos*, speak the word)" (NIV). We could also translate Hebrews 13 like this: "Trust in your leaders who speak the truth. Imitate them.

Yield, support, and give deference to them because they watch over you and must/will speak the truth of God's Word to you."

Follow those who follow the Lord (1 Cor. 11:11).

Mutual submission = Believers support leaders

Why should believers submit to (get under and support) their leaders? Because leaders, "Keep watch (stay awake) over you (your soul, your mind – *psuche*) as men who must give an account (#3056 *logos*, speak the word, NIV). Perhaps we could say it like this, "TRUST in your leaders and yield to them for they watch over you and must/will speak the Word to you."

We are not COVERED by people. But we do submit (get under and support) others.

SUBMISSION IS A VOLUNTARY, MUTUAL, AND RECIPROCAL ACTIVITY.

 To submit means that we uphold others and that we do not undermine them by criticism, or by gossip.

"Don't listen to a complaint against a LEADER that isn't backed up by two or three responsible witnesses" (1 Tim. 5:19, MSG).

Another scripture often misused is Titus 3:1. Please follow in your Bible as we break this verse down: "Put them in mind to be subject (*hupotasso*, be UNDER) to principalities (*arche* – meaning ORIGIN and beginnings) and powers (*exousia* – mis-translated, should be author-ities), to OBEY magistrates (obey is an added word not in text), to be ready to every good work." What Paul probably had in mind here was that believers must yield to Him WHO was the AUTHOR, (beginner and origin) of their faith and obey Jesus and those He puts in charge.

The pre-eminent New Testament concept of submission to just *authority* is unquestionable. YES, WE ARE TO SUBMIT TO *AUTHORITY*. That never means being a mindless "doormat."

Submission = to voluntarily defer our preferences for the benefit of another person or another cause. Notice this primary definition did not mean to become "subordinate," but rather to voluntarily cooperate and yield.

NOTICE THIS! It's all about mutual submission! BELIEVERS SUPPORT LEADERS. LEADERS SUPPORT BELIEVERS. The word for submission (*hupotassomai*) is nearly identical in *meaning* to the word *agape* – which is

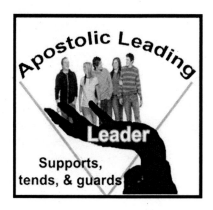

Apostolic Leading

Leader

Supports, tends, & guards

*All
leadership
must be
underneath
PUSHING up.*

the God kind of love! We defer and prefer because we WANT to do it. With NO EXPECTATION OF RETURN!

Submission literally means to "get under and PUSH UP with support."

Submission speaks of a mutual alliance, a compatible rapport of interdependence with another person – one that promotes complimentary harmony. Submission to Godly *authority* becomes an "adjustment ethic," which means that we CHOOSE to cooperate. Submission to just *authority* should not require an evaluation of every circumstance. Willing submission should spontaneously arise from a yielded heart.

True surrender requires discriminative choices concerning who you entrust with this task. Submission allows you to covenantally cooperate with someone. It means we allow them to see us as we are, without hiding behind a mask.

What is the criteria for finding those you can trust? Genuine spiritual mentors promote their disciples' self-worth and self-respect. Rather than insisting on absolute compliance with their opinions, they encourage the right to inner inquiry – which should drive you to personal discipline, actualization, study, and search.

THE PATTERN is MUTUAL SUBMISSION

*Submission
is mutual.*

The defining difference is – yes there's governmental *authority*, but government is NOT a "covering" from the top. Apostolic leadership is the foundation or UNDERNEATH. It supports everything else.

We choose to do things BECAUSE WE WANT TO and not because we have to. That way, our motive is right and our will is left intact.

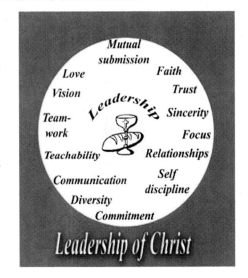

Properly aligned, the foundational Apostolic *AUTHORITY* is the perfect picture of submission. True submission upholds, supports, and under-girds ministry by standing firmly beneath. Notice how true *authority* is parallel to the proper definition of "submission" (the getting under and giving support).

The task of a wise leader is not to try to run the church alone, but to determine how the Lord wants to do it and appoint and train others to have *authority* also. Godly *authority* operates from a clear motivation to enable and enhance other people's lives with Divine purpose.

SECTION 7

What Was Lost & Why?

What Were the Consequences?

Authority Lost Through Hierarchy

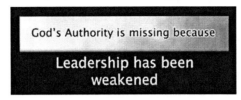

God's Authority is missing because

Leadership has been weakened

"The primary mission of Jesus was to tear down religion as the foundation for people's connection with God and to replace it with Himself – the Divine coming to us in our own context and our own form. This is what Jesus called the 'Kingdom of God.' It is God and His people living together the way He originally intended." (Pastor Bruxy Cavey, from "The End of Religion," p.23)

It's hard to comprehend how the ideas about church *authority* became distorted for centuries. This crisis has been studiously ignored until now. We find that some early ecclesiastical leaders caused many doctrinal problems concerning *authority* - and these ideas are commonly perpetuated today.

Hierarchical government (from the Greek, "*hieros*" = sacred, and "*archos*" = ruler) is the most typical type of government for the church at this hour. This was patterned after the churches under Papal and Episcopal forms of government where the Pope, Cardinal, or the Bishop represented the "one person ruler" OVER the group. *Authority* is invested in that one person.

We usually think that the beginning of Hierarchal government started with the Remnant Theory. That theory says that the first Church started out wonderfully until the wicked, self-centered Church Fathers deliberately led everyone astray. Everything they did was evil and wrong.

The problem with that thinking is that *initially*, the hierarchical government of the church was set up to maintain unity and order and the love and cohesiveness of the Church. Originally, these dedicated men tried to establish a government that would prevent people from spreading alternative ideas which could cause disruption and mayhem. They didn't know a better way.

- The encyclicals of St. Ignatius (about 110) tell how he believed that there was a Divine origin for hierarchy and priesthood – in order to "protect the precious."
- The first instatement of formal clergy was intended to maintain the unity of faith and to protect the preciousness of the Gospel.

As we know, their idealism was disrupted and the principles of true apostleship were lost. History tells us, man-made ideas began to interweave into the church. Still, our biggest resistances to governing *authority* stems from this past misuse of *authority* – especially during the Medieval era where fanfare and vestments increased. Human energy and efforts could not produce the glorious Kingdom. UNTIL WE CORRECT THESE long held ERRORS, WE LABOR IN VAIN.

1. In about 300 A.D., strict governmental structure was established to maintain the status quo of the church – so that things wouldn't change. This is the beginning of hierarchy.

- Scriptures were only interpreted to confirm what the Church Fathers established. If contradictions emerged, then the interpretive writings of the Apostolic Fathers were chosen *above* the Scriptures.
- Everyone was expected to accept what the Church (the custodian and absolute official interpreter) said about Scripture – as that interpretation was official.

2. The Catholic Church established itself as the holder of all truth and insisted upon rigid conformity to excessive church order and rule. The installation of the succession of "Apostolic *Authority*" upon those elitist Church Fathers placed them on the highest of pecking orders. Their "spoken words" became equivalent (equal to) that of Divine Scripture.

Priests insisted that "Apostolic *Authority*" was intrinsically patriarchal, (meaning that it was limited to certain men).

Church statements concerning the *AUTHORITY* of the pope is where "hierarchy" really began to go astray:

- "As to papal *authority*, the Pope is as it were God on earth, sole sovereign of all the faithful of Christ, chief king of kings, having a plenitude of unbroken power, entrusted by the omnipotent God to govern the earthly and heavenly kingdoms."
- "The Pope is of so great *authority* and power, that he is able to modify, declare, or interpret even divine laws."
- "The Pope is of so great dignity and so exalted that he is not mere man, but as it were God, and the vicar of God."[1]
- The Roman Church claimed that Peter had the *authority* and position as the first Pope. However, Paul's last letter (Second Timothy) is dated around 68 AD. Most Scholars agree that Peter died in Rome by at least 66 AD. That means Peter had already died two years before Paul's last letter from Rome.[2] The writings of Paul do not state that Peter was the Bishop of Rome.

---

1. http://www.lightministries.com/id523.htm
2. These quotes are from The New Unger's Bible Dictionary. Originally published by Moody Press of Chicago, Illinois. Copyright © 1988.

These priests decided that the Spiritual Gifts once distributed to everyone, were for the priests only and could no longer be used by the general assembly. Now, only the elect priesthood could interpret or mediate. Only designated "priests" could receive revelation and hear the voice of God. All others were silenced.

3. Only a few select scholars of the Church were qualified to confer with the mystical meanings of this magical oracle. Medical and scientific research were considered ungodly. Superstition prevailed, and neither laity, nor the religious, really understood the Scriptures that remained hidden away in monasteries.

4. In the Middle Ages, the Church Fathers ruled with tenacious control. Prohibitions increased and taxes were levied. Indulgences were sold and MANDATORY GIVING was demanded. This church amassed fortunes. The established priesthood ruled with absolute *dictatorial authority*. The select and elite "clergy" vehemently suppressed all "laity" (common people).

5. For centuries, Church TRADITION was exalted as the only truth, which placed the words of the Church Fathers above Scriptures (called Apostolic Doctrine).

6. The Apostolic Fathers' viewpoint defined and contained ALL acceptable human knowledge, both sacred and secular. Their unbending views began to be severely questioned during the 17th century when the new astronomy findings of people like Nicolaus Copernicus (1473-1543) and of Galileo Galilei (1564-1642) challenged the known system of thinking.

The Reformation brought a renewed appeal for the Scriptures to be the final *authority*. They decided that the church should be built upon Scripture and not the other way around. (Mt. 15:6, Mk. 7:8-9). Biblical scholars began contradicting ancient religious traditions.

The development of the printing press during the Reformation also brought a renewal of learning that sparked greater inquiry. Information spread into an intellectually starving civilization that had been steeped in centuries of ignorance and superstition.

The emerging Protestant Reformation sought to teach the priesthood of the believer.[1] Following that we find a series of revivals and movements that gradually began to change the dynamics of church government.

The Protestant Revolution brought new emphasis on having a personal experience with God. Finally, some new theologians pressed beyond blind prejudices. Faithless lack of reasoning slowly gave way to a more accurate approach to the Bible.

---

1. See my book, "From Enmity to Equality" for more information.

- The early Protestant concepts of the *"Priesthood of all believers"* was for men only. Especially selected male authority figures still maintained absolute control and spectator-performance-type meetings.
- The pyramid pattern continued into the Protestant renewal – and is still the only structure commonly taught.

The beginning of the 20th century opened many variations of Bible translations beyond the King James of 1611. Later, we will study the more about the wrong consequences of this hierarchal development.

1940-50's brought the restoration of the office of "Evangelist." The Gifts of the Spirit became more used by the general believer. The Latter Rain movement and the "manifest sons" teachings began.

1960's brought the restoration of the office of "Pastor." Renewals ignited and Spirit-filled believers birthed many new ministries.

1970's was the restoration of the "Teacher" and the era of the Word of Faith groups, believer's *authority*, confession, and cell churches.

1980's showed us the restoration of the office of the "Prophet." The church began to hear more about the Tabernacle of David truths and hear the voice of the Lord as many waters. Teachings of dominion emerged and intercession increased. Greater signs and wonders occurred in the church. This also began greater understanding of the Third Day.

1990's began the restoration of the office of "Apostle" with glimpses of new governmental order.

2000's bring forth the realization of the corporate Body ON EARTH, the consummated Bride, Manchild company coming forth, Apostolic Destiny, greater dimensions, unheard frequencies, etc.

The quest today is to re-discover God's original intention concerning authority.

We are moving into an era of the Corporate Christ revealing Himself within the Body. All the believers must establish the awareness of their Royal Melchizedek priesthood and begin to possess the Kingdom (Dan. 7:22). This global priesthood is free from prejudice and is swallowed up into the revelation that the blood of Christ has already made us one (Gen. 14:18-20; Heb. 5:10-14, 7:1-18; 1 Pet. 2:5; Rev. 1:5-6, 5:10).

The danger in these previously mentioned governmental styles is that ONE person usually has no "checks and balances." This hierarchy was the beginning of the "pyramid structure" in church government.

The Pyramid

By the thousands, believers are searching for greater definition, purpose, and direction. These people are rethinking traditional ministries and migrating toward new apostolic reformation and revolution.

Now, a new pattern for effective ministry is rediscovered. It's not really new. It's the apostolic model that pioneered the great early Church. A couple hundred years later, we find change already starting.

Hierarchical governmental structures replaced the intended pattern by setting up clerical church roles of command and management. (See pyramid diagram.) We replicate this type of government mainly because it is all that we have ever known.

Pyramids don't work in government. Even the disciples had to learn about the positions that they would receive from Jesus. "Now there was also a dispute among them, as to which of them should be considered the greatest" (Luke 22:24-30). This NEEDING to be the ONLY Number One is common. Jesus answered that their question of seating priority was a wrong seeking of *AUTHORITY*.

This pyramid formation was NOT the style of government of the first early Church. The original apostles led with governmental *authority* and influence but not with authoritarian control (Eph. 4:11-12).

Hierarchy church management tends to be a self-centered phenomena. The problem with this style of government is that those on the lower ranks always want to get "up there" to the "higher" leadership. They want titles and position rather than responsibility. The members strive to be elders, the elders want to be on the board, others think they should be the pastor. It is a DOCTRINE of "BESTING" which presents a

CLOSED SYSTEM of management. Everyone involved is focused on personal promotion and advancement to the #1 spot. Everyone "needs" to have a pulpit ministry and their optimum goal is to be THE pastor.

The first church was not run by one person. The current term "pastor" is more defined from a traditional experience than a Scriptural one. Building another pastoral leadership program is insufficient in affecting the hour in which we live.

Jesus didn't build His church upon the foundation of pastors – but upon Apostles and Prophets – He Himself being the chief cornerstone.

What happens in this closed system is that the pastors tend to be in rival competition with the church down the street. The seeds of dissatisfaction and competition are reproduced all the way down the pyramid ladder. This ambitious striving for position breeds quickly among the membership. Therefore, dissatisfaction fills the ranks. Leaders want to be elders. Elders want to be pastors, etc. There is a constant jockeying for prominence. Innumerable people have been hurt because of this squabbling and infighting.

Hierarchical church government causes everyone inside the structure to posture the same way the leader does. And that means down deep no one really wants to assist, help, or play "second fiddle." Everyone wants to be NUMBER ONE!

> Diotrephes seemed to exemplify this kind of ruling (3 Jn. 9-10). Diotrephes-like government systems are those with one person ruling everyone else. He would not receive the apostles. He spoke against them maliciously. He forbade the others in that church to receive the apostles. He excommunicated those who did receive the apostles or any other traveling ministry (3 Jn. 6, 9-10).

The attitude in the heart of a one-leader contending PYRAMID system is duplicated all the way downward. Striving fills the membership. Everyone wants to be "important" and noticed. Everyone vies for an acknowledgment or the exalted "position of honor."

The Jethro Solution
MOSES

captains
1000 – 1000
100–100–100–100
50–50–50–50–50–50–50
10–10–10–10–10–10–10–10–10–10
Over all Israel

The Jethro solution is an example of a pyramid (Ex. 18:17-27) style of leadership. He had a "good idea" of placing captains of tens and hundreds. But remember. THAT IDEA DIDN'T WORK. As much as we try to make the pattern work (and we still continue to try to duplicate it), it won't work for long.

> Jethro's idea is not in the Bible for us to follow the instructions. It is there to see that this idea didn't work!

Finally, Moses complained to the Lord, "Why have I worked so hard and not found favor in your sight. Why is there such a burden from all the people? How can I feed them? This is too hard." (Num. 11:11). The Lord told him to assign seventy to lead (11:16-17) and they prophesied.

The concept of pyramid is the way the Levitical system worked – this is the wrong PATTERN. However, most churches still insist on using Levitical models and particularly Levitical worship.

The Levitical priesthood is a type of caste system that we do not need to replicate in the SEASON of renewal. The original meaning of castes in India (known as *varna*), was a permanent identification of a life-long hereditary system of social stratification.

The Levitical Pattern

Many church members have lost hope because this singular rulership style fosters perpetual immaturity and dependence. They just keep waiting for someone "high up" to tell them what to do. Eventually, these floundering and ill-equipped believers will tire of being treated like children and run away from home – wanting to make their own decisions.

- A One-person organization tends to expect unflinching obedience to some sort of "superior clergy" rulership.
- One person operations tend to devalue, view as competitive, and/or underestimate the leadership potential in others.
- One person cannot possibly meet the needs of a whole flock.

It's not about the "pulpit" but about what is being produced.

Look at this pyramid diagram and ask, "Where is God in this structure?" He is uninvolved... in distant view – just not intricately WITHIN the plan. He's always somewhere "out there" and not within the Body. Like the old song, "God is watching, from a distance."

Apostles are not SENT to create subservience or cause a bondage of superiority. Nor do they need others to be dependent on them.

Just as the Lord led Israel "OUT FROM" the land of pyramids (hierarchical systems, and oppressive rulers), the LORD continually searches for those who want Him to be the only # 1!

THE CHICKEN COOP

A pyramid is fastened to the ground – there can be no lift off. A pyramid cannot move. Advancement in this kind of structure is only by a "PECKING ORDER." The birds (believers) that are involved with this type of pecking order system are usually confined.

> The PYRAMID type of government does not allow for migration.

We make this analogy because we were told to notice the storks and migrating birds – but never the chickens. Chickens represent the unhappy believers that always strive to be Number One.

CHICKENS DON'T MIGRATE – in fact, they can barely fly. But... the odd thing is that chickens have everything they need to migrate. They just don't. Instead, chickens run around making a lot of clucking noises and complaining about circumstances. Chickens are capable of migrating – they just can't! When we get tired of being in the house and not going anywhere, we call it "being cooped up."

Pyramid systems are led by "restrictive" leaders who rarely recognize, raise up, or release others.

Worse! Because chickens are generally caged within a confined space (a farm, a chicken coop, or a barbed wire fence) and that confinement produces a lot of bad odors.

To be at the top of the "pecking *order*" (deemed most successful) means that a "particular" chicken eats first. The top chicken can peck all the other chickens. In this system, a bird pecks the bird who is of lower rank, and submits to being pecked on by all who are above it in rank. The age-old custom of being hen-pecked has its counterpart in social hierarchy.

Chickens are fully equipped to migrate – they just don't!

Tradition insists that we maintain the "traditional" concepts of church *authority* and by that phrase they mean—the way it's always been. But, today's congregation has become tired of false *authority* that is based in CONTROL and manipulation.

 The Kingdom cannot fully fill the earth until God's authority is established in our thoughts, actions, and motives.

CHICKENS ARE LED BY ONE ROOSTER

"To lead people, walk beside them... As for the best leaders, the people do not notice their existence. The next best, the people honor and praise. The next, the people fear; and the next, the people hate. When the best leader's work is done the people say, "We did it ourselves..." – Lao Tzu

Rooster types preach grandiose sermons that tickle our ears and yet fail to ensure that those Biblical concepts are incorporated into lifestyles. They strut around assuming unearned positions that lack heaven's endorsement. They are more concerned with the size of an altar call and the size of their church. These self-absorbed charlatans give lip service that does nothing to change lives.

The Rooster is the strutting peacock-type leader of the chickens – usually preening his big feathers and puffing up his chest trying to impress and dominate others. Roosters are exceptionally observant and seem to have eyes in the backs of their heads! They are always knowledgeable of what others are doing around them.

This type of leader is usually a quick thinker. Rooster types tend to be perfectionists – especially concerning their appearance. Their primping and posing can seemingly go on forever! Styles and material possessions always matter, regardless of the cost. Being noticed, admired, and deferred to is their aphrodisiac – and they love being seen by a following of adoring chickens. Rooster types can be extremely competitive and boastful, with a strong egotistical need to constantly be the center of attention at any function.

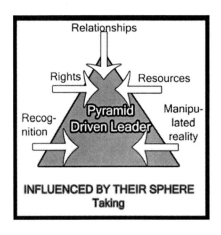

"You do not lead by hitting people over the head -- that's assault, not leadership." Dwight D. Eisenhower

The lead rooster possesses a powerful personality and is notoriously dominant. He attacks anything that may be construed as threatening to what is "his." In groups, all roosters are loud – but there will be only one big lead Cock.

The COCK is always the "Big Boss" and usually views strong, competent newcomer leaders as threatening rivals. Rooster-type leaders are aggressive debaters able to sharply refute any opinion. Often, they are impeccably neat. Their need to be in total control (of their pyramid) will often cause them to say flattering things to control behavior.

Roosters enjoy nothing more than being in the company of lots of adoring chickens! Attempting to get their attention causes much jealous competition among the flock.

> *"Does the eagle soar at your command and build his nest on high?"*
> Job 39:27

The sphere of *authority* for a Rooster-type leader is limited to their courtyard. Their identity is enforced by others around them. Listen to them loudly crow. "Cock-a-doodle-doo!" They call out trying to attract more subservient followers – expecting to be in total control of their surroundings. Many of the congregation of the rooster-led pyramid style often just end up squawking – feeling henpecked, and having feathers flying.

This rooster type of pastor dictatorially tries to fill all five of the ministry positions and is usually not close with any peers. This out of order form of government results in confusion, strife, and deception.

The remedy for anarchy cannot be dictatorship.

Rooster-led congregations make their followers feel like "Chicken Little." If you remember the story, Chicken Little tried to take a trip – but couldn't interpret the "signs" and always thought that the sky was falling on his head. He was convinced that the world was coming to an end and all would be lost. "The sky is falling, the sky is falling," he insisted. Chicken Little had not been mentored or prepared for getting outside the barnyard on his own.

- Prairie chickens may wander – but they usually get lost. They aren't prepared for life beyond the chicken coop.
- Chickens won't migrate – even with a strong leader.
- The only realm of influence this type of "rooster" really has is when the people show up and preaching is part of the entertainment.

These kinds of pastors (in a pyramid structure) fear joining with other pastors because each (rooster) one needs to be "in charge!" Their own insecurities foster a bickering competition. Everyone in this organization wants to be in charge of someone – they fight for the pecking order of position. In hierarchical systems, you mindlessly follow orders from those who are placed above you (1 Pet. 5:2-3, AMP).

In these less productive situations, *authority* is associated with the position or title – but not necessarily with character.

In Scripture, "cock crowing" is related to denial: "Assuredly, I say to you that this night, before the rooster crows [or crows twice, Mark 14:30], you will deny Me three times" (Matt. 26:34; also Luke 22:34; John 13:38).

QUESTION: Do you prefer serving over the world's definition of success? Are you dissatisfied with what has gone on before? As a leader, are you willing to take risks and pay the price to serve?

Believers do not connect with leaders in order to make the leader look successful; people connect so that leaders will make *them* successful in life.

People want to follow those with character and a heart of passion and compassion.

People follow those who care about and encourage them.

People follow those from whom they can receive.

People follow those who empower them.

People follow those who bring change to their life for the better.

People follow those whose destinies are intertwined with vision and purpose.

People follow those who co-labor with them.

QUESTION: Why be a leader of a disempowered group?

 Leaders who know how to genuinely serve one another will not have an ATTITUDE of arrogance and superiority OVER anyone.

Lord, please show us how to change Your community from being merely emotionally driven spectators and consumers of spiritual products to being mobilized and activated participants. Teach us how to facilitate real, permanent life changes. Teach us how to reproduce SONS who will turn the world upside down!

Hierarchy Caused Equalizers

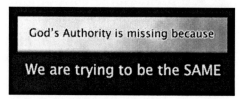

God's Authority is missing because

We are trying to be the SAME

"Let me now be partial to no one, nor flatter [any] man" (Job 32:21).

The unfortunate consequence of hierarchy was to build a PYRAMID structure of government. Leaders emerged with grandiose mentalities and excessive ATTITUDES of arrogance and superiority OVER anyone.

There were several adverse reactions to this pyramid-hierarchal type of leadership. One of the most unfortunate reactions is this mind-set of EQUALIZING. This attitude refuses the "pecking order" by insisting that we are "all equal."

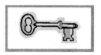 Sure we are equal. Galatians 3:28 is totally egalitarian! No divisions of race, class, gender in Christ. But, we can be egalitarian and still choose to allow delegated people to speak into our lives.

Equalizers oppose authority and leaders. There's a huge faction of believers who insist that everyone is an equal leader.

Here's where the big debate lingers – right here at this touchy place of opinions based from bad experience, competition, hurt, and wrong motivation!

GOING BEYOND EQUALITY

The message of racial and gender equality is still basically unresolved issues in most of the church. This huge problem must be addressed. But, beyond concepts of genuine equality lies the commandment of UNITY. Unity can never be accomplished until we understand that everyone has a particularly unique function and that we fit together as different parts of the Body.

We are equals in God's love. However, we are not all the same.

We are created to be different.

Embracing freedom, equality, and dominion must never become a license to randomly live without structure or government. No organization can succeed as a free-for-all, or a group that requires a consensus of opinion to decide each matter. God's government is a Theocracy not a democracy. It isn't about voting on what *we* want. It's about agreeing upon what *God* wants. Within our assembling, there needs to be effectiveness, efficiency, and order.

Within this concept of unity is the fact that we are not now nor ever should we become the same. Even though God is no respecter of persons, he chooses leaders. Abraham was selected to head a nation. He chose Jacob and hated Esau – even before they were born Rebecca was told, "The elder shall serve the younger" (Rom. 9:11). At one time, God elevated the tribe of Levi to the priesthood and not the others. He raised up certain people to lead, to be judges, kings, and prophets.

> A believer is a priest and king – but not every believer is called to be a five-fold ascension gift.

You are not someone else. Comparing yourself with others is unwise (see 1 Cor. 4:2, 6-7; 2 Cor. 10:12). You are unique and part of the corporate Body of Christ. The foot (a very necessary part) should NOT say, "Because I am not a hand (a 5-fold gifted ministry), I do not belong to the Body" (1 Cor. 12:14-15).

Leaders gather believers into purposeful groups to accomplish greater works and INFLUENCE.

This is a difficult concept – particularly for those who strive. It just means that some are called to lead in church and some are leaders in other arenas. But, without question, we do not all have an equal measure in all the gifts of the Spirit – some have phenomenal signs with huge miracles. "Are all apostles? Are all prophets? Are all teachers? Do all work miracles? Do all possess gifts of healing? Do all speak with tongues? Do all interpret?" (1 Cor. 12:27-30). Let's emphatically say the answer together now... "NO!" When we recognize the different capacities and aptitudes in a variety of people, we are not showing partiality or lack of equality.

The original apostles were told they would judge the twelve tribes – that's not partiality! But... it is different work from the rest of the leaders. Difference allows us to work together for the good.

DO WE NEED LEADERS? Yes. It is our only PATTERN. Are all Christians ministers? Yes. Everyone has a full-time ministry – of living a precious life. But, is everyone called to be a five-fold minister set apart to lead and govern in the *ecclesia* full-time? Can every believer exclusively dedicate their life to Biblical study, caring for the flock, and prayer? No!

EQUALIZERS

The reactive response attempts to EQUALIZE everyone (=). It's preached in progressive groups – let's all band together and become the nameless, faceless mass that meets in homes and mystically conjoins together rather like some New Age metamorphism.

This idea of the "equalization mentality" brings to mind that horrible old movie, "The Equalizer." In the depressing future of the post-apocalyptic world, a new-age warrior tries to usurp the powerful regime by killing everyone who opposed him.

 EQUALIZERS try to make everyone be at the same status as themselves. But equality, by itself, will never create unity. Unity requires relationship and valued diversity. Unity is built through integrating diversity and not by leveling everyone into the same mold.

This whole reaction to the invalid pyramid-type church government has caused many believers to think that they don't need the church anymore. They even decide to not have leaders anymore. Many of them say, "I long for the day when you won't need me to lead you any more."

To EQUALIZE means to make level, to make the same, to even out.

"The heart of modern paganism is to attempt to make equal what God has made unique.... God is hung up on individuality or distinctiveness."
Dennis Peacock

Comparing both incorrect ideas: the pyramid structure and the EQUALIZER mentality.

BIGGER PYRAMIDS	NEED TO EQUALIZE
Pecking order	Jealousy and envy
Besting of everyone	Lack of respect
Arrogance	Lack of leadership and direction
Controlling mentality	Familiarity
Wrong Pattern	Lack of structure and order
Lack of SONS	Smaller groups
Hurt members	Weaker leaders
Rigid Doctrine	Rebellion
Can't MIGRATE	Can't MIGRATE

Church EQUALIZERS claim loudly that it's "not a one-man show" anymore. They really work hard to claim that everyone is the same. And, most of them are so sweet and sincere about their beliefs. They insist that every leader is equal (in *authority*) to all the congregation. They refuse to acknowledge any ministry titles. The bottom line is that a lot of this thinking is driven by hurt, insecurity, positioning, individual Kingdom building, jealousy, and envy.

Cain resented the fact that God accepted Able's sacrifice – and not his. Scripture says that Cain's countenance fell (pouting) – and sin was "at the door" (Gen. 4:7). This envious and jealous positioning is the same emotion that drives much of today's church. Envy disconnects believers from the power of *God's authority* and disrupts them from their destiny. Envious comparison causes them to abort their vital process of development and growth.

 The MOVE toward equalization can't sustain MIGRATION – but it paralyzes and stagnates leadership because of jealousy and envy.

The quest for equalization all started with Lucifer (Is. 14:12-14) who wanted a throne like God, etc. An incorrect insistence on "equality" creates bitterness and even tyranny. Yes, we all have individual *authority* in the sight of God. No. We do not all have the same job functions in the local church. Not everyone is equally trained to lead a local church – nor should they want to be.

> Like it or not, we are NOT the same.

Some people are born with greater abilities than others. Some can play the piano by ear and some can never do that.

 YES. Each person has a ministry of equal importance – whether it be marketplace, finances, teaching, etc. Whether it be large or small. But, we don't need to overlap or equally do the same jobs in order to be satisfied. YES. God loves us equally, but He has a different destiny in mind for each one of us.

This kind of equalization thinking is not new. Carl Marx attempted to advance his fundamental ideas for Communism by forcing equality into being. Communism sees all people as equals and tries to accomplish this by government rule.

- For example, the revolt in China caused all those who were educated to be killed in order to start a race of equals – they called it the "People's Party." That left no professors, no doctors, no professional people. Just a working class. China transitioned into Socialism 1953-67. This, of course, left the nation powerless and at a standstill for the last generation. Only now are new leaders growing up and beginning to emerge.

- Socialistic mind-sets cloak the church with ineffectiveness. True justice aligns our expectations to who God says we are in

His Word rather than unwisely trying to measure ourselves against each other (2 Cor. 10:12).

"No one believes more firmly than Comrade Nepoleon that all animals are equal. He would be only too happy to let you make your decisions for yourselves. But sometimes you might make the wrong decisions, comrades, and then where should we be?" -
George Orwell, Animal Farm, Ch. 5

Exaggerated ideas of equality are a BIG DEAL because they can keep others from being able to receive instruction. It also causes an OVER FAMILIARITY that discredits and dishonors leaders. Many of us know what it is like to have been regularly "served up" as part of the dinner conversation. (This topic of needing to be equal is more thoroughly covered in the second book section, "*In Defense of Titles.*")

As we said earlier, familiarity is the EQUALIZER that attempts to justify being as good as someone else. Equalizers want to present leaders through their filter of personally predetermined criteria.

The price of equalization is conformity, uniformity, and cookie cutter Christianity.

Listen, we can't sit at our own feet and learn very much! There should be those who can teach and advise us. And, if we don't respect them, we won't learn much. Giving respect doesn't exalt ministry leaders above church members but it does help open hearts to learn from those who teach and minister.

Unbelief is the product of familiarity.

We see only too often how two people can hear the same thing and one can receive while the other one (because of trying to be a peer, a critic, a judge, etc.) cannot. Like we mentioned, Jesus faced familiarity in His own hometown (Mat. 13:53-58) when he could do no "mighty works." People tried to say anything to strip Him of His *authority* in their eyes. Therefore, these neighbors were unable to receive.

Many "equalizers" have stopped going to their church and now go to a HOME CHURCH. Now this is certainly not true of all home churches. However, there seems to be a prevalent problem.

Let's differentiate the significance of what we're saying here. Each believer must determine why they want to gather. If it is to be without leadership, then that's the problem! Many believers meet in homes because they are mad, frustrated, hurt, independent, and/or rebellious.

> Silent rebellion diminishes POWER in the church.

We must be wise in this New Order. Some Home Churches are wonderful. The problem with *some* in the current "House Church" is rebellion against the established *leadership authority*. Now, we're not talking about problems with Cell groups of a larger church –

but about individual tiny groups with no outside influence, external instruction, or accountability.

What needs to be determined is WHY ARE WE GATHERING? Small meetings can often offer greater individual attention, intimacy, and personal activation, etc. The incredible value of small groups is that they provide essential, personalized relationship. Small groups allow everyone to participate in a verbal part of what God is doing.

However, if you continuously meet in little homes in order to reproduce the early church – you're missing it. Most of the "homes" where they met were palatial estates – and they also met in amphitheaters, such as the one in Ephesus that seated 30,000 people!

The Jerusalem Church model was to teach "house to house" (Acts 2:46). They enabled a processing of discipleship training. Small groups are vital to our growth. This group was called to their locality of Jerusalem and did not expand past that. They were a single nationality – (Acts 2) all Jews, whereas, the Antioch church was multi-ethnic.

Some great things happen at some House Churches... but remember, they can become inbred and myopic unless they align apostolically and report to accountable leaders. Don't become limited and separated from the contribution to the momentum of changing this world. Listen... God didn't fill us with the Holy Ghost so that we would just prophecy back and forth to each other every week! Let's think BIGGER!

New apostolic leaders must be proactive to overcome reactive and hurt people.

Strongly directed groups can provide the necessary impetus to get things done for the Kingdom. Leading visionary groups is part of a whole new methodology – and that's what we're talking about here. Groups directed by strong leaders can change and influence culture and impact nations for the Kingdom.

The Issue Of Covering

God's Authority is missing because

We have COVERED instead of UNCOVERED

Hierarchy caused Pyramid formations of Government. One of the greatest problems today in the traditional Church is the idea of "covering."

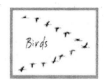

Sometimes, stork's heads and necks are totally bare and often scabby. However, during the migration season, the uncovered bare spots become the most dignified and distinctively noticeable part. They get a new COVERING of vivid colored feathers far brighter than their old feathers.

THE MANTLE

A spiritual mantle is the sign of authority. It represents the unique GLORY that COVERS US with God's sacred responsibility. In the Old Testament, many of those with spiritual authority wore a MANTLE which represented their distinctive calling, reputation, and effectiveness.

Authority carries effective influence.

There's a HUGE difference between a MANTLE and a "covering!" (We will discuss "covering" as the next subject.) A mantle (*addereth*) is a garment, cloak, or robe (clothing) such as used in 1 and 2 Kings. Elijah threw a mantle onto Elisha right before he went up in that chariot. This mantle "represented the glory" of the office that Elijah walked in as a prophet. The mantle was the visible identification of Elijah's *authority*. When Elisha used the cloak, power happened for him, too.

- Elijah's mantle became the focus of Elisha's life.
- Gehazi disqualified himself and never received the mantle from Elisha.

All believers have a mantle of *authority* that reaches out and affects their family, their lives, and their circumstances. The spiritual mantle we wear is the WEIGHT of *authority* that we have been given to accomplish specific assignments. Spiritually speaking, we have to pick it up and wear it. If we don't walk with our mantle, we can't operate in full capacity.

According to Webster's Dictionary, a "mantle" is a symbol to designate preeminence and the "*authority*" of a person. A natural mantle is symbolic of the job someone holds. A spiritual mantle is the weight of what we wear in the realm of fulfilling our destiny assignment.

> **Authority has weight and force. It can be observed.**

When we walk in the mantle of our *authority*, we feel and act uniquely confident. We sense a bold pioneering spirit, a courage to suddenly "pursue, overtake, and recover all." Nothing can stop us. There were many different mantles (that which defines function):

* Mantles were special garments worn by the priests – each item having prophetic and futuristic symbolism. Ancient leaders dressed in mantles to identify the office they represented. Kings and queens wore fine cloaks that spoke of their natural *authority*. Military people wore mantles or garments designating their authority.

* The first Apostles were clothed with the Holy Spirit (endued, saturated, with the miraculous, Lk. 24:49) and were also clothed with God's favor.

* Joseph wore a GOVERNMENTAL MANTLE that caused his brothers great jealousy. The Pharaoh gave him new garments. Potiphar's wife tried to take away Joseph's coat, which was a mantle of *authority* (Gen. 39:1-20).[1]

A mantle flows out from you, over you, and around you with strength.

> A "mantle" is the *symbol* of someone's "metron" or measure of authority and influence.

Using this analogy, there is a GIFT OFFICE mantle that sweeps around our spheres of influence. Different people have different mantles. Some apostles are sent to develop foundational truths. Others have the spiritual garments for signs and wonders, etc. It is said that some apostles wear the 5-star Generalship uniform! That means they rule in war and strategy.

Prophets are clothed with a mantle of insightfulness and SEEING eyes. Some apostolic ministries (particularly the evangelists) wear the cloak of gathering others to follow them.

The transfer of our spiritual mantle should go to our spiritual SONS.

---

1. For more information, please study the article on Joseph's coat in my book, "Connecting."

A mantle is not the same as a person "covering you." Mantles are worn upon our SHOULDERS. Apostolic mantles are generally governmental in nature (the government is on His shoulders, Is. 9:6). That means mantles are a sign of the apostolic *AUTHORITY* that rests UPON US (as a cloak) and it comes from WITHIN US (from the Divine SOURCE of our gifting) sweeping forward as we move.

A well-defined and properly fitting mantle takes away the "fear of man" and opinions of others. You know who you are. Spiritual mantles encircle, enclose, delineate, represent, portray, and define our function – which is our duty, task, assignment, capacity, capability, aptitude, endowment, objective, and purpose of our Gift Office.

 FAITH brings us to new levels of authority. As we grasp it and walk in it – a greater scope of our mantle comes to us!

COVERING

My intention in writing this is not to cause a revolt but to begin to restore right perspective and right order in the Church. The truth of the matter is the word "covering" does NOT appear in the Bible under the context that it is expressed concerning leaders being "over" other people.

Okay. So, I know all your arguments to the contrary. Covering ideas have been taught to all of us for generations. In fact, I've personally "covered" many churches and ministers in the past. That's the way it was done! But, like Priscilla and Aquila, we begin to understand "a way more perfectly" (Acts 18:26).

Of course, most of us don't recognize the real concern about this term "covering." This concept is generally quoted by most well-known ministries and it is well "covered" by selective Biblical garments.

Now, before jumping to conclusions, let me say that there are many well-respected and genuine ministries who honestly believe in "covering;" they think that covering provides a safety and protective mechanism for their people. There may be instances where this idea could be legitimately used. Perhaps some young believers coming off drugs or inappropriate life-styles may need strong "covering!" Young ministers just learning may need someone to protect them and kept them safe.

The problem with much of the past teaching about covering is that it has frequently been used by Illegitimate types of leaders who have deeply injured lots of believers. Some of the leader's personal agendas have caused offense and wounding. They have instituted "covering" to control every move and have not allowed their flock to grow up. Rather, "covering" tends to keep believers immature, dependent, and unable to hear the voice of the Lord for themselves.

➤ The Scripture never discusses covering people.

Currently, the church uses this *catch phrase* about "covering" so much that everyone seems to understand it. Countless times, believers glibly repeat the "who-is-your-covering" question. They say that every believer needs a "covering" and every local church needs a "covering." Like Waffle House hash browns, we just gotta' be covered and smothered – somehow it's the thing to do.

It's true! Babies need to be covered!

This COVERING idea began with the hierarchical-type government structure that we studied previously. It typifies the need of being #1 – or the "top banana!" We've nearly made a mantra with talk like, "I'm UNDER your covering" – and "I'm the covering OVER you."

Spiritual "covering" has become one of our biggest "Sacred Cows." As Fred Sandford said, "This must be the big one, Elizabeth!" Hold on tight, because here it comes again!

The Chicken Coop scenario showed us the consequences of the misuses of "covering-type" ministries that are rooted in an ambitious desire for preeminence. Covering could be fueled by the need to "CONTROL."

The current usage of the church phrase "covering" is a misnomer. Accurate leadership for mature believers doesn't need to cover, dictate, restrain, have power over, control, or constrain.

Just consider that yes there's governmental *authority* – but accurately, it should NOT be a "covering" from the top.

Apostolic Leading
Supports

PEOPLE SHOULD NOT COVER OTHER PEOPLE. Repeatedly we have demonstrated how leadership should NOT flow downward, but should be upward.

Upholding apostolic SUPPORT should be under-girding (from beneath, FOUNDATIONAL). Proper *authority* is fully satisfied in the establishment of God's PATTERN. Properly functioning in governmental *authority* doesn't require a "covering" to be effective. But each of us MUST be accountable to someone - not out there alone!

Let's remember how we learned that centering together AROUND Christ and His presence is optimum positioning. And, before you ask, Yes! Someone's in charge - it's not supposed to be a free-for-all.

WORD STUDY:

 After the Fall, the first couple "COVERED" themselves with leaves. Covering began in order to hide in fear.

We haven't understood that leaders are supposed to be UNCOVERING. That means we are to release believers to be all they can be. It means that believers are not supposed to be improperly dominated, intimidated, or coerced.

Ministry is a temporal job of FUNCTION not RANKING.
The issue is not position but service.

We are covered over with a robe of righteousness (Is. 61:10).

In searching the scriptures we find what was really covered: The ark had a covering (or roof, Gen. 8:13). The cherubim wings covered the mercy seat (Ex. 25:20). The priest wore special underwear as a covering (Ex. 28:42). Goats' hair and rams' skins dyed red covered the tabernacle (Ex. 27:7, 14). The leper had to cover his upper lip and cry "unclean" (Lev. 13:45). Censers were used to cover the altar (Num. 16:38). Every open vessel in the Tabernacle was to be covered (Num. 19:15). Jael covered Sisera with a blanket before she killed him (Judg. 4:18-21). Michal covered (hid) an idol trying to deceive Saul (1 Sam. 19:9-17). A woman covered a well's mouth to hide her husband (2 Sam. 17:19).

Clouds covered (Job 22:14; Ps. 105:39). Solomon's chariot (SOS 3:10), Judah (Is. 22:8), and death (Is. 28:20) were covered. Isaiah told about the rebellious children not covering themselves with His Spirit, adding sin to sin (30:1). Sackcloth covered those in iniquity (Is. 50:3). Wings covered the body of Ezekiel's vision (Ez. 1:11, 23). The King of Tyre (Lucifer) was covered with every precious stone and later called a "COVERING CHERUB" (Ez. 28:16). Waters cover the sea (Hab. 2:14). The ashamed and disgraced cover their faces (Micah 3:7). A basket with a lead cover carries sin (Zech. 5:8). The altar of the Lord being covered with tears (Mal. 2:13). God hates a man covering himself with violence (Mal. 2:16). Etc. Love covers sin (1 Pet. 4:8). Clothes cover (Rev. 3:18). Atonement covers (Heb. 9:5).[1]

Jesus said that princes of the Gentiles (or world leaders) exercise dominion over their subjects. They desire to control those that follow them. The Greek word for exercise is *katexousiazo*, (#2715, Strong's) from Greek 2596 (*kata*) and Greek 1850 (*exousiazo*); to have (wield) full privilege over and exercise authority. Here we see how heathen leaders dominated in their authority over their followers. This was not good!

---

1. See my book, "From Enmity to Equality," for complete discussion of head coverings and women being covered, etc.

GOD COVERS US WITH HIS HAND

Ezekiel 37 tells us four times, "GET UNDER THE HAND OF THE LORD - and He will BRING US OUT!"

The greatest force in the universe– is being BROUGHT OUT (Ez. 37:1) in the spirit! We do that by "getting under" the cover of God's hand.

"Therefore humble yourselves UNDER the mighty hand of God..." (1 Peter 5:6).

WE GET UNDER GOD'S HAND

Romans 14:12 states it as directly and succinctly as it can be stated: *"So then EACH OF US shall GIVE ACCOUNT of HIMSELF to GOD."*

Dunamis is the POWER to "BRING UNDER."

SUBMISSION is the powerful principle "OF YEILDING or GETTING UNDER."

God covers us with His hand. Then He gives this promise... that He will "bring us out" (Ez. 37) and "lift us up" (1 Pet. 5:6). He covers us with His BLOOD. He covers us with His LOVE. He covers us with His NATURE and His PRESENCE. He covers us with His GLORY (Ex. 33:22). He covers us with HIS *AUTHORITY.*

EXAMPLES of COVERING IN THE NEW TESTAMENT:

VERBS:

Kalupto - to cover, to veil, to hide. Don't *cover* a light in a bushel (Luke 8:16). Waves *covered* the boat (Mat. 8:24). Everything *covered* will be made known (Mat. 10:26). Escape and cry out for the hills to *cover* you (Lk. 23:30). *Cover* a multitude of sins (Jms. 5:20).

Epikalupto - to cover up. Sins are *covered* (Rom. 4:7).

Epikalumma - to cloak. Don't use freedom as a *cover* up for evil   (1 Pet. 2:16).

Perikalupto - to cover around, to overlay. A blindfold *covers* eyes (Mk. 14:65, Lk. 22:64). Gold *covered* the ark (Heb. 9:4).

Sunkalupto - to cover together, to cover wholly. Nothing *concealed* that will not be disclosed (Lk. 12:2).

NOUNS:

Katakalupto. Custom of *covering* for her head (1 Cor. 11:6-7).

Shepasma - Clothing *covered* (1 Tim. 6:8).

Peribolaion - "something thrown around" (1 Cor. 11:15), "a mantle around the body, a vesture," (Heb. 1:12).

Skepasma - "a covering" like a roofing or shelter (1 Tim. 6:8, "raiment").

Most of us already know how Paul quickly clarifies the whole veil/covering debate concerning women. He tells the Corinthians not to be contentious about this matter (1 Cor. 11:16), explaining that Jews have no such practice of covering veils, NOR DOES THE CHURCH OF GOD.

The Scripture never discusses covering people.

Then, Paul rebukes them (vs. 17) because they had come together "not for the better but for the worse..." This church wanted to assert control over their women.

Paul says, it's up to them—they can veil if they want. Permission to veil (being covered) isn't a command to do so... or a principle to follow for centuries—even in other nations. Rather, Paul told the Corinthian church: "Never mind. This is only a custom – wearing material on your head really isn't a big deal – but if it matters to you, then wear it." He also says that women don't need a special covering, neither of cloth, nor another person. Ideally, women should unveil before God, men, and angels who enjoy seeing women worship.

If Paul had disapproved of women teaching and preaching he could have easily expressed that opinion here, but he didn't. Paul concluded, "You can all prophesy one by one..." (veiled or unveiled, I Cor. 14:31). When viewed as a synopsis concerning church government, we see that Paul's advice assured that all things be done decently and in order.

Leaders WATCH OVER those who follow them (not RULE OVER).

He continues, "Nevertheless, in the Lord woman is not independent of man nor man of woman; for as woman was made from man, so man is now born of woman and all things are from God" (I Cor. 11:11-12). This shows the fitting together of believers as part of the One Body (I Cor. 12:26). Paul projects a new vision of the body of Christ, envisioning the personhood and interdependence of men and women existing together in Christ – a breakthrough in the first century that soon went askew.[1]

- Women frequently appeared unveiled in public under the Roman Empire. Jewish women normally didn't wear veils. But veiling was a significant ethnic social problem to the Greeks (in Corinth), to whom this Scripture is addressed.

---

1. Please see my book, "From Enmity to Equality" for a complete study concerning veiling.

- In 1 Corinthians 11, Paul wasn't establishing a practice of "covering" until the end of time. The issue here was the cultural practice of Greek women covering their faces with veils. His comments were not intended to be a universal mandate concerning women needing to be covered by men! Nor was it about certain pastors covering others.
- "No one lights a lamp and hides it in a jar or puts it UNDER a bed. (Lk. 8:16, NIV). The Lord wants to display you.

SUMMARY:

Although many leaders meant well with this idea, there's a "better way" for us to pursue.

- Young believers need mentoring and parenting in order to become grown-up sons who can receive a covenantal transference or receiving of your legacy.
- Bringing SONS into maturity demands an accountable releasing attitude rather than a hierarchal smothering.
- Each of us needs to find someone who has successfully traveled down the road before us, who can help us and give us advise and opportunities to be accountability.

 There's NO Scriptural support for anyone to need another person's "covering." The term, "Spiritual covering" is at best, a poor choice of words! The better term is "accountability" which provides a spiritual force-field of relationship parenting and mentoring that brings direct and indirect protection and blessings.

The Kingdom of God consists of interrelated relationships

True spiritual ACCOUNTABILITY comes from the genuine relationships we are in and that we keep!

True ACCOUNTABILITY networks believers together in order to release of their individual and corporate destiny.

THE WHOLE IDEA IS TO BECOME UNCOVERED!

Jesus came to UNCOVER us. He takes the leaves of our lives and the sin of the Garden off His people and fills us up with Himself. Yes. It is all about the unveiling of Christ IN US. The word "Revelation" (*apokalupsis*) actually means "to uncover!" The Book of Revelation is "the uncovering of Jesus Christ." As Christ is uncovered in us, we won't be bogged down with the doctrines of men. But, we will mutually defer to one another for the sake of the Gospel!

The law veils us. "Even to this day when Moses is read, a veil covers (*kaluma*) their hearts (*cardia*, mind, thoughts, or feelings).[1] But whenever anyone turns to the Lord, THE VEIL (*kaluma*, covering) IS TAKEN AWAY.

Now the Lord is the Spirit, and where the Spirit of the Lord is, there is FREEDOM (meaning legitimate liberty, from Strong's #1658, no longer a slave, unrestrained, exempt from obligation or liability. Hence, no need for covering). And we, who with UNVEILED (*anaklupto*, uncovered) faces ALL REFLECT the Lord's glory, are being transformed into his likeness with ever-increasing glory, which comes from the Lord, who is the Spirit" (2 Cor. 3:15-18, NIV). Oh, precious Lord, let's read that again! How can we reflect glory if our faces are covered?

The un-veiling of the BRIDE

After the wedding, THE BRIDE IS UNVEILED! Jesus is all about UNCOVERING us.

Paul continues about being unveiled/uncovered. "And even if our gospel is veiled (*kalupto* #2573, covered), it is veiled (*kalupto*, covered) to those who are perishing... (God) made his light shine in our hearts (*cardia*, thoughts or feelings) to give us the light of the knowledge of the glory of God in the FACE of Christ" (2 Cor. 4:3-6, NIV).

I guess my question to you is, when is your marriage? In heaven? Or is it now? Will you become unveiled into the Kingdom?

Imagine his thoughts as she stood at his side –

The one he had longed for – at last was his bride.

But, envision his shock as he looked at her face.

How had she tricked him to take Rachel's place?

But, she had been veiled... until it was done

Now, nothing could stop them – Now they were one.

Still, Rachel awaited with her eyes open wide –

Till the timing was right and the seasons collide.   kjs

1.See my book, "Whole and Holy," to learn about the heart being the mind.

Leah was veiled and was not the chosen Bride. But, at last (after SEVEN YEARS) the UNVEILED BRiDE of Christ is slated to come forward. Rachel comes forth. Rachel's name means seven sevens or perfection. The time has come. The process of unveiling the promised True Bride of Christ has arrived – and she will be revealed to the world in glory and majesty.

QUESTION: Do believers need a covering? Do churches? Pastors?

SUMMARY:

* The Church is supposed to exercise great authority.
* Each believer has authority to govern their lives, minister with power, and preach the Gospel.
* God chooses some to have authority to lead, mentor, and govern. Accountability does not insist on blind obedience.
* Church authority structure will no longer work through old-wineskins of hierarchy.

Leaders can govern in authority, but they will only function through relationships of accountability.

True leaders teach those they love how to hear the Spirit of the Lord for themselves. Apostles must learn how to allow those they have covenant with to have differences of opinion.

Not just any leader can provide this kind of relational accountability – not if you want the best! It must be genuine and practical. Accountability must flow to and from the specific leader 1). who cares for you, 2). who is chosen by the Lord, and 3). who has the Christ-like anointing to accomplish the task.

REMEMBER - the Lord will not and can not bless arrogant independence. We are to be linked as joint and marrow to one another. Ask the Lord to provide the right spiritual parent for you. Stay with them and never walk away from Godly relationships. Be covenantal.

WE LEAD BY "GETTING UNDER"

God's Authority is missing because

We have misunderstood
SUBMISSION

What lies ahead for the Church will surely invalidate all our previous ideas. The Church is heading for a civilizational change – an internal repositioning. We have to CHANGE – because most dogma that we've held dear is changing. The cloud is moving! Wrong methodologies concerning submission and spiritual *authority* don't work anymore. We can't put new wine in old mentalities. We can't move ahead and hold onto wrong thinking. But we can gather our strengths and agree to migrate together into new dimensions of understanding.

Nothing can happen until someone makes a decision to lead – and then teams of others choose to follow. Remember, in teams we can go farther, go faster, and belong! It happens through submission. Perhaps we can remember this definition by thinking of the natural division of the word "sub," which means under, and "mission" that means "to get under for a purpose." Submission holds teams together.

Submission is probably the most ignored concept in our culture. It seems to conjure up images of waving a white flag while hearing the loud orders to run out of a building, "with your hands up!" For most of us, submission means admitting defeat, being humiliated, being weak and dependent, and non-thinking.

There must be a differentiation between a mindful surrender that purposefully complies in order to grasp deeper dimensions of covenant truth and mindless submission which is a deadening dependency.

> Submission is easy for migrating birds – they want to fly together and follow the strongest one.

Etymology (the study of words in their original application) shows us that "submission" originally was a military wartime expression of how the leader chosen for the frontal attack would carry the greatest responsibility for the success of the campaign. Those leaders involved in adjoining maneuvers would "assist" or submit to the first leader.

 Submission happens not because of superior rank but mainly out of a desire to accomplish the essential mission of the Kingdom.

We cooperate for the GREATER SAKE OF THE CAUSE (like flying farther). That doesn't mean that one person is *better* than another. Mutual submission is an adjustment ethic critical to the perpetuation and expansion of the Kingdom.

The wrong use of submission is said to be what God HATES! "Revelation 2:6 and 15 give us examples of the OVERPOWERING type of "clergy" leadership: "God HATES" (present tense) the conduct as well as the tenets of the Nicolaitans. "*Nike*" means to conquer or triumph, and *laos* means the common people (the word for *laity*). In principle, the Nicolaitan ministers ruled over and remained separate from the common folk. God hates a haughty and conceited leadership.

Hierarchical systems like those of the Nicolaitans demand that their followers unflinchingly obey their orders. However, in a setting built according to God's PATTERN, those with Godly *authority* are motivators that inspire others to willingly follow.

> The terms "laity" and "clergy" are NOT Biblical concepts, but were later introduced. However, LEADERS and FOLLOWERS are Biblical concepts.

How can leadership encourage submission to be effective?

- Leaders should not expect mindless obedience.
- They allow believers to grow up so that they are not dependent upon the apostle but have learned to live under the *authority* of Christ and the leading of the Spirit.
- They prepare for the day when those they have led and cared for will leave in order to have their own ministries. They look forward to a new level of relationship with them as a co-laborer and friend who will reproduce their dreams.
- Believers want to be guided by strong leaders.

 A basic principle of submission is that leaders respect the rights of others. Leaders should give opinions and then allow informed and well taught believers to have the right to make decisions without guilt or inter-ference (that is not a lack of submission). Leaders should not bully others into conforming, nor attempt to exercise *authority* not delegated to them.

True "submission" is voluntary! Hierarchical systems demand obedience – that is not voluntary.

SUBMISSION INSTEAD OF COVERING

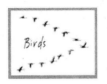

Migrating birds utilize the principle of RIGHT POSITIONING. When one bird tires, another simply takes the lead. This rotation of strength provides for consistent strength in the leadership.

In this new day, we must lead a new way. This idea is primary to accomplishing our destiny. As the set-leader delegates, elders must learn to "take OVERSIGHT" as necessary (1 Pet. 5:2; Acts 20:28; 1 Tim. 3:5). We have misunderstood this assignment thinking that we have to be "over" someone (or the boss) in order to take "oversight." We've talked before about oversight meaning to "go before, or support." Vines Dictionary also describes this word as not being a matter of assuming a position, but of the accomplishment of vision. It means to TEND and GUARD (part of our original Garden commission).

Every leader must become firmly aware of what Christ has already accomplished for all humankind.

Did you know that your concept of submission and obedience directly relates to your interpretation of the topic of covering? Submission is an eternal truth. We must submit to God and to one another. But, we don't need to BE a covering for another person any more than we need to HAVE a covering of another person. Jesus is the ONLY covering. Jesus gives us His MANTLE (covering) of authority. However, each person does need firm accountability, mentoring, parenting, and teaching. We are not to be isolated rebels.

Apparently, others had that problem of taking charge and using God-given *authority*. The following verse is another key to the duty of *authority*. Paul told Peter, "Take the *oversight* thereof" (1 Peter 5:2). This understanding is absolutely huge! Remember, the word "OVERSIGHT" (*episkopeo,* often translated *bishop*) also means to look carefully upon or to contemplate.

This empty guilt of needing "covering" causes inherent weakness and impotence. This victim mind-set vacillates in indecisiveness, unnecessarily wavering in uncertainty. Now is the day for change.

It is clear that Titus had this issue as well. Paul wrote to Titus about ruling strongly and correctly using Godly *authority*. Titus 2:11-15 says: "For the GRACE of God that brings salvation has appeared to all men. It teaches us to say 'NO' to unGodliness and worldly passions, and to live self-controlled, upright and Godly lives in this present age...THESE THINGS, then, are the things you should teach, encourage and rebuke with all *AUTHORITY. Do not let anyone despise you*" (NIV).

Leaders should take authority over certain unGodly issues. Let's now consider the last part of verse fifteen, "*medeis sou periphroneito.*" It is translated, "Let no man despise you." Some commentaries say, "Let no man think around you." This word *"periphroneito"* is used only this one time in the Bible. Perhaps it could better read, "Make it clear to everyone that salvation comes only through Jesus. Be certain that no one can get around that imperative truth with their tricky and manipulative words. Your job is to teach with *authority*."

Elders are shepherds who protect the flock of God (Acts 20:28-31). They help tend and guard for strange teachings that could distort truth.

 Solid apostolic leaders position themselves in proper "oversight," which "TENDS and GUARDS."

Being "uncovered" never means you should stand alone, but rather function as part of an integral team of strong ministers who provide checks and balances without lording over. The church needs those who can work shoulder to shoulder, and who are able to communicate fresh insight into roles of positional leadership. Leaders must securely anchor with a readiness to minister with effective influence.

We see the example of the primary church leaders. Apostles didn't gloat about being "over" a bunch of churches. They had no secret need to promote themselves as super-clergy "spiritual covering." Rather, they considered their disciples as their SONS. They SERVED their SONS in wisdom and dignity. They passionately cared and helped them.

> Remember... submission to the authority of just leadership is the freedom to voluntarily yield by preference to those who are veterans in the truth – that's Biblical.

Leaders should lead from BENEATH (foundational leading). And because they do, we should willingly CHOOSE to mutually submit in love to one another (Eph. 5:21). "I urge you, brothers, to submit to such as these and to everyone who joins in the work... (1 Cor. 15:16). Accountability (answerability through proper submission) is safety.

 The best definition for submission means that we each volunteer to GET UNDER and SUPPORT.[1] Apostles support. They are foundational.

Deferring to delegated leadership is a choice that we all make in order to get a job done more efficiently. Participating in proper relationships to *authority* should become a foundational principle. Ideally, ministers should find other seasoned ministers to advise them – mutually submitting one to another in the bond of peace.

---

1. Please see my book, "From Enmity to Equality" for a full study of the word "submission."

Spiritual *authority* can only operate in an inner-relationship between those who agree to be joined together for God's purpose. A disciple (literally, a learner) wants to learn from others.

Becoming a disciple means to maintain a sense of necessity to bond or essentially to learn from someone that which no one else has been able to impart to you.

The disciple grants the leader an access into their lives with the purpose of awakening and fulfilling their destiny.

Proper Apostolic accountability provides the essential order and guidance that matures Christians. It brings capability, responsibility, and competency. It releases others to develop and achieve. It enables activation. It unveils new revelation knowledge to the Church. It blasts away at ingrained thoughts that have been held captive in religious minds. It's the battle-axe (Her. 51:20) that breaks down the forbidden archives of entrenched tradition (the way it's always been).

 Do we promote rebellion, anarchy, or self-rule? Of course not! Is there governmental *authority*? Absolutely. Account-ability? You bet! But does it "cover" you? NO. Let's say it again and again until we really get it! Accountability supports you. It's not OVER you; it is UNDER you. "...Built on the FOUNDATION of the apostle, prophet" (Eph. 2:20; 2 Tim. 2:9, 1 Cor. 3:10), The foundations supports.

This is the current pattern.

Headship -HOW THESE COVERING IDEAS BEGAN

Your concept of "headship" determines how you establish governmental patterns.

Hierarchy resulted in the pyramid type of government style where one person is in charge of everything (the Pope, or the Bishop, etc.). This graphic to the left shows how the pyramid structure caused leaders to think that being the "head" meant to be "the boss, chief, in charge." Because ministers were taught that they were the "head" (boss, top, and in charge), church government styles have been mis-applied.

The reason for the incorrect "covering ideas" and also this pyramid model of government was because we have misunderstood the word "head" and "headship" (*kephale*). We may have been sincere in our motives, but the information we built upon was wrong. *Kephale* does not mean the one in "*authority*" – it means that from which flows all else.

Those to whom the Scriptures were written fully understood this word *kephale* to mean ORIGIN/SOURCE.[1] The SOURCE is the beginning – everything that pertains to the life and nature of Christ becomes enlivened.

The ONLY PATTERN is that Jesus is the SOURCE and CENTER of all things. He is the HEAD. True HEADSHIP means that God is the SOURCE of your life. We submit to the authority of others who will guide us to the SOURCE.

NO PERSON is "the HEAD, the boss, in charge" of another person! True "headship" releases authority!

Jesus is the only SOURCE (the origin and center) of the church. No person is ever the "head." You have one head – and that is God.

Jesus is the HEAD or SOURCE and CENTRALITY of everything. He is HEAD of the Church. Headship speaks of the source of Rulership, *Authority*, government, and kingship. Jesus is the HEAD (SOURCE) for every believer, individually and collectively (1 Cor. 11:3).

"*It is the Source that more than fully supplies the whole body, knits it together and makes it grow... (Col. 2:19 Source).*

HE is the HEAD (SOURCE) of all principality and power (Col. 2:10). "And he is the HEAD (SOURCE) of the body, the Church; He is the beginning (*arche*, first in order, time, commencement, rank, and origin) and the firstborn (first one, foremost, apostolic type) from among the dead (Col. 1:17-18, NIV).

- *He is HEAD over ALL THINGS to the Church (Eph. 1:21-23).*

Many theological changes will occur as believers begin to move into the emancipation of God's liberty. kjs

"The CHURCH of GOD HAS NO SUCH PRACTICE AS COVERING" (Paul, 1 Cor. 11:16).

---

1. See my books and articles – particularly, "Understanding Headship" and "From Enmity to Equality" for full explanation of *kephale*.

SECTION 8
Going the right direction

The Right Direction

Recorded observations of migration date back 3000 years. In the Bible, Job asked (39:26), "Does the hawk fly by thy wisdom and stretch her wings toward the south?" How does God give wisdom to a hawk to know where to fly? WHERE DO BIRDS MIGRATE? They go north to breed and they go south for winter.

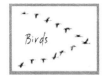

Cranes are one of the most ancient of birds. For thousands of years, their unexplained memory allows them to follow the exact same route as their ancestors.

Some of us are beginning to remember – we've had amnesia it seems, but finally we remember where we are supposed to fly – and how to live in dominion and rule. This truth has always been there. The early church preached it – and now we begin to remember how to follow the SAME ROUTE AS THESE EARLY BELIEVERS.

God's perpetual design flows from the dawn of humanity until our day. He clearly authorized and decreed His precise eternal plan – that of effective Kingdom ministry dynamically working together to impact the world.

1. Birds OBSERVE THE STARS and the heavens for signs of where they are. True apostolic leaders observe the times and signs from heaven.

2. Birds USE THE RADIATION from the sun for guidance. Good leaders KNOW their own location – where they are.

3. Birds use their SENSE OF SMELL – there's a SENSE of where to travel.

4. Most importantly, studies show that birds have MAGNETIC FIELDS consisting of tiny grains of a mineral called magnetite in their heads. Most migratory birds have a built-in sense of direction and know innately which direction they need to travel. While researchers have long known that migratory birds use the earth's magnetic field to choose their flight path, it is now known that such orientation capability is present as a potential in all birds (even chickens that do not migrate). This sense to use magnetic fields to find their way was not developed extensively enough through use to be functional in some breeds.

I don't know about you, but I don't ever want to use a GPS system. One of my favorite things to do is "dead reckon" across an unknown city or even through the forest. Ever since childhood, I've enjoyed "sensing" my way to a destination. My friends in Guam who are island fishermen can still navigate the oceans by a "sense of knowing" where they are.

APOSTOLIC LEADERS POSSESS THE AWARENESS of what is happening around them. They know the signals from other people and from their environment. They just "SEEM" to know where to go next. They recognize the color of the sky in the mornings. They possess an intrinsic ability to discern the time and SEASON and the *kairos moments.*

"In the evening, you say, 'it's fair weather: For the sky is red!' And in the morning, 'it will be foul weather today; for the sky is red and lowering'" (Mat. 16:2-3a).

- When we see a red sky at night, it means that the setting sun is sending its light through a high concentration of dust particles – basically good weather follows.
- A red sunrise could indicate a potential storm system may be moving toward the east. A deep red morning sky means rain is on its way.

Knowing Where to Go

One view of Biblical prophecy speaks of the return of Jesus with a dynamic and powerful people who will usher in the Kingdom. Their leaders will be unified in vision and filled with dynamic purpose and energy. This new breed will manifest the authorization of God's intentions. They will be those who the whole world has longed to see (Rom. 8:19). They are the elect who have the ability to defy all opposition. They will have spiritual power to accomplish the purposes of God.

> An apostle must know the SEASON and where to go.

Habakkuk tells of these people, "Behold... and regard, and wonder marvelously; for I will work a work in your days, you will not believe, though it were told" (Hab. 1:5). Paul expanded on this statement in Acts 13:40-41): "These will be the ones who APPREHEND THEIR *AUTHORITY* to do the greater works that the Father be glorified in the Son. If you shall ask anything in my name, I will do it" (Jn. 14:12-14).

Apostles BUILD the Body by healing, teaching, and empowering others toward God's intentions.

Historically, all the offices of the primitive church innovatively used leadership positions to accommodate specific assignments. These functions still seem to differ greatly within each successive era and from one geographical sector to another.

We know that the apostle, prophet, evangelist, pastor and teachers are GIFTS FROM GOD "for the perfecting (*katartismos* – complete furnishing, or equipping) of the saints, for the work of the ministry, and for the edifying (*oikodome* – architecture, or building up) of the body of Christ." Leadership equips God's people (Eph. 4:11-13) to the measure (*metron*) of Christ. They tend and guard the believer until they are mature.

What exactly is the "WORK of the ministry?" The NIV translates this portion to say, "to prepare God's people for works of service." Vines Dictionary describes "work" as toil, employment, a task, or "work with the idea of enterprise."

- Apostolic leadership enables believers to function within their distinctive expression of God's image – and to "do the work" of the ministry. That work doesn't necessarily mean that every believer gets to share in pulpit ministry every Sunday morning!
- Preaching in the pulpit must not be viewed as the only "work of the ministry." It is not the greatest positions or the goal of all ministry.
- The "work" required includes all that is necessary to cause the ministry to function in authority.

Apostolic/prophetic leaders release a transference so that EVERYONE "catches the local vision" and becomes a mutual partner in achieving shared goals. Maintaining the well-defined direction toward PURPOSE becomes the cause. It's about being effective. It's about accomplishing the true WORK of the ministry – to save the lost, to heal the sick, to grow and mature the believer, to love the unlovely, to provide answers for the poor, to reproduce likeness, and develop a heart of compassion, etc.

We're talking about how to migrate in the right direction. As the Church repositions on the sure foundations of maturity and wholeness, then believers will anxiously choose to allow dynamic LEADERS in *authority* to unlock their individual and collective destiny. Leadership provides the essential order and direction that enables believers to mature and find answers. Delegated leaders inspire the congregation by teaching, redirecting, and encouraging them with spiritual and natural insight.

Real Christianity is about transformation.

True spiritual *authority* encourages mutual participation. Those of us who have been leaders in the past will have to open our hands and raise them in surrender to the transformation from our obsolete and rigid mind-sets into a re-connection with glorious new principles. On this new frontier are new paradigms of RELEASE. The follies of escapism theology, arrogant and self-oriented ministry, obsession with hierarchical positions, and false operations must give way to stability and truth.

The critical job of the set-leader is to discern the optimum vision, strategize, and maintain the momentum (migration) toward key goals over time. The leader's job (without being inflexible or unreceptive) is to adhere to an apparent and sustained forward focus of the team and congregation.

As in any organization, there are always alternative suggestions from others – and lots of those ideas will be INCONSISTENT with the God-given organizational strategy. That's why a focused leader is vital.

In that way, the primary leader is in charge of direction – but that doesn't make him/her/them any "better" or more important than others – no one has a higher VALUE – but rather, a set-leader becomes a MANAGER who is a MENTOR. The set-leader is the CHIEF AMONG EQUALS and this person should be a part of an integral team who provide checks and balances for one another.

GETTING A BIRD'S EYE VIEW

"Revelation is the definitive SOURCE of Biblical Authority"
Bishop Kirby Clements

 Most birds have incredible eyesight – we sometimes refer to that as a "bird's eye view." Because birds fly in a V-pattern, they can see farther ahead and at wider distances – just as Leaders in teams should see far in advance of where they are going. That's PURPOSEFUL vision.

A bird's eye view is the wider view. It is time to survey the surroundings of the upcoming, yet to be explored, terrain. We must set the objectives to bring the others into position.

KINGDOM PURPOSE isn't building bigger church buildings, establishing a new program for the kids, the youth, having a TV ministry, etc. These are projects or programs (some of which may work great), but they are not God's PURPOSE for you or His Church. They will produce – but not necessarily demonstrate Kingdom authority and progress.

> Clarity of PURPOSE sets the right VISION.

Walt Disney's purpose: "To make people happy."

Henry Ford's purpose: "To mass produce, mass distribute and have cars mass consumed."

Andrew Carnegie's purpose: "To manufacture and market steel."

Mother Teresa's purpose: "To care for and comfort ⟍
and needy all over the world."

We must not confuse our purpose. Without correct purpose ⟍
accurate vision. Without vision, our goals can be indiscriminat⟍
undirected. Purpose should be the underlying core that gives ou⟍
direction and meaning.

QUESTION: Do you see the big picture? Can you step back and main⟍
perspective and objective evaluation – in spite of problems? If you ha⟍
purpose you can set vision.

"When the vision is unclear, the price of commitment is always too high." John Maxwell

Leadership is the capacity to translate vision into reality.

VISION: What makes your ministry innovative? You can only achieve what you can conceive. PURPOSE causes your vision to stick like glue inside your heart – when everything has changed. Your mind naturally gravitates toward your real vision even when you're thinking about something else. Habakkuk says to write that vision down so that when they SEE it, THEY can run with it. That means our vision isn't just for us. We need to make it clear for OTHERS. That means we draw pictures, make diagrams, and use words so others can see and understand. We see the greatest moments of LIFE in the future as though they are in the NOW.

PURPOSE is revealed by God.

Prov. 29:18-20 says: "Where there is no vision the people perish. Where there is no REVELATION, the people cast off restraint." This familiar verse often is misunderstood. In Hebrew, it literally reads, "where there is no prophetic vision, the people perish." (The RSV is correct, where there is no prophecy (hope in the future – people die). Hopelessness is not a strategy. Where there is vision (made plain and kept in view), people are compelled to go forward together.

PURPOSE reveals the understanding of the supernatural purposes of God. It is the magnet that COMPELS and LEADS others to come along with us. It establishes corporate vision concerning Divine concepts, priorities, and values necessary to accomplish God's intent. His vision for us is always huge – far more than we can do on our own. Vision demands that we become productive to re-establish the 5-fold mandate to be fruitful, multiply, fill the earth, subdue, and take dominion in order to build the Kingdom.

Purposeful vision moves forward. It energizes and it does not maintain or restrain.

Vision directs and re-directs migration toward purpose and cause.

Revelation flows both from Scriptures and the prophetic in various and different directions for each new SEASON.

...*ITY* is increased by focusing upon **PURPOSEFUL VISION.**[1]
...(aiming) the **SOUL** (mind, will, and emotions) is essential.
...he definition of "focus" as you concentrate on your vision.
...ns:

- ...vergence point of rays (as of light, heat, or sound).
- ...ustment to find distinct vision; a clear image, or a
  ...on permitting perception or direction.
- ...e center of activity, attention, the point of concentration.
- The place of origin.

Apostolic vision was how the first Church spread into new worlds. Acts 16:4-5 tells us that increase to the Church came as a result of agreed relationships that brought forth the revealed message. The decree of the Jerusalem council was delivered by SENT apostolic teams to each city. "While they passed through the cities, they delivered DECREES." The Jerusalem council communicated to the churches through real relationship with the sent ones. As the churches were "strengthened in the faith," they grew in number each day.

Because the city church of Jerusalem turned together in a specific direction, they were able to change history and influence the world.

Perfecting the saints is almost impossible without the input of a completely unified team of five-fold gifted ministries, all of them moving toward the same goals as an integrated team.

As believers gather and support corporate vision, Apostolic-leadership should also rally around the personal vision of each individual. They guide toward setting Biblical goals and objectives that produce LIFE. They train to bring believers into maturity, teaching them to accurately hear and respond to the Holy Spirit (Matt. 28:19-20, Eph. 4:11-15).

Apostolic leaders MUST maintain PURPOSEFUL vision because they carry an essential, deep-seated and far-reaching message.

1. Vision allows leadership to move forward with definite purpose. Apostles must work with specific assignments. They ask: What is our message? Who can we reach? What is our motive?

2. Vision allows others to run (migrate) with you in a team. Vision is a problem for those who just want a non-structured environment. The Saddleback Church has a good motto: "We welcome you here only if you are willing to serve. If you intend to just sit around, we'd rather save your seat for someone else."

...the poor, sick
...e have no
...ly vision
...tain
...e

...ues a
...alid chance
to actually
accomplish
the
PURPOSES of
God.

No one will follow you if you don't know where you are going!

---

1. See "Connecting" for more discussion of poising the soul and focus.

3. Belief in the vision allows others to be commitment to your plan and convinced of their own personal Divine placement.

4. VISION DEFINES OUR RELATIONSHIPS. Mutual vision and compatible goals is what draws us together. When correct relationships are established and believers support the vision of the house, their own personal vision will also be accomplished.

 The purposes of Corporate vision have a greater scope and, therefore, require the necessity of priority in co-operation beyond the personal vision of an individual.

VISION ENABLES TEAMS TO WORK TO COMPLETION

This new time of reformation demands a heart change. It is built on revelation of strong and precise leadership that joins others around a common cause. Nehemiah learned how to forge people into mighty warriors. That learning came from the place of great difficulty. They were at the halfway point of a 52-day project of rebuilding the wall when the people said: "We've done too much. We are tired."

LOSS OF STRENGTH = LOST VISION = LOSS OF CONFIDENCE

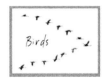 A Swedish legend claimed that a stork encouraged Christ during His crucifixion by crying "Stryka! Stryka!" This means "Strength! Strength!" Strength comes from working with others to help bear the load.

Nehemiah knew it was necessary to KEEP FAMILIES TOGETHER (4:13). Family togetherness strengthens people to fight better for their own family. Next, he gave them GEOGRAPHICALLY DEFINED POSITIONS – they didn't just build and fight anywhere they wanted to be. They learned triple PURPOSE: 1) to work, 2) while also being on guard, 3) so that they can fight.

The NEHEMIAH PRINCIPLE is to RENEW single-minded VISION and PURPOSE EVERY twenty-six days. This can't happen when vision is vague or when people are working alone. Apostolic leaders must guide with authority toward vision and purpose. The Body is held together by a commitment to a common cause and PURPOSE. Nehemiah's purpose was clear... to provide a safe place for the return of the people to their temple. Nehemiah had to change mind-sets in order to facilitate restoration. He knew how to finish his task.

"So they continued the work with half the men holding spears, from the first light of dawn till the stars came out. They stayed dressed and guarded. They kept their weapons on guard even when drinking water"
(Neh. 4:21-23).

Loving Care

God's Authority is FOUND because

We have true relationships

As we move into this new season with a different **PATTERN** of government, we see that it is all about relationship and care for others.

"Even the migratory birds are punctual to their SEASONS. Yes, the stork [excelling in the great height of her flight] in the heavens knows her appointed times [of migration]... But My people do not know the law of the Lord [which the lower animals instinctively recognize in so far as it applies to them]" (Jer. 8:7, AMP).

There are two kinds of storks in Palestine. They stand about three feet high. When they fly, their long, red legs stretch out far behind them. Migrating storks make a definitive sight in the sky. The unusual strength of their vast wings readies them to ride the thermals for long distances. Many people in Bible times watched the storks, noticed their habits, and observed their customs.

David looked high in the fir trees that towered up above all the rest ... and way up near the top of the fir tree, he saw storks sitting on their nests. He said, "The stork makes her nest in the fir trees" (Ps. 104:17). The stork seeks the high places. As we observe the stork, we should be reminded that it is our privilege and obligation to nest in the high places. (Please study Col. 3:1-2, Eph. 1:3). As leaders learn to reside here, we can teach others how to live "in this heavenly relationship" because we have determined to "set our compass of affection upon the things which are above."

Each creature does best in their own environment.

Jeremiah was a great bird watcher. Essentially, he said, "You know, that stork has more discernment than God's people" (Jer. 8:7). He says, "That stork understands the will of God because he knows when to move and where to go." My friend, now we can be as wise as the stork. We can understand the will of God and know when and where to go next!

Another amazing phenomena about storks is that they were known to carry groups of smaller birds on top of their wings as they migrated. Little birds too small or frail to travel, RODE on the wings of the stork.

From the ground, it was oftentimes difficult to determine what was actually flying through the air – because it had lumps on it. But, there were always lots of smaller birds riding on the wings of the stork.

The stork bears the little birds on her wings. Scripture tells us to observe these birds in their travels and learn from them how to better interpret the intention of the Lord. Sometimes we can lead best by carrying others along with us for awhile.

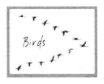

Notice the parallels. Birds trust in their food provision. How much more the Father cares for us! Jesus said, "take no anxious thought for tomorrow." Don't worry. Jesus didn't prohibit planning for the future – just not to worry. Not one sparrow will fall to the ground without God's knowledge (Mat. 10:29, 6:26-30).

Jesus observed nature and taught us how birds move to where there is food, they collect their food, and they feed themselves from what God provides. "CONSIDER THE BIRDS" (Lk. 12:24).

Birds need places to stop over places to rest and refuel. Birds do not fly non-stop. They will land in a safe place and find food so they can continue with their trip.

Leaders must gain control over their negative emotional responses and reactions. They must be settled and strong when opposition comes. Hardships make us strong. Overcoming offenses serves as the Divine "crucible" of refining. If we back up, we have to start again.

One of the most common reasons for failure is quitting before the finish line.

DON'T QUIT!

The arctic tern has been tracked with satellite radar as flying over 20,000 miles a year. Some cranes are capable of migrating as far as 2,500 miles per year, and the barn swallow 6,000 miles a year. The great albatrosses have life spans of up to fifty years and some are calculated to have flown over five million miles during their lifetime.

THE APOSTLES WERE STRONG AND TOUGH! Difficulties did not hinder the Apostles from accomplishing their assignments. If you ever have a chance to travel along the route of Paul in Asia Minor, you would be totally amazed at the gigantic mountains he traversed. The distances and difficult weather in northern Turkey winters. It's absolutely staggering to consider these trips on horseback or on foot. Ministry isn't easy.

Apostolic ministries will be tested, tried, and proven. The Bereans tested Paul's word by the Scriptures they had. No one is infallible. True ministers are never afraid of being examined and even admitting mistakes.

- Paul described apostleship by saying that God has set forth the apostles last... "We are weak, we hunger, thirst, are naked, are buffeted, have not sure dwelling place, we labor with our hands, we bless when we are reviled, we are persecuted and suffer. We are defamed as the filth and offscouring of the world" (1 Cor. 4:10-11).

- Paul described his life: "I've worked much harder, been jailed more often, beaten up more times than I can count, and at death's door time after time. I've been flogged five times with the Jews' thirty-nine lashes, beaten by Roman rods three times, pummeled with rocks once. I've been shipwrecked three times, and immersed in the open sea for a night and a day. In hard traveling year in and year out, I've had to ford rivers, fend off robbers, struggle with friends, struggle with foes. I've been at risk in the city, at risk in the country, endangered by desert sun and sea storm, and betrayed by those I thought were my brothers. I've known drudgery and hard labor, many a long and lonely night without sleep, many a missed meal, blasted by the cold, naked to the weather. And that's not the half of it, when you throw in the daily pressures and anxieties of all the churches... I feel desperation in my bones" (2 Cor 11:23-29, MSG).

Being an apostle is complex, and many will bring accusation against them. There will always be faultfinders.

> We must go through the "process" to arrive at our destiny.

Paul spoke boldly, but many who heard became obstinate and publicly maligned the Way (Acts 19:8-19, NIV).

They were persecuted (1 Thes. 2:15).

Crowds questioned their *authority* to do what they did (Acts 4:7).

They were accused of being "MAD" (meaning crazy, Acts 26:24-25).

Authority seems to increase in proportion to our ability to overcome difficulty.

Leadership is painfully difficult. Those who are leading the way often suffer extreme loneliness, isolation, and unjust accusations from those to whom they once were close. Overcoming hindrances and obstacles are part of how we become broken to the opinions of others and finally get stronger in order to build the character that doesn't quit. We must endure. Our strengths come through overcoming sufferings, rejections, failures, betrayals, and challenges. It is what we overcome that we remember.

Women Flying Like Storks

God's Authority is FOUND because

We have effective leadership

A PROPHETIC INTERPRETATION

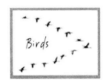

Pliny wrote that it was a capital crime in Thessaly to kill storks, because of their work in slaying serpents. The early Christians regarded the stork as a symbol for Christ because storks frequently ate snakes (which represented Satan and his demons).

To sum up all of what we have learned, let's look at the fascinating parable that Zechariah tells concerning leaders at the end times. Zechariah's name meant "The Lord remembers." His ministry was to prophesy to those returning from the Babylonian exile – many brought with them the problems of living in that sinful nation,

We can look at what Zechariah writes as also being prophetic to us as we begin to move out from the Babylonian system that the church has engendered for centuries. This demand for the purification of His Body is found throughout the Scriptures.

Zechariah chapter 5 describes two women with WINGS LIKE A STORK who are called to carry out God's final consummation of the age and judgment upon Babylon (Zech. 5:9-11). "Then the angel who talked with me came out and said to me, 'Lift your eyes now, and see what this is that goes forth.' So I asked, 'What is it?' And he said, 'It is a basket that is going forth.'"

These two women fly like storks carrying a basket BETWEEN HEAVEN AND EARTH. They head for the Plains of Shinar (Zech. 5:11). "Shinar" was the city built by Nimrod in the land of Babylon. In the early manuscripts "Shinar" and "Babylon" are interchangeable. In this land the Tower of Babel (the first unified people group) was destroyed by confusion. Babylon was known as the center of the pagan world where false goddesses had built their temples. From here, the world has remained confused, religious, and ego-centered.

These two WOMEN in Zechariah's vision had big wings – strong enough to SOAR through this long journey.

These TWO WOMEN represent the ONE true Church grafted together. They also represent the spotless Bride (Eph. 5:22-33), the two Hebrew midwives (Ex. 1:18), the grafted branch, the ONE CHURCH, etc. They can typify Israel (Is. 62:1-5) and the Church (Eph. 5:22-23), Old Jerusalem and the New Jerusalem, the two witnesses (Rev. 11) who reign with Christ.

This Scripture in Zechariah shows a fulfilment of the Garden promise when the Almighty said to the serpent, "I will put enmity between you (the serpent) and the WOMAN... SHE will bruise your head." This happens because of what the cross accomplished. The WOMAN (the Church who is like a stork) is victorious over the wilderness and wickedness.

She is clothed with the sun. Her raiment is the light from heaven. In her hair is a garland of 12 stars. She stands with the moon under her feet (Rev. 12:1-6). She is the Bride of Christ. The Dragon stands to devour her child, to persecute and pursue her. The Dragon drives her to the wilderness. This is the Lamb's wife. The Bride adorned for her husband. She is the Holy City where the names of the twelve tribes are inscribed upon her gates.

Zechariah goes on to say, "*This is their resemblance throughout the earth:*" The NIV translates this, "*This is the iniquity of the people throughout the land.*" This is what happens to sin. The Church (like storks) will carry sin away.

"*Here is a lead disc* (ephah) *lifted up.*" The lead disc were units of measurement and symbols of commerce (*ephah*) or measure of evil going forth. The "Ephah" was a commodity measure for dry commodities, such as flour is now measured as "bushels." The hugeness of the basket portrayed the immensity of "sin" being carried away.

(Zech. 5:7-8) "*There is an evil woman who sits in the basket. This is Wickedness!*" The third woman sits in the basket. She represents the weight of wickedness, sin, lust, greed, materialism, and dishonest gain. The Hebrew word for Wickedness is feminine and is probably why a woman personifies evil in this vision.

WHO IS THE WOMAN IN THE BASKET? She represents the counterfeit bride. For our study, let us say that this woman is also a type of the Church that is or has been directly or indirectly connected with sin, impurity, ungodliness, unrighteousness, and wickedness. She is the Church that is not pleasurable to the Lord.

The harlot bride is clothed in purple and scarlet and wears gold, precious stones, and pearls. Cloaked in religious garb, she rules over the kings of the earth (Rev. 17:18). Ten kings hate her and visit her with plagues, death, and destruction. She is the Mother of Harlots and the abominations of the earth. She is full of wickedness. She is drunk with the blood of the saints and martyrs of Jesus. This woman rides upon the Beast (Rev. 17). She is that great city of iniquity. All the nations drink of her fornication (Rev. 14:8, 18:2).

"They (the stork women) thrust her down into the basket, and threw the lead cover over its mouth." The two stork-winged women (the true Church) are capable of removing wickedness from earth and put a lead lid over it. Lead is a symbol of judgment. (vs. 9-11) The wicked woman in the basket and sin are returned to Babylon.

The stork women (Church) have total *authority* over evil.

The cup of iniquity is full – contained beneath the leaded lid.

Wickedness is suspended between heaven and earth awaiting final return back to Babylon where materialism and confusion began – and where it awaits destruction.

What is this great city of Babylon (Rev. 19)? She is "Mystery." That's because we have not recognized her as the religious system that we've been so near. Yes, we have "shared in her sins" (Rev. 18:4) throughout history. False ministries "make merchandise of her." She is spiritual in nature (political and religious) (Jer. 44:16-19). She has no remorse about her outrageous behavior. Babylon is needs oriented. Double tongued (1 Tim. 3:8). Scandal upon scandal. Hireling. Razzmatazz services. Apostate. (Rev. 18:23-24). Gone the way of Cain.

This "Hallelujah" in Revelation 18 is the only time this word is mentioned in the New Testament – heard at the demise of this wicked woman (19:1-4).

> In Zechariah's visions, the wicked woman is the unfortunate product of the wickedness that is weighed and measured. She is imprisoned by the merchandising and carnality that have fueled and energized the pyramid government pattern for centuries.

"When it is ready, the basket will be set there on its base." A "base" is thought to be a pedestal for an idol. The stork-women re-set the idolatry of wickedness and evilness where it belongs. The good news is that we've fully come to a time of migration. Soon, the rising Church will band together as the two women and begin to move like a stork. This flight is not backward or around in circles, but forward and upward – purging.

The angel said to Zechariah, *"This is the bushel moving forward!"* Those two women soar like storks and move forward:

> Forward toward effective leadership

> Upward to impact civilization

> Advancing toward greater character and reproduction of sons

The woman (the TRUE BRIDE) ascends to gather and purify the Church.

CHACIYDAY

The Hebrew word for stork is *"chaciyaday" (chaciydah)* which means loyalty, kindness, and love. Did you ever wonder why the stork was used in this analogy? Perhaps it's because the stork is the only bird, as far as ornithologists know, that shows dedication, attachment, and devotion to its family throughout its entire life. As the true meaning of stork, she (the Church) begins to soar with "loving kindness."

Many species push the little birds out of the nest to fend for themselves, but the stork maintains that family relationship. Even after the storks leave their nest and live on their own, they return to take care of the old parents. Perhaps this is why God selected this word *chaciydah* to describe them.

People will never behave like birds, but people can behave like God.

Storks represent *loving kindness* in leadership.

Watching birds helps us see more clearly the beauty in life all around us. A bird can help us love with our heart, instead of always analyzing with the mind. Learning to love is the most important thing to learn of all.

The Antioch Church thrived during times of persecution, famine, poverty, and victimization (Acts 11:20). It was marked by compassionate and benevolent caring.

"Successful people are always looking for opportunities to help others. Unsuccessful people are always asking, 'What's in it for me?"
Brian Tracy

They emphasized walking in the "purpose of heart" toward the Lord (Acts 11:23). This PURPOSE-driven group emphasized loving kindness to one another. They emphasized group goals over individual goals. They were concerned with the Kingdom rather than just material convenience.

When either success or discouragement come to ministers, the first thing to leave is usually this quality of loving kindness. We tend to put up walls and isolate ourselves. Paul maintained the right heart condition and was "affectionately desirous" towards those he served. He didn't go on missions just to preach. He loved them with his SOUL (1 Thes. 2:8) - all of himself.

We mentioned earlier that storks were a symbol for Christ because they rid the environment of snakes and pests. Storks were also Christian symbols for vigilance, meditation, contemplation, prudence, seriousness, and chastity. Aristotle taught that the jealous male stork would put an unfaithful mate to death for her transgressions.

Storks remind us of God's attention, God's consideration, and His love for those who belong to Him. With everlasting loving kindness He continually draws us (Jer. 31:6). Why is the stork called *chaciydah*? Because it never forgets. When Zechariah looked to the sky and saw the vision of the women flying as storks, he knew it was to take care of their families and the family of God.

Zechariah's name reminds us that God never forgets. His love never exhausts itself toward us. "God will never forget YOU." The Lord remembers. The soaring Church must also remember that Her destination is to ascend up out from wickedness and cry out as a deliverer.

> We are left with a complete
> feeling of awe and
> wonderment that thousands
> of birds are undertaking migration
> somewhere on
> the earth at this very second.

God's Authority is FOUND because

We apprehend it

BOOK 2 - RESPECT, HONOR, & TITLES

God's Authority is missing because

We lack RESPECT
for those in authority

Tackling this subject of respect and titles while going against the tide of present church ideas is not easy. However, to me this is one of the *most important subject* I've considered. For years, I've felt like the lone crier on this subject of respect. Know this... I'm not writing about titles or positions but rather about the motivation of our heart that causes us to be able to fully function as apostles.

So far in this book, we have studied about WHY AUTHORITY IS MISSING in the church today. In this section, we will study *WHY authority is missing* from a lack of respect.

It is my strong conviction that the lack of respect and the gaining of familiarity is a large contributor to why the power of God's authority is missing in the Church today.

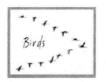

In review, let us remember that Jeremiah was an avid bird watcher. In the previous sections, we learned that birds can tell us about how to govern in this new season. Essentially, Jeremiah said, "You know, that stork has more discernment than God's people" (Jer. 8:7). He says, "Birds understand the will of God because they know WHEN to move and WHERE to go." Now, we can be as wise as the stork. We can understand what God's will is. We can know when to move. We can know where to go next.

If we want to live as leaders in authority, we HAVE TO MODIFY THE PRESENT THINKING THAT THE JESUS WHO LIVES WITHIN US IS NOT AS GREAT AS THE ONE WHO IS TO COME. We must deliberately embrace Him as LIFE in us today. The Gospel of the finished work requires that we live as an example of the finished work.

As we gain authority as we realize the increasing necessity to respect the authority that the Lord allows us to use.

R.E.S.P.E.C.T.

Rodney Dangerfield loved to say, "I don't get no respect." And like Aretha Franklin sings, it's all about "R.E.S.P.E.C.T."

But... these days, who can we respect? Too many believers have been wounded by false *authority* situations. And perhaps you may also wonder, who to honor and TRUST? The respect that we should have for the Bible goes without saying, but what about having esteem and admiration for those leaders to whom congregations are committed. We are commanded to "esteem" (highly regard) those who lead us (1 Thes. 5:12-13).

THE PENDULUM SWINGS... Lawlessness increases. You and I both know that we live in a day when the pendulum of American INDEPENDENCE has swung far from center. Our independence – which once indicated glorious liberty and freedom – now swings our civilization into greater arrogant detachment and self-willed lawlessness.

We live in a scandalous society of disrespect. Our media and newscasts are filled with over familiarity and social impertinence. Rebelling against *authority* has become a national disaster. Meanwhile, our kids are losing respect for older people, their teachers, and their church leaders. The problem is pandemic.

We see the pendulum swinging too far both ways for many church leaders. Too many ministers still revel in being small despots ruling over their co-dependent groups. They strut around as the "Grand Pooh-Bah" and expect others to grovel.

THE PENDULUM SWINGS

INDIVIDUALITY	INTER-CONNECTED	CO-DEPENDENCE
No accepted authority	Moving together	Controlling authority
Rugged independence	Focused direction	Lack of expression
General disrespect	Releasing of Sons	Discipleship movement
Lack of direction	Mutual respect	Lack of freedom
Isolated groups	Building the Body	Hierarchy
Anti-local church	Christ revealed	Pecking order

The other side is just as bad - - the independent isolated believers who insist on being equal. Many of them disrespect leadership in general.

The increasing deterioration of presenting Christ to the world through the believer is staggering. The world looks to us - and we are at war.

The decay of morality and values is basically caused leaders modeling the wrong image and believers being jealous of one another. We can only help counteract it by beginning to reestablish proper character within the leaders of ministry – it really can start with us.

WHAT IS RESPECT?

Firstly, it's not about us. It's all about the Lord. We often find Him in greater dimensions THROUGH ONE ANOTHER. Believers are the image of God. They are to show forth His glory upon the earth.

> RESPECT releases greater authority.

Respect is defined as feeling or showing esteem to another. It means to show appreciation, value, and honor to everyone, particularly those who have sacrificially laid down their own preferences in order to serve us as our leaders.

In Divine order, though all are equal in value as believers and SONS with the Lord, God has set in the church first (*proton*) apostles, prophets second, then teachers, and so on (1 Cor. 12:28-29). False religion opposes systems that present strong leadership. However, the wisdom of God set the 5-fold in place (Mat. 23:34, Lk. 11:49).

These ministers are to provide guidance and direction. As a general rule, they do not tell others what to believe or what to do. No leader is infallible. Churches in the New Testament we LED and GOVERNED by apostles and elders. These leaders settled doctrinal issues (Acts 15:1-10; 22-23). Prophets are not generally called to govern, unless they work harmoniously with apostles.

Those whom we respect are not better, above, or more spiritual than others. We respect them because they lead, serve, and instruct by example. They have influenced others for good! Showing respect toward leaders is not a return to the "clergy/laity system (Rev. 2:6, 15), and will not rob the corporate Body of unity.

Honoring one another releases favor from God and man.

 The Bible is about people from another era who lived lives totally different from ours. One of their strongest Jewish social customs was RESPECT.

RESPECT COMES FROM RELATIONSHIPS

RESPECT demands RELATIONAL ABILITY. An old pastor once told me, "Ministry is temporal, but relationships are eternal." That statement totally impacted my life. While on this earth, ministry is a grace gift for building relationships with the Lord and His people.

Relational affirmation is a basic force which most believers need. Speaking honorably to leaders of the church gives members a sense of BELONGING TO THE FAMILY – belonging to the HOUSE! Respect should first come out of relationships.

My family is built upon relationships. And notice this... My kids don't call me by my first name. And yet, being called "mom" doesn't make me "feel" egotistical or feel more important than my kids. The title of "mother" connects me with these children more than with all the other children in the world. These kids are part of me.

My husband always calls me "mom" or "your mother" around our kids. He says, "Ask your mom if she's almost ready." Am I his mom? Of course not - he does this for the sake of respecting this family relationship. Now that our children have become ADULTS, they STILL call me "Mom." It's about the relationship of belonging as a UNIT.

It's goes on. My grown up children call my brothers "uncle" even though these "uncles" are some of their best friends. RELATIONAL TERMS JOIN US AS A FAMILY. My grandkids (who live with me) fondly relate to and address all my children as "uncle" and "auntie." They do this ALL THE TIME. Our family ALWAYS address our favorite people by relational titles – it's our expectation and custom.

 Using continuously chosen words of relationship promotes a sense of togetherness, mutual covenant, and belonging. It strengthens our UNIT.

RESPECT COMES FROM SERVANTHOOD

Leadership is a gift to serve but not to LORD over.

Looking again at Mark 10:42 -43, "And calling them to Himself, Jesus said to them, You know that those who are recognized as rulers of the Gentiles LORD IT OVER THEM; and their great men exercise *AUTHORITY* over them..." (NSB - see also Luke 22:24). Leaders are never to have intrinsic or limitless *authority* OVER others. Godly leadership with *authority* is not to manipulate and control. It was (and is) an *authority* given by GRACE to function.

Paul said he was a "bond slave for the Lord Jesus Christ." One translator said that being a bond slave is as "one whose will has been swallowed up in another." Servanthood of Christ is not bondage but a liberty of serving.

Jesus came to serve and not to be served (Mat. 20:28).

Jesus carefully defines this necessary ATTITUDE in His selected leaders, "You know that the rulers (*archon*) of the Gentiles Lord it over them (with subjugation and control), and their great men exercise *AUTHORITY* (wield full privilege) OVER them. It is NOT so among YOU, but whoever wishes to become great *among* YOU shall be your SERVANT, and whoever wishes to be first *among* YOU shall be your SLAVE (Mat. 20:25-27 NASB). In the Kingdom, God transforms His servant apostles by turning upside down their previous concepts of importance.

> Become GREAT?
> Be a SERVANT.
>
> Desire to be FIRST?
> Be a SLAVE.

Notice that Jesus never rebuked them for wanting to be *great* or *first*. He merely told them that the way to do that was to serve and to be a slave to others.

Servanthood (*diakono*) means to run errands and do tasks (this word is often translated as deacon). A "slave" (*doulos*) is one involved in both voluntary and involuntary serving. There is a great price to obtaining Kingdom position (the cup). There is a greatness to serving. Leaders want to help people not stir up an audience.

"But he who is greatest AMONG you shall be your servant" (vs. 11). Notice also that Jesus said that greatness came from being "among" them, not "over" them.

"For you I am bishop. But with you, I am a Christian. The first is an office accepted. The second a grace received. One a danger, the other safety. In them I am gladder by far to be redeemed with you than I am to be placed over you. I shall, as the commanded, be more completely your servant." Augustine, 354-430

Leaders should always hold a towel.

At the final Passover feast. Jesus defined servanthood by removing His outer garments and with a towel and a basin He simply redefined the greatness of leadership as servanthood (Mat. 20:20-28, Mk. 9:35; 10:35-33; Lk. 9:48, 22:24-27; Jn. 13:14). Flawless and limitless Christlike authority is reproduced by serving.

> The SECRET to
> GREATNESS =
> Your metron of
> Kingdom *authority* is
> proportional to
> service.

After washing their feet, Jesus asked, "Do you understand what I have done for you?... I have **SET AN EXAMPLE** that you should do as I have done for you. I tell you the truth, no servant is **GREATER** than his master, nor is a messenger **GREATER** than the one who sent him..." (Jn. 13:12-17). Leadership is not about us being greater or better than anyone else.

Wise leaders lay down their lives and pick up the work of Christ.

> A servant
> "gets under
> and supports."

Servant leaders genuinely love people! Jesus, the holder of all power and *authority* displayed it by washing feet (Jn. 13:14). Because of His *authority*, He loved us enough to die for us. *Authority* must always be connected with love and compassion.

A leadership culture of *authority* operates in a servant system that responds to "what God wants from us for His people in order to expand the Kingdom!"

NOT LORDING

"Be shepherds (be a shepherd/guardians) of God's flock that is AMONG your care, SERVING AS OVERSEERS (elders/guards) – not because you must, but because you are willing… NOT LORDING IT OVER those entrusted to you…" (1 Pet. 5:2-4).

This verse above makes it really clear. OVERSEEING is not LORDING OVER. Leaders are "among" those people that they lead. Leaders are the elders *(episkopeo)* who SERVES.

People don't rule or have dominion over any other person. All humanity was given rule over this earth! But, there is only ONE LORD *(kurios)* and He is Lord over all (Ps. 12:4; Rom. 10:12). Leaders are not to "lord over." This is the word *katakurieno* (which comes from *kurios*) and means "to take dominion over or to try to control or subjugate someone else" – which is forbidden (Ex. 24:4; Mat. 20:25-26; Mk. 10:42-25; Lk. 22:24-25).

This attitude was what God hated about the NICOLATANS: "But you have this in your favor, you hate the practices of 'those who LORD IT OVER THE LAITY', which I also hate" (Rev. 2:6, DVP).

"Don't aim at being a dictator, but be an example of Christian living in the eyes of the flock committed to your charge" (1 Pet. 5:3, PHIL).

Servant authority opposes the ambitious "Nicolaitans" attitude.

Governmental *authority* in the church should provide supportive guidance concerning the affairs of the Kingdom. Having *authority* must never elevate us; we are not to revel or "lord over" others with our *authority* – like the Nicolaitans did. This "lording over" mentality is that of the world systems.

God HATES" (present tense) the conduct as well as the tenets of the Nicolaitans. "*Nike*" means to conquer or triumph, and *laos* means the common people (the word for *laity*). In principle, the Nicolaitan ministers ruled over and remained separate from the common folk. God hates a haughty and conceited leadership.

Leading is not about "LORDING OVER" being "GREATER," or "BEING FIRST."

Another time, Jesus sat down and said to the twelve, "If anyone wants to be FIRST, he must be the very last, and the SERVANT of all." This kind of striving for position isn't new! That's the problem with our pyramid hierarchical church structure. Someone always wants to be number one – every time! If we want to be first, then we first must serve.

To illustrate the proper ATTITUDE, Jesus took a little child in his arms and said, "Whoever welcomes one of these little children in My name welcomes ME…" (Mk. 9:37).

Paul tells us to "*esteem* others BETTER than" ourselves (Phil. 2:3). How do we do that? Paul calls himself "the least of the apostles" and "not worthy to be CALLED AN APOSTLE" (I Cor. 15:9). He also claimed he was "less than the least of all the saints" (Eph. 3:8). Yet, Paul continued to affirm his apostleship in almost every epistle. This gives us a clear window into Paul's thinking. Yet, he continually establishes his *authority* to rule and speak for God.

Everyone needs a leader. Even leaders need leaders. In order for someone to lead as a servant, it means that those following must choose to acknowledge the one God "sent" and "set in place" to lead and "serve" them. When you agree that someone can lead you, it releases them to bring supernatural resources upon your life. Then, that leadership can advance you into your destiny.

- Servant leaders genuinely care about those they lead, and therefore, bring them into identity and purpose.
- Servant leaders train others to be leaders. People follow those who serve them.
- Ultimately, servant leadership is about passionate co-laboring relationships, not rules and regulations. People follow those who are passionate about what they do.

RESPECT RELEASES AUTHORITY

In the late Middle Ages, wealthy European families were trained in the "ART of respect and manners."That generation developed a *courtesy book* which contained the guide for the behavior of "gentlemen" concerning honor, respect, and concern for those less fortunate. There was a famous saying in these days, "Is chivalry dead?" Or, what happened to manners and respect?

All modern day social etiquette is based on chivalry – introductions are made according to age, then gender, and then social status. Respect and manners have always been highly valued by civilized people. Respect is an effort to have deference, to be considerate and politely express efficacy towards another person – *especially* those in leadership or are older.

 This theme of respect runs throughout the Bible, appearing in such words that are rendered into the English commonly as "fear," "regard," "honor," and "respect." We have everything to gain by giving respect because it greatly aids our progress in preparing for His Kingdom.

Romans 13:7 makes this explicitly clear: "Render to all men their dues. [Pay] taxes to whom taxes are due, revenue to whom revenue is due, RESPECT (esteem, honor, give deference and dignity) to whom RESPECT is due, and HONOR (value, esteem, money) TO WHOM HONOR IS DUE." Here we actually find mandatory commands to give deference, not because we want to, not based on whether we think they deserve it, but simply because they fit a certain description in our lives.

- To define more fully, honor means "to give high regard, respect, and esteem to; to bring respect or credit to; an outward token, sign, or act that manifests high regard, and to provide money." Respect means "to treat with propriety and consideration; to regard as inviolable."
- We can respect, honor, and be in covenant with someone and not agree with them on every little issue.
- The Greek word translated "honor" in Strong's Concordance, *(timao)*, means "to prize, i.e. fix a valuation upon; by implication, to revere." Showing honor, means treating another respectfully because we value them highly. Synonyms according to the Thesaurus for "honor" are: "esteem, respect, pay homage to, assign value to."
- "Welcome him in the Lord with great joy, and *honor* (respect) men like him" (Phil. 2:29, NIV).
- Wives *respect* your husband (Eph. 5:33).
- Live your daily life may win the *respect* of outsiders (1 Thes. 4:12, NIV).
- Elders must manage their own family well and see that his children obey him with proper *respect* (1 Tim. 3:4). And IN THE SAME WAY, their wives are to be women worthy of *respect* (1 Tim. 3:11).
- Teach older men to be temperate, worthy of *respect* (Tit. 2:2).
- Show proper *respect* to everyone (1 Peter 2:17).
- Always be prepared to give an answer to everyone... but do this with gentleness and *respect* (1 Pet. 3:15).

So strong is this Biblical theme of respect that we find calamity comes if respect is not given. Remember the time some kids saw Elisha and jeered at him and called him "baldheaded" (2 Kings 2:23-24). Elisha "turned around, looked at them and called down a curse on them in the name of the LORD. Then two bears came out of the woods and mauled forty-two of the youths" (NIV).

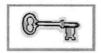

God is the giver of all authority (Rom. 13:1), and it is out of respect for the God-given office that respect can be shown.

RESPECTING OLDER PEOPLE

"Teach the OLDER men to be temperate, WORTHY OF RESPECT, self-controlled, and sound in faith, in love and in endurance" (Titus 2:2, NIV).

So far, we have determined that honor and respect is due to everyone. Next, let's talk about those who particularly deserve it – like older people. The Bible demands respect and dignity toward the elderly. They not only deserve our respect, they should behave worthy of respect.

Respect goes both ways.

I was raised to never call adults by their first name. That is my culture and generation. I still do not call someone older than me by their given name. I call older women in my congregation "Auntie," or "Ms." My physician friends are always "Doctor." The same goes for giving someone a shortened nickname without their permission. Families have that kind of familiarity – but we don't – without agreed permission.

Calling an older person by their first name could cause them to not feel valued. It is called the manners of THEIR generation.

In most civilizations, age is honored – and yet in the West, respectful behavior toward anyone is lessening. Isaiah predicted that the time would come when, "Everyone will take advantage of everyone else. Young people will not RESPECT their elders, and worthless people will not RESPECT their superiors (Isa. 3:5).

- "RISE IN THE PRESENCE OF THE AGED, SHOW RESPECT for the elderly and revere your God. I am the LORD" (Lev. 19:32, NIV).
- Solomon exhorts his son, "Harken (listen)... and despise not your mother when she is old" (Prov. 23:22).
- Because Elihu was the younger of Job's friends, he waited until the older men had spoken before he communicated with Job in admiration and RESPECT (Job 32:4-5).
- "Gray hair is a crown of splendor" (Prov. 16:31, 20:29),
- "Do not rebuke an older man harshly, but exhort him as if he were your father" (1 Tim. 5:1, NIV).
- Jesus repeated Exodus 20:12. It is the only commandment with a promise: "Honor our father and mother, that our days may be long in the land which the Lord your God gives us." In Mark 7:10-12, we find Jesus saying, "He who speaks evil of his

father and mother, let him surely die." Jesus did not address His mother by her first name.

Leaders should remember that the elderly have a tremendous wealth of wisdom to share, experience to entertain and teach us, expressions and advice on life to share. It is a shame to neglect the counsel and advice of the elderly. Let them amaze you by their wisdom, humor, and guidance. All too soon they pass from our midst.

 Age carries with it this precious promise – that they deserve the respect, dignity, and honor that is due.

WHEN RESPECT IS NOT THERE

Even though Saul didn't seem to deserve respect, David honored Saul for His position of *authority*. Luke tells us to honor Caesar and pay him what is due (Lk. 20:25).

Peter, in three words, taught this same difficult concept by commanding believers to "Honor the king" (1 Pet. 2:17). He was talking about honoring Nero! the heathen Roman emperor and madman who mercilessly tortured and killed hundreds of Christians in various demeaning ways. Nero even crucified his own mother and used her as a human candle for one of his garden parties! And yet, they were commanded to *"honor* the king."

A king is to be honored because he represents the *AUTHORITY* given him by God (Rom. 13:1). No matter his character, he is king, and we must honor him as such. Paul calls the civil authorities "ministers" or servants of God (vs. 4).

Even though some of America's presidents have not conducted their personal lives well, it still pales besides Nero's life. Regardless, Peter said to honor them. It is this same concept regarding our parents. We must honor them that "our days be long" – regardless of their life choices. If we give honor, not only will our days be long, but we will have life and LAND!

* Jesus said His "Father will honor" those who serve and honor Him (Jn. 12:26).
* Honor embeds in our heart. The more honor we give, the more honor we will also receive.
* We should make it our aim to recognize someone in life who we need. We should give double honor to those who lead us.

Honor is a LIFESTYLE.

"As you select (LEADERS) ask, "Is this man well-thought-of?" (Tit. 1:6-7).

The elders who direct the affairs of the church well are worthy of DOUBLE HONOR (compensation), especially those who preach and teach (1 Tim. 5:17).

Respect has great importance in our everyday life. Most American children are taught to respect our parents, our family traditions, our school teachers, the school rules, traffic laws, other people's rights, our country, our flag, our governmental leaders, the truth, and the differing opinions of others.

The concept of possessing respect is also called having dignity – which is an infinite concept since it can represent one of the highest human values. According to Webster's Dictionary, the word "dignity" means the quality of being worthy of esteem, honor, worthiness, or highly valued. The ability to walk with dignity (to be respected) is subjected to a variety of judgments from others. Therefore, this infinite concept becomes reduced to measurable traits, virtues, accomplishments, etc.

> Respect
> helps develop all people
> to their full potential.

Respect is the essential and foundational attitude necessary for effective conversation, cooperation, and mutual collaboration. Jesus always interacted with respect toward different and diverse people as individuals. Because each person is created in the image of God, we as leaders are called to profoundly respect the dignity of every person as an individual. Such respect is enforced and demonstrated by kind words, money, benevolent actions, and just policies.

"Be beautiful if you can, Wise if you want to... But be respected - that is essential." Anna Gould

Believers are commanded to give actions and words that manifest respect for the Lord and for one another.

Familiarity

God's Authority is missing because

FAMILIARITY diminishes authority

"And I will give you pastors according to mine heart, which shall feed you with knowledge and understanding" (Jer. 3:15).

In my opinion, the most dangerous and deadly PLAGUE facing today's church is familiarity. Some believers seem obsessed to find the fleshly weaknesses that could make their minister EQUAL with them. This attitude is reflected in conversation and attitude, even though the pastor has been given the Divine responsibility of caring for and teaching them.

Familiarity can be the greatest deterrent to effective spiritual authority.

Familiarity is the direct result of a lack of respect.

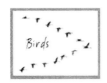

Familiarity CLIPS THE WINGS OFF LEADERS – and keeps them from soaring. Clipping a birds primary feathers prevents a bird from flying. A wing-clipped bird cannot migrate, cannot lead, nor can it get away from predators. Equalization can't sustain MIGRATION – it paralyzes and stagnates movement.

The lack of respect and familiarity cause some of the main problems in almost every church. The sin of familiarity hinders the flow of the Spirit from coming forth in fullness. We don't need a Word of Knowledge to know what's wrong. Familiarity strips leaders of their God given *authority* to LEAD.

People who are familiar don't want to be told what to do.

People who are familiar don't like to be corrected – even though they may need it! If the are corrected, they usually go out of their way to find fault. Familiarity is a BIG DEAL because it can keep others from being able to fully receive from leaders. OVER FAMILARITY discredits and dishonors leaders. Many of us know what it is like to have been regularly "served up" as part of the dinner conversation.

As we said earlier, familiarity is the EQUALIZER that attempts to justify and not make anyone worthy of respect.

Equalizers want to present leaders through their filter of personally predetermined criteria.

It never ceases to amaze me how two people can be at the same meeting but come away with different messages. One can receive phenomenal healings and visions while the other one (because of trying to be a peer, a critic, a judge, etc.) just wants to go home and watch TV! This usually happens because of familiarity caused by lack of respect.

Listen, we can't sit at our own feet and learn very much! There should be those who can teach and advise us. And, if we don't respect them, we won't learn much. Giving respect doesn't exalt ministry leaders above church members but it does help open hearts to learn from others.

IDOL Mentality -- by David Chandler

"I must admit, I'm entirely fascinated with American Idol. I love the first weeks of the show with the interwoven tryouts of both the amazing, the shockingly good, and the horrifyingly bad.

Don't we wait with baited breath for Simon to say something horrible, but still generally well deserved, to the clueless? I often find myself cringing there in my lazy boy chair as Randy starts laughing and trying to hide his face, or when even Paula can't even think of something falsely nice or encouraging to say.

The judges have the little dance steps of the formula down for enduring, but then every once in a while you get a real gem, a golden talent shining out from the crowd.

I watched a recent episode where one girl was mind numbingly bad. She brutalizing the song, and the audience alike. Then, to top it off, she had a chip on her shoulder... and in spite of being totally tone deaf, had decided that SHE was "the next American Idol." Her proletarian agenda didn't qualify based on skill, but on her perception that she was on all other levels as good as or better than any American Idol.

She was devastated when she found her activist stance (that anyone could be the Idol "with or without talent") was shot down. I remember thinking, "how could she be so sincerely deluded?" And how sad and scary she was in her self righteous indignation that they wouldn't see her worthiness! She missed one little fact which Simon then pointed out to her, "Why enter a singing competition when you can't sing?"

I think further on the shocking number of people who seem to honestly think they deserve a place in Hollywood. I can't imagine putting myself forward like that. And being so self deluded as to think I'm a world class singer. There is an amazing need for people to rightly judge their talents, and to honestly view their own strengths and weaknesses. Do I have talent? Do I lack talent?

Over the years we saw the same thing repeatedly in our church with people who just decided that because they loved music that they were some how singers. The level of self delusion being outrageous – but they continue to strive for a forum to "entertain and bless" others.

I Cor 11:28-31 "But let a man examine himself, and so let him eat of that bread, and drink of that cup. For he that eats and drinks unworthily, eats and drinks damnation to himself, not discerning the Lord's body. For this cause many are weak and sick among you, and many sleep." "For if we would judge ourselves, we should not be judged."

I know the context of this passage specifically deals with communion. I'd like to conceptually extend this a bit – that it is the lack of discernment of the Lord's body – not just in communion but in everyday Christian life. That if we judge each other unjustly, or if we don't judge our own place in the body accurately, we will be weak and sickly or perhaps even die.

It's interesting. If these prospective singers on the show would just judge themselves they would not be judged. Not just by the contest judges, but the entire nation. I know the show would lose much of its attraction if people would just do this for themselves.

As Christians, the body of Christ, it is so important for success and life to rightly evaluate ourselves, and to not think more highly of ourselves than we ought to think. Romans 12:3 "For by the grace given me I say... Do not think of yourself more highly than you ought, but rather think of yourself with sober judgment, in accordance with the measure of faith God has given you."

While we may all be able to physically sing, if we could just step back and away from our ego we'd see some of us are good singers, some are amazing, and some of us are horrible. And on the show, out of the multiplied thousands who auditioned there are only one or two who are honestly world class.

We are all (physical limitations aside) able to draw or paint. My mom recently gave me my (well kept) second grade book report on the Dr. Seuss, "Green Eggs and Ham" fully illustrated. Many of us doodle and scribble while on the phone, but most have given up even rudimentary finger painting - unless of course your therapist has you doing it as an exercise. We can honestly evaluate here in this realm how few of us are a Picasso, a Rembrandt, or Monet. How does our double minded approach allow us to see them as the "masters" they rightfully are, but at the same time not afford even this same consideration to those with whom they co-labor in the Body?

I've seen over the years so many efforts to be inclusionary in the Body of Christ. The effort on the part of both leadership and the general body to make everyone feel both a part, capable, and empowered. But how much stronger and greater would the Body be if we could just back away from our opinions of ourselves and others long enough to honestly evaluate who and what we are. That way, we can enjoy the Gifts we have.

Too many times over the past few years, I've heard the phrase, "no more lone rangers," and "no more superstars." I keep looking in the Bible for examples and types of this actually being the case. Where is the type and shadow of this?... I wonder, using the example of American Idol experience, if perhaps there aren't actually "Gifts differing," at various levels of skill. (Rom 12:6).

For example, let's say that one day dentistry is the new vogue in the Church. That collectively we've come to decided that everyone is as good as any dentist. And all of us have the same capabilities and capacities as any dentist, thus we are just as good. Sorry, but just because you know how to brush and floss your teeth doesn't mean you are a dentist. Not to be rude or anything, but don't think for one moment I would let any self-professed dentist near my mouth. Nor for that matter, a self professed prophet near my destiny!

Perhaps we really are the BODY of Christ, and some of us are ears, some mouths, some hands, some lungs, some legs (I Cor 12). And perhaps if we'd determine what we were actually individually created to be and to do, we would be more content in life. Not striving for pre-eminence as is the manner of some, but rejoice in yourself alone, and not in another (Gal 6:4).

Rest is realizing that I'm not in competition with anyone else in the Body, nor do I have to drag another down to achieve my destiny. And maybe - just maybe, God was big enough in His creation of me, that my place in His will and Kingdom will not intrude on yours. That in His house are many mansion, and there is room enough for each of us to do what God has prepared us to do.

I need to be secure in what I'm called to do, and to rationally evaluate that place accurately. Only "SOME" are apostles, prophets, evangelist, pastors and teachers. While some believers may have evidence in their lives of the nine gifts of the Spirit, others have maybe administration and helps, or some such (Rom 12:6-10). We've placed such a separation on the big five (Eph 4:11), that the return swing of the pendulum in recent times has been the near denial of five fold and the refusal to recognize the differences in us all.

I happily recognize those who are different from me – which is every other person in the world! I see that some are greater in gifting, some are lesser. Some have different gifts, and shockingly I don't actually have all of them entirely in me (which would thereby render others less useful). I think that to see an accurate release of God through anyone else, we need to see their expression as unique and right individually - just as they are.

I've no reason to despise any other part of the body, nor to count myself as less because I am jealous of the contents of another vessel.

A specialized tool can be very expensive and in a specific set of circumstances it may be irreplaceable. But at the same time it is nearly useless in most day to day living chores. In the grand scheme, the more exotic things are less useful.

"I would that the body would rightly divide itself and to rightly judge itself. Let's be more healthy. To not judge the time of (insert favored thing we want to declare finished) having been passed because our experience or gifting is not within that realm. I would that each part contributes what it may that the whole be strengthened and be synergistically greater than the added sum of its parts". (Eph 4:15-16).

"I don't want to be the self deluded one who ends up with a great announcement that I didn't use my talents – that I buried them in favor of something else on the final day" (Matthew 25:24-30).

I keep thinking where Paul says that all may prophesy, and how this has been abused. Not much unlike the poor deluded girl, too many believers think that this means they are all essentially the next American Idol."

End of article.

DULLING THE AUTHORITY FOR MIRACLES

MY STORY: Truth is – in the early days, I never believed in using titles. That is until the day when I arrived at our church to find out that everyone else was already there. They had decided to have a meeting WITHOUT ME! That had never happened before! And the purpose of that gathering was to vote on their decision to stop calling me "Kluane" and start calling me "Pastor."

"But, why?" I answered stunned at their plot. "I don't need a title!"

"We want this town to gain respect for who you are and all that is happening around here. So, that's the way it's going to be from here on!" Then they laughed and celebrated their big surprise!

I thought it was silliness – maybe it would all go away!

But it didn't go away. They continued with their plan. After awhile, and to my amazement, several productive changes began. Quickly, my leadership gained greater support. The church banned together with greater energy and momentum. We rapidly grew in numbers and in effect upon the community. Direction clarified.

It's not that using titles is even the issue. But... titles can help focus vision and purpose. For all of us, maintaining a well defined direction must become a cause. Direction causes effectively accomplish ministry – to save the lost, to heal the sick, to grow and mature the believer, to love the unlovely, to reproduce likeness and image, to develop a heart of compassion, and so on.

For us... the difference was amazing.

ATTITUDE OF THE HEART

Refusing to respect and follow someone else is not the appropriate relational heart attitude. Unity does not occur just because we can all do the same thing.

> When we dare to treat others with respect, our own self-respect will increase.

Miriam and Aaron questioned the *authority* of their brother and they were stricken with leprosy! Leprosy is the dis-EASE of familiarity. It is highly contagious and difficult to cure. Jesus (the greatest minister of all time) faced familiarity in His own hometown (Mat. 13:53-58) when he could do no "mighty works" in HIs own home town. Therefore, they were unable to receive.

"Familiarity" in this usage is defined as: "An improper or indecorous act or remark, especially an unacceptable use of words not suited to circumstances. Impropriety and undue or uninvited intimacy. Informality. Impertinency. Unwelcome and presumptuous intimacy."

'Though familiarity may not breed contempt, it takes off the edge of admiration." William Hazlitt

Why are people everywhere resistant to leadership and those in authority? It is a common problem, even for Jesus.

Neighbors tried to strip Jesus of His *authority* by being overly familiar. "We've known him all hIs life – he's just a carpenter's son," they claimed. "He's no different – he's just a man LIKE US! We even know his mother's name, and his brothers, and sisters!" (vs. 55-56). They actually viewed Jesus in their minds and hearts as someone who could do nothing special. Their comments were an attempt to make themselves EQUAL to Jesus! Therefore, they were unable to receive from Him!

 Unbelief is the product of familiarity. Will those closest to you receive from you? Or does familiarity stop it?

Jesus' neighbors spit out their judgmental evaluations, "... Where did he get all these things?" (vs. 56). The modern day scenario is the same, "Does our pastor really hear from God?" "I read a book last week that was different...!"

> Respect releases authority.

All objects go unnoticed by too familiar a view.

- Familiarity demoralizes leadership and weakens the anointing resident within Gift Offices.

- We should honor the God-given Gift Offices.
- Respect allows us to draw from the Gift of the office.

Alluring, charming, magnetic personalities often disappoint us.

 Leadership is God's GRACE GIFT to those in the church. It's a form of envy, pride and jealousy to NOT ESTEEM another minister more highly than yourself. We all need to respect someone for knowing more than we do. We all need to be teachable. Leadership is supposed to deal in our lives. SOMEONE NEEDS TO BE ABLE TO SPEAK INTO YOUR LIFE. WHO IS IT?

"Excessive familiarity is the bane of social happiness," William Godwin (in his book, The Enquirer, written in 1797, pg. 86).

"Familiarity doesn't breed contempt, it is contempt." Florence King

"Only fools think they are always right in their own mind" (Pr. 12:15).

Let's review the problem with the pyramid government (see earlier section in *"Apostolic Authority"* for details). The problem is NOT just because they use TITLES. The real problem is:

Competition - wanting bigger pyramids

Control and manipulation

Arrogance

Members are hurt

Besting systems develop

Covering is stressed

Rigid doctrines increase

Secondly, the pendulum swings the other way and we have a HUGE OVER REACTION *against* the Pyramid Government. This group is one we'll call the EQUALIZERS. They want to make everyone EQUAL – meaning to make level or to make the same. The weaknesses of this system are manifold. Some problems are:

Lack of structure and government.

Smaller groups.

Ineffective and weaker leaders.

Rebellious and angry members.

Lack of respect and familiarity toward leadership.

Familarity must not be used out of hurt, insecurity, jealousy, and envy.

We see Biblical equality of personhood in statements such as, *"So Mephibosheth ate at David's table like one of the king's sons" (2 Sam. 9:7 NIV).* Mephibosheth was accepted as an equal member of the family, but he was not in line to become "KING."

NOT EVERYONE IS A GENERAL

How we relate to others is very much a part of being Christian. Though a brand new believer is "proportionately equal" to all other believers in the Kingdom, we must remember to regard those who have gone before and paved the way.

Valuing others keeps us from striving to be like anyone else. If we should have ever met Billy Graham, should we have contended to be equal with him? Of course, we don't idolize him – but we should regard him as a powerful influencer who was mightily used.

God's Generals always have Rank in His Army! We need to acknowledge spiritual position as part of God's Kingdom plan. A general realizes that the war can't be won without all the ranks of all his military might working together! It takes everyone working together to bring forth the Kingdom.

Striving for position causes us to loose our zealousness, passion, and motivation. *And we should not try to compare ourselves with others (2 Cor. 11:12-18).* Why would those who have never won a soul posture in a way to be viewed as an equal to someone like Rev. Billy Graham? Our goal is to serve God – and we're all in this together.

HONORING WITH TITLES

It's just plain old good manners to defer to those in authority.

FIRST NAMES

This section is not intended to be a mandate - but to offer another side to the idea of using first names. Now, wait before you shut down this idea... let's take it farther! Most of these believers honestly think that USING "FIRST NAMES" REPRESENTS THE ORIGINAL BIBLICAL CONCEPTS of a New Testament. However, this kind of presumption was never assumed in the early church – I can assure you, if a poll were taken, most of these people (who insist on first names) don't speak fluent Aramaic (which a great share of the New Testament was written), nor do they comprehend the culture and customs of the Bible lands.

- Jesus spoke Aramaic and occasionally quoted scriptures from ancient Hebrew. Yet, many of our Bible translations are translated from Aramaic into Greek, then into Latin, then into ancient English. Do we really understand everything?

- The Old Testament Hebrew that Jesus quoted was basically written with all consonants and no vowels and with no spaces between the words, leaving many of the exact meanings to a translator's decisions.
- Up until recent years it has been impolite in the Western world to refer to people by their first name.

Church titles do not make God's servants more important than other members. We use titles to distinguish what God has set in order for His Church to function best. Every person and position in the Church matters.

If we don't give our church leaders respect, then our children will fail to do that as well. Instead, they listen to our disgruntled disrespect and move further and further away from truth. Disrespect is affecting the entire next generation. Many leaders concur that the use of titles helps maintain leadership and greatly reduces problems of over familiarity.

We are in a Renaissance of new ideas concerning leadership development. We have finally figured out that our traditional methods aren't working well and methodologies must change before the crisis increases. But what are the alternatives? Let me ask you... is your leadership enhanced by encouraging familiarity?

Giving someone a title merely validates that we have given them permission to operate in specific areas of work. Titles do not necessarily imply exceptional giftedness. But, the use of titles can often help release expectation and faith.

Is the answer to error taking away everyone's title?

Consider: Could the insistence refusal to call someone else by a title signal that we think of ourselves too highly?

 The protocol of giving respect is an attitude of celebrating someone that the Lord has allowed in your life.

We all know how all military personnel on the job consistently use titles to assure team work and clear accountability. Someone has to lead and that leader is always clearly defined... not only with titles, but with insignias, uniform variations, etc. It is standard that no fraternization occurs between officers and enlisted people. An apparent chain of command is essential for there to be efficient follow through. Who will we die for? Who can we trust? It is EFFECTIVE to keep function clear.

Respect and honor inspire people to give their lives for what they hold dear.

The military also teaches enlisted people to not fraternize with officers. For example, my son is a Marine officer while my son-in-law is an enlisted Marine. When visiting at home, they are friends and family – at work, they don't fraternize.

In much the same way, it is possible that verbally acknowledging true Spiritual *authority* could, in exchange, offer the chance to be mentored into maturity – and to be given accountability.

 SUMMARY: Most servant leaders who carry *authority* are not consumed with posturing authoritarianism. They are polite, considerate, prudent, dignified, deferential, respectful, humble, compassionate, and unassuming with others. They do not pursue ambition but are fully consumed with helping humanity.

It is the job of apostolic leadership to consistently reassure and make certain that their flock understands why we think our teaching can truly deliver such great value to their lives!

IN DEFENSE OF "TITLES"

This section opposes the way most "enlightened" believers are conditioned to think these days. But, I'm convinced that much of what is happening now needs to be corrected – and soon. Many of the modern trends oppose leaders USING TITLES. This opposition stems from the long term observation of the problems caused by the controlling hierarchy and the inappropriate division of clergy/laity.

Many of the 'equalizer type' people (especially in the Western or American churches) seem to relish in NOT addressing people as "pastor" or even "reverend" and insist on using their first name -without asking first! Many just were never taught better – while others have absolutely NO hesitation about humiliating, embarrassing, or being insultingly discourteous to a minister – even though that minister has lived a long life of dignity and genuine intentions.

Not much is said about what could be some GODLY ADVANTAGES to using titles. Now granted, here again there has been a lot of misuse and arrogance about titles – but is there ever an intrinsic value to using them? Is the use of titles ever Scriptural? Let's examine further how the use of titles can cause greater activated *authority* to be present.

 The reason this subject of titles is important is related to the loss of Godly authority. We're not talking about the false arrogance or the well known cheap imitations of the apostolic. What is defended here is the genuine benefit of respect. Respect should be an essential part of true apostolic ministry. What we really need to do is look for the BALANCE concerning titles, recognition, distinctions, and appreciation of function.

I'm not saying that you should or should not use titles. But, I am calling for tolerance and understanding on both sides. This portion of the book will defend that right to use titles, because in my opinion there is far more Scriptural and historical evidence supporting the use of titles than not. I know that many disagree, but this topic does need to be examined further.

What is comprehended as respect for one person will not necessarily be the same for another. Titles should not be used to draw attention or exalt ourselves above others, but call us into service. Titles can give a sense of purpose and belonging... this is "my pastor."

RECEIVING THE FUNCTION

God isn't impressed by our job function, but He does allow us to represent Him and to help others. Titles help identify how we can help. As the church now responsibly redefines herself, it can no longer benefit from a rigid pyramid of *authority*...but rather become a community that respects one other's assignments. Titles can describe where we fit and how we belong.

We do know that our traditional concepts of "pastor" and "bishop" are clearly unscriptural. However, the word "pastor" before a person's name is universally understood to simply indicate that he/she is a vital minister of the gospel. It should bear no significance to personal superiority, hierarchical importance, visibility, or prominence. "Pastor" can be a loving relational term. This also applies to "Bishop," "Elder," "Reverend," etc.

Some terms are by their very nature genuine and functional in helping establish relationship and promote governmental order within that relationship. For example, I never spoke to (or about) any of the pastors who worked with me in my local church without calling them "pastor." There were times when they lived IN OUR HOME... but regard toward their office remained.

Kingdom relationship is a partnership with spiritual authority.

It is important to emphasize that such terms as "apostle" and "pastor" are functional terms; they are not to signify lofty Christian Guruism. These terms are descriptive of one's task. Recognizing and calling forth the God ordained purpose of someone else in your live can release vital living value into your life.

Titles can represent the relationship we have with others – and reference or defer to the *authority* they have because of the power that backs them up – whether it is the government, the country, or civil officials. Those in charge of ships are "Captain." We address a judge as

"Your honor," a Queen as "Your Highness," a policeman as "officer." Our school teachers are "Mr., Mrs., Professor" etc. That helps them maintain order. Some honorific titles often have prefixes to them (such as Mr. Mayor, Madam President, or Rabbi) without attached surnames. The "Associated Press Stylebook and Guidelines" states that usually "These titles mentioned above, in effect, BECOME THEIR NAMES."

We need to recognize that some people have full time jobs leading the church and some have full time jobs doing other necessary things. Those who lead the church can reasonably be called or "*pastor*" or "bishop" without diminishing those who work in the marketplace. It's the minister's job to be in relationship with the flock – and therefore, they have "more delegated *authority*" in that certain arena – just as a judge ("Your Honor") would have in a court room.

 Tell me, if the Queen of England invited you to a palace dinner – would you presume to call her by her first name? Is every position EQUAL? Do you really think *you* should also be addressed as "Your Majesty? Or "Your Excellency?"

We should be comfortable calling people what they deserve to be called.

- Proverbs 24:21, "Fear GOD, dear child – *respect* your leaders; don't be defiant or mutinous."
- Ecclesiastes 10:20, "Don't bad-mouth your leaders, NOT EVEN UNDER YOUR BREATH, And don't abuse your betters, even in the privacy of your home. Loose talk has a way of getting picked up and spread around. Little birds drop the crumbs of your gossip far and wide" (MSG).

Ministers aren't any more important – titles should lovingly affirm relationship function.

The point is that titles can make the job of leadership more effective and easier. Leaders give themselves to the ministry of the church full time. This is a job worthy of respect (as many other jobs are as well). Giving respect is an ancient landmark that should not be moved (Prov. 22:28).

SPEAKING A FUNCTIONING TITLE

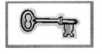 Calling a Gift Office out by words puts a spiritual demand of faith upon the Gift of that Office to fully respond and operate from that Office. CALLING A GIFT OFFICE OUT BY WORDS PUTS A DEMAND of FAITH UPON THAT GIFT TO OPERATE FULLY TOWARD YOU. Honoring the office (name, prophet, righteous man, etc.) of a minister can help you tap into that GIFT. Many people cannot receive because they do not honor the God in the person who brings their blessing.

Like I mentioned earlier in the book, I used to prefer just being called by my first name, but then I had an insight. When someone calls me "pastor," it is NOT A TITLE, but my role in their life. I am honored and willing to be that under Christ. It is also about relationship. "Pastor" is a warm, affectionate and caring word. I like it. After 25 years of being called "Pastor," it has literally become my name. At every moment in my life when with others, I am *always* a pastor.

Calling out function brings the GIFTS OF THAT OFFICE to bear upon the situation. It's not meant to self-exalt anyone. For example, when someone calls me "Pastor," it means to me that they trust me to guard and teach them – and it causes me to immediately respond in that way. It means that they want to be in relationship with me and are not looking at my weakness of the flesh but are regarding me in the spirit (Rom. 8:4, 2 Cor. 5:16). If someone calls me "Apostle" it means to me that they regard and recognize the impact of my life and doctrine upon the Church.

 Matt 10:41-42 He that receives a prophet in the NAME OF A PROPHET shall receive a prophet's reward (Mat. 10:41-42, KJV). That's gift recognition. We attend meetings where prophets prophesy because we want to receive from that GIFT. (And we well know that not every prophet has that gift equally.) The idea here is in RECEIVING. If we do not receive the fact that a person is coming in the NAME of a prophet, we cannot receive the reward. If suspicion and disrespect fill our mind, we won't receive.

In Hebrew, the word NAME in this Scripture is *onoma* and is used in general of the "name by which a person or thing is called. A person's name represents "the title and dignity" of who they are... for all that a "name" implies, of *authority*, character, rank, majesty, power, excellence, etc., of everything that the "name" covers and its attributes. *Onoma* is used to represent the *AUTHORITY* of Christ" (from Vine's Expository Dictionary of Biblical Words).

That means, if you RECEIVE me in the GIFT OFFICE that God gave me, (without being judgmental, or mistrusting) then, there will be ministry FOR YOU (the reward).

Just leadership escorts believers into the fulfillment of becoming who God intends them to be. And finding this positional alignment with authority should release an even greater freedom to collaborate and work together. The church doesn't need rebels, but a cooperating and effective Body that recognizes the indwelling gifts of the Holy Spirit.

WAYS TO SHOW RESPECT

"We must build a new world, a far better world - one in which the eternal dignity of man is respected." Harry S. Truman

There are many ways to show respect and regard: you can help people, imitate and follow them, cooperate with them, give them credit for contributions, protect them, and provide for them. You can speak to them (and about them) in ways that reflect your value for their worth. You can treat them as though they are special to you and not just one in a crowd. You should respect those leaders who are decent, honorable, and honest. You must deal with each individual impartially on the basis of whatever is relevant to their particular situation.

 As society changes in regards to customs of respect, we discover that believers should choose to reflect the Kingdom rather than the world.

Showing respect is a learned socialization skill that varies within cultural factors. If we want to emulate the early church moving in *AUTHORITY*, then we need to understand their culture of respect.

The best thing a leader can do to encourage honor is to affirm others and then affirm them again. The Scriptures teach us to give honor to those we consider least (Mat. 25:40).

There will be those who follow the corrupt desire of the sinful nature and despise authority (2 Pet. 2:10).

TITLES IN ANCIENT TIMES

We rent a "Ben Hur" movie or watch the "Passion" and think that we understand ancient life. But, watching a few movies doesn't give us great insight into the Middle Eastern mind of 2000 years ago. To think that we can fully comprehend or appreciate how the first church lived or what they thought about titles would surpass the grasp of all possibility.

 Regarding this topic of respect and titles, what must be considered above all is that Jewish culture most certainly respected their leaders and their elders. Hebrew is an extremely honorific culture and language. The Jewish perspective of respect has always been their basis for human interactions. Their concept of actively valuing and honoring with deference the life of others is the reason why the Jewish people established welfare institutions thousands of years before the rest of the world ever considered it.

A title is merely an appellation of dignity, honor, distinction, or consideration given to a person by virtue of rank, office, age, or attainment. A spiritual title recognizes the capacity in which the Lord has assigned a person to serve.

It is almost laughable that we should try to validate our brazenly libertine ideas of Church Government by inserting our Western notions and definitions into their ancient culture of respect. Does using titles matter? Yes and no.

 If being called by a title makes YOU feel superior or better than someone, then it's wrong for you to be called by a title.

If needing titles is based in PRIDE, then God hates it (Pro. 6:16-19). All that is in the world is not of the Father (1 Jn. 2:16). Pride is self-centered, ambitious, and haughty.

The Lord sees pride differently than we do – not just as arrogance. There is also a spiritual pride... the more revelation we have, the closer to God that we've been, the more we pray than others. Pride is independence; the Lord would have us become dependent upon Him and interdependent with one another.

Pride acts without clear instruction from the Lord. It takes ministry into our own hand. Pride is repelled by servanthood concepts. Pride gets upset over the success and position of others. Pride does not want to recognize other ministry positions.

 If giving titles helps you to acknowledge and give respect of those who spill out their lives for you, then, yes, IT MATTERS – because then, it is right.

Truth surpasses our limited ideas and notions.

HONORIFIC LANGUAGES

In the Jewish world, language was built around relationship, status, title, and position. Honor of God is particularly noticeable. In the Old Testament, nobody dared speak HIS NAME – it was what is known as the Tetragram, YHWH (Yaweh).

Moses asked God's NAME; And God said unto Moses, "I AM THAT I AM: and he said, Therefore, you shall say unto the children of Israel, I AM has sent me unto you" (Ex. 3:14).

Much of the Old Testament refers to God with the four character tetragram YHWH and JHVH – and nobody spoke the sound. (The actual pronunciation no one knows to this day.) Some theologians have better translated this as, "I WILL BE WHO I WILL BE," or "The Ever Changing and revealing God of Covenant."

We mention this because in Jewish tradition this principle of respect was so profound that it became a SIN to speak or even to write the HOLY name of God. Indeed, the Third Commandment says, "You shalt not take the NAME of the Lord your God in vain..."

Later, because they still didn't want to take God's NAME in vain, around 300 BC, the letter combination of "YHWH" was substituted by the word,

Adonai which simply meant Lord. This practice continued through all the Greek and Latin translations such as the King James Version. It wasn't until the American Standard Version (1901) that translators went back to translate JHVH as Jehovah.

 A most significant thing about what Jesus taught was that God could be called something... they could call Him "Father." Father is a relational title.

- Jesus said, "I have made your NAME KNOWN and will make it known" (Jn. 17:6). In what we call the "Lord's prayer, Jesus taught them to say, "Hallowed be thy NAME" (Math 6:10).
- "God for the first time turned his attention to the nations to take out of them a people for his name; people who are called by my NAME, says Jehovah." Acts 15:14-17
- "Hallelujah" is a form of the Name "Yaweh,"

The current disuse of the honorific language was primarily caused by the massive import of foreign words into the early languages which leaves the ancient traditional customs of everyday speech of ordinary citizens and even the official languages to be forgotten.

> The Hebrew and Aramaic languages were honorific.

There's no getting around it... Hebrew and Aramaic cultures and languages were honorific!

All over the natural world honor is given within language structure. Many subtle changes in the pronouns and verb forms (honorific protocol) go unnoticed in translations. Asian languages all tended to be honorific and some still are. Honoring one another has long been the natural part of their ordered environment including: Chinese, Keigo (the honorific Japanese language), and Korean; most Islamic languages; Arabic and ancient Iranian; most all the dialects from India and Vietnamese: island languages such as the Micronesian, Chammorro, Tongan, and Pohnpein languages. Early Indo-European languages. Many African dialects. The Himalayan languages, the Charyan languages, to list a few.

- Quakers didn't use first names ("thee" and "thou," etc.).
- Read any good novel and discover that just a century ago friends called each other "Mr." and "Miss." "Sir" and "Ma'am."

 Read the Bible through the eyes of God so that the barricades of culture, time, and space are transcended.

If we want to capture the energy and experience similar results of the early Chris-

> Apostolic leaders neet to consider important issues through a Biblical lens – rather than depending upon what is happening now.

tians, let's not overlook the situations they faced and their feelings of honor and commitment.

Then, we may possibly discover, not only WHY the power of God was released in their midst, but also learn how that power might come in greater measure into our midst. The process asks how do we project our understanding across this gap of twenty centuries, and understand what the early church thought about titles?

Mostly, the earliest Christians focused on living fully in the light of the gospel message – their doctrine was much less elaborate than in later formulations. In other words, the first Christians weren't particularly interested in hair-splitting word searches. Instead, the true believers exhibited a fervency of faith that catapulted them into greatness. The early church was a SOCIAL ORDER of the Roman era. Their messages were about supernatural revolution and relevant change.

What we do know about the leadership in the early church is that it was strong. Those leaders were highly esteemed and prized by the followers. Followers related to leadership in deference and honor. The Jewish tradition and culture (as well as many other cultures around) centered on the virtue of respect – respect for life, the family, the temple and ceremonies, the Law, and tradition. How the New Testament church lived with "fear and honor" toward God and respect for one another is almost unfathomable to our modern mind-set.

WE ARE IN DIRE NEED OF LANGUAGE REFORM. We need to study and not just accept what everyone is saying but to find truth. Those of us who have been leaders in the past will have to open our hands and raise them in surrender to the transformation of our obsolete and rigid mind-sets into a re-connection with glorious new principles. I believe that on this new frontier, we will see new paradigms of respect releasing greater authority.

 We can legitimately give honored deference to Five-fold Ministers who have established or earned genuine ESTEEM. Respect doesn't come from any hierarchical "*positioning.*" This true kind of esteem toward established and attested ministers brings dignity and honor toward their God. This respect is not only considerate, but is also fitting, appropriate, and Scriptural.

"But we request of you brethren, that you appreciate those who diligently labor among you, and have charge over you in the Lord and give you instruction (admonition, warning, correction) and that you ESTEEM THEM HIGHLY IN LOVE BECAUSE OF THEIR WORK"

(1 Thes. 5:13).

RIGHT OR WRONG?

Paul says it was appropriate to have *deference* toward leaders based on the spiritual giftings, wisdom, and leadership ability that they demonstrate. 1 Thes. 5:12-13 says, "Now we ask you, brothers, to RESPECT (acknowledge, appreciate, and highly regard) those who work hard among you, who are OVER YOU (*prohistemi*, which is a combination of two words: *pro*, in front of or gone before and (2476) *histemi* which means to stand) in the Lord and who admonish (warn, remind, gently give instruction, teach) you.

Hold them in the highest regard (greatest ESTEEM and affection) in love (intelligent and sympathetic appreciation) because of their work." In other words, "RESPECT THOSE WHO STAND AS HAVING GONE BEFORE YOU BECAUSE THEY DESERVE RESPECT AND REGARD."

Jesus said, they were "all on the same level as *brothers*" (Mat. 23:8, LB), (literally meaning from the "same womb"). This meant they belonged together at the same level as family. When we each realize that we are all Kings and Priests, there is no more rank or class system. We can be "brothers" of DIFFERENT SKILLS belonging to the same family.

There will be a day when we can gratefully acknowledge one another for their particular and unique giftings and anointing. We will respect those in our family who carry greater responsibility or have gone before us and can teach us. We will value their help and instruction. We value and respect them and still not be "less than" – in any way, because we are family!

 QUESTION: To whom are you related to as family? Not COVERED by... to whom are you JOINED (in *koinonea*)? To whom are you accountable? With whom do you labor?

A title is a designation of esteem, admiration, deference, or recognition of accomplishment given to a person.

QUESTION: Do titles take away from the Lord being our all in all? Let's agree. The last thing we would want is to offend The Lord. God is Holy and reverent. Notice the only occurrence of "reverend" and how it is used: "He sent redemption unto his people: he has commanded His covenant for ever: holy and reverent is his name" (Ps. 111: 9). God deserves to be called reverend because of his essential nature and deeds.

In saying this, we must also ask ourselves, "Is any person creditable, honorable, or deserving of our respect? If the Lord fully dwells in us, we can say that another person is holy because Jesus has already made them holy[1]... and each and every one of us is commanded to be holy.

And just who do we think we are calling ourselves "reverend?" Why, perhaps we think we're getting more and more like Him. We do represent the Reverend God, we want to act like Him and care like He does. Just like we are "little Christs" (Christians), can we become "little reverends?"

BIBLICAL RESTRICTIONS ABOUT TITLES

There are three instances in the New Testament that give instruction concerning not using "titles." They are spoken by Jesus to His disciples. If you will examine them again, you will also see that they do NOT restrict using titles – just using them incorrectly. Please read Matthew 23:1-10 in your Bible as we study it out verse by verse:

"They sat on Moses' seat" (vs. 1) The first thing we notice here is that Jesus is still in the temple as he addresses the crowds and his disciples. He says that the scribes and Pharisees "sit on Moses' seat." Moses, of course, was respected as the great lawgiver. Sitting in "Moses' seat" may be metaphorical, or it could even be possible that Moses' seat was actually a piece of furniture at the front of the synagogue.

This is an account of the age old problem with abusive *authority*. In Jesus' time, much like it is in our time, so-called ministers took for themselves the right to sit at the seat of Moses. From this lofty position these men could speak "from God" to the people. Because of their falsely perceived position, they were able to mislead and abuse their followers.

We cannot put a man in Moses' seat of *authority*. And, we must not look upon any person as holding *authority* beyond their capacity. Titles are not meant to over-exalt or to wrongly portray a person. Titles are supposed to identify the person who has already distinguished himself in the capacity and function that the Spirit has assigned him.

What is important about this 'seat of Moses' is that it refers to the "assumption of religious and cultural *authority*" by those men. These Pharisees presumed to sit in Moses' seat as deciders of religious matters (and we all know that God's Word is the decider). At the same time, they bound people by their Jewish traditions and their own outdated interpretations. Jesus said that they were seated in improper positions of *authority*! They weren't to compare themselves to Moses!

 Spiritual leaders are given the right to exercise authority for God. They are not to overestimate their abilities or self-exalt their position unworthily.

(Vs. 2) Do what they tell you to do, but don't do things like they do them. Let's not miss this next part. Then Jesus said to the crowds and to his disciples, *"The scribes and the Pharisees sit on Moses' seat; therefore, DO WHATEVER THEY TEACH YOU AND FOLLOW IT; but DO NOT DO AS THEY DO"* (vs. 3).

 In spite of their personal failings (which Jesus lists later), the disciples were supposed to LISTEN and FOLLOW what these scribes and Pharisees said (they had some truth).

"BUT DO NOT DO AS THEY DO"

They were to do what they taught, but not do as the do! This is the point! What did the Pharisees do wrong? "They do not practice what they teach" (v. 3c). When it comes to teaching, nothing is more detrimental than being a bad example! As teachers, these men had a special responsibility to model lawful behavior. Their personal conduct should have provided a visible lesson – they should have shown the community what lawful behavior looked like and the benefits that it could bring. But these men who taught the Torah failed to practice what they taught. Their lack of integrity undermined their work.

This is what Jesus said! Their teachings were good – but their *AUTHORITY* was not the same as Moses. They just weren't that important. Jesus tells the disciples to listen to them and do what they say but not to be like them.

WHAT DID THEY DO WRONG?

"For they bind heavy burdens, hard to bear, and lay them on men's shoulders" (vs.3). Jesus had no complaint against anyone teaching the law, but He didn't like their binding interpretation of the law.

"They made others work hard, but they themselves were unwilling to lift a finger" (v. 4). The Scribes and Pharisees required others to conform to a higher standard than they themselves lived. They spent their days debating the minute points of the law – which would only burden the people more.

- Contrastively, Jesus offered an easy yoke, a light burden, a fulfillment of the Law, and rest for the soul (11:29-30).

"They did their works to be seen by men" (vs.5). Okay. But, what could that mean? It sounds contradictory to what Jesus told the disciples (in Matthew 5:16), "Let your light so shine before men, that they may SEE YOUR GOOD WORKS and give glory to your Father who is in heaven!" Paul "boasted" to the Corinthians about what he had done. Visible good works shows the glory of Christ living in us...

The scribes and Pharisees were guilty of seeking the glory that rightly belongs to God. What is condemned here is the prideful motivations of these particular deeds.

"They made phylacteries broad and enlarged the borders of their garments" (vs. 5b). Their phylacteries (also known as *tephillin*) were leather boxes that contained one or more scrolls inscribed with passages of scripture.

- In the Old Testament phylacteries and tassels helped people, particularly pre-literate people, to remember and to understand spiritual truths. The wearing of the phylacteries was okay – but the showing off wasn't.
- "Do nothing from selfishness or empty conceit, but with humility of mind let each of you regard one another as more important than himself; don't look out for your own personal interests, but also for the interests of others" (Phil. 2:4).

These Pharisees and Scribes puffed around in ridiculously ornate garments in front of mostly illiterate people who did not have access to the precious scrolls even if they could read.

- Robes (like mantles) came to have distinctive decorations to show the rank of the wearer. It's not the robe that was wrong – but the prideful over-estimation of themselves (wearing of robes that did not match their calling). Their actual standing in God's *authority* did not match the perceived grandeur of their apparel.
- David knew not to wear Saul's armor because he knew that was not his calling or his assignment (sphere of *authority*).
- After 200 AD, the clerical robes were worn to hide the individuality of the person in order that God would be exalted.

"They love the place of honor at feasts and the best seats in the synagogues" (vs. 5). Does this Scripture mean that we shouldn't sit at the speaker's table at the church dinner or to sit on the rostrum during the service? No. Again, what Jesus forbids is the prideful seeking of positions of visibility. He told us to take the lower seat (Lk. 14:7-11) and wait until the host may invite us to the higher place.

"Called themselves RABBI (teacher)" (vs. 7-8). The word "Rabbi," (*didaskalos,* used in Matt. 23:9) simply means "teacher" or "leader." We may wonder what's so bad about designating someone as a teacher? We do that all the time. Now, surely you know that Jesus is not saying we can't call ourselves teachers or leaders?

This word *"didaskalos"* was a very common term. It is used for words translated as teacher, leader, and rabbi. *Didaskalos* is also frequently translated as "master." It is "straining the gnat" to never call anyone

"Mr." Mister means master, and Jesus said these men called themselves "*didaskalos!*"

Didaskalos was an every-day term of address and role designation (Jn. 1: 38; Matt. 22: 23; 23: 32, etc.). *Didaskalos* was a word being used by all the Jews and Christians at that time (and afterward). Jesus regarded this title *didaskalos* as normal form of address for Himself (Mt. 7:21, 23:7-10, Lk. 6:46):

- Jn. 13.13: "You call me *Teacher* and Lord, and you speak rightly" (Jn. 13:13).
- Before the final Passover, Jesus told his disciples to... say, "The *Teacher* says, 'Where is the room where I may eat the Passover with my disciples?'" (Mk. 14.14, Mt. 26.18, Lk. 22.11).
- John called Jesus by this title, (1:38) "...*Rabbi*, (which is to say, being interpreted, Master,) where do you live?"
- *Didaskalos* in some translations is also rendered as "doctor." in LK. 2:46, "And it came to pass, that after three days they found him in the temple, sitting in the midst of the doctors (*didaskalos*, teachers), both hearing them, and asking them questions."
- *Didaskalos* is a form of the word, *didache*, which is translated 29 times in the New Testament as "DOCTRINE."

Truth is, *didaskalos* was just a common word used to refer to someone who was a teacher – it wasn't a big issue – one way or the other. The statement in this Scripture concerned the inordinate desire to gain prominence and control – and that was the issue.

In fact, Jesus was not ruling against someone being called a teacher. The fact that He said they were "all brothers" didn't forbid any one of them from being a teacher or being referred to as one – if they really were one! Many other scriptural references encourage us to be teachers. The apostles were appointed by Jesus to be "authoritative teachers."

"We are all brothers" (vs. 8b). This Scripture is fully discussed in my book, "Apostolic Authority." Tim Early explained it this way: "So, while we are all brothers on a horizontal plane, with Jesus Christ as the Head of every man, nevertheless, THERE ARE THOSE AMONG US WHO ARE WORTHY OF DOUBLE HONOR. THEY DESERVE OUR RESPECT for who they are in Christ and in our lives. We are to obey (outward actions) and be submissive (inward attitudes) to them and to their legitimate, delegated spiritual *authority.*"

"Call no one FATHER" (vs. 9). Was Jesus really suggesting that it is wrong to call one's biological male parent "father."

- Jesus insisted that the disciples first mission was to love HIM more than their own family (Matt. 10:37).

- He stated that those who do His will are His real family (Matt. 12:48-50; Mark 3:33-35; Luke 8:21).

However, when a rich young man asks Jesus what he must do to inherit eternal life, the Lord includes in his answer, "Honor your father and mother" (Matt. 19:19; Lk. 18:20 - quoting the Ten Commandments, Ex. 20:12; Dt. 5:16).

- Paul said, "There aren't many fathers willing to take the time and effort to help you grow up. It was as Jesus helped me proclaim God's Message to you that I BECAME YOUR FATHER" (1 Cor. 4 MSG).
- When Jesus hung on the cross, His great concern was that John take care of Mary – and that she become like a mother to John" (Jn. 19:26).

Jesus NEVER spoke against or showed that He had a problem with anyone showing true loving, relational esteem, or attachment towards a family member. He also never suggested that it was wrong for one's spiritual son or daughter to acknowledge their spiritual parent "father." In fact, Paul called Timothy his "son in the faith" (1 Cor. 4:17). This parental connection connotes belonging and it also infers accountability (which we must have). And notice that when Paul wrote the epistles to "his son" Timothy, he called himself an apostle (1 Tim. 1:1; 2 Tim. 1:1).

 Paul's full authority with Timothy surfaced "at the point of" his greatest relationship of Fatherhood.

This statement is joined with the former statement – of not calling people "teacher." The earlier explanation applies here as well. Of course, we should not elevate the position of those who don't deserve it.

 Jesus NEVER intended to stop all KINSHIP TIES and honorable references to those who are meaningful in your life. In the New Testament, the term "father" is a title applied to God (63% of usage) but is also used to refer to the patriarchs of Israel, to fathers of children, to Jewish leaders, to Christian leaders, and even to the Devil (the Father of Lies). Every New Testament book except 3 John uses the word "father" at least once. Obviously, Jesus didn't mean that we couldn't refer to anyone as "father!" Certainly Jesus' prohibition against calling anyone "father" does not preclude the honor due to natural parents.

- When the rich young man asked Jesus what he must do to inherit eternal life, our Lord replied, "Honor your *FATHER* and mother" (Matt. 19:19; Luke 18:20).
- Sixteen times Stephen referred to the crowd's ancestors as *FATHERS* – and once he addresses his audience as "brothers and *FATHERS*."

- Paul addressed the angry crowd in the Temple as "brothers and *FATHERS*" (Acts 22:1).
- 1 Thessalonians, refers to Paul "as a *FATHER* exhorting his own children" (1 Thes. 2:11).
- Elisha calls Elijah his "*FATHER*," though they were not related (I Kng. 19:20; II Kng. 2:12).

Well after Jesus died, Paul called leaders in the church "fathers"

- "You have in Christ ten thousand *teachers*, but not many *FATHERS*..." (1 Cor. 4:15).
- Christian men were addressed as fathers: "I write to you, *FATHERS*, because you have known him who is from the beginning" (1 Jn. 2:13-14).

Here, we have a clear authorization from Scripture concerning the privilege to call our family and religious leaders "father or mother" while at the same time we are given an admonition not to let any human being become as important as God. Yet, we should continue relating to certain Christians as our spiritual parents.

Inspiration without instruction only produces frustration. Everyone needs a guide to help plan how to achieve their goals.

Proper relating to those who mentor you has absolutely nothing to do with "Lording over people."

"*They called themselves TEACHER*" (continuing Mat. 23:10) A different Greek word is used here, *kathegetai* which means guide or teacher. Once again, it is not using titles that Jesus was complaining about, but giving people titles of positions of authority beyond that for which they qualify! Jesus is saying that just using their titles doesn't actually put them into Moses' seat of authority. Why? He lists what they did that the apostles were not supposed to do:

They were hypocrites (vs. 13) keeping men from the Kingdom of heaven. They didn't possess the Kingdom for themselves either. (vs. 14) They took advantage of widows, and made pretentious long prayers in order to be noticed. (vs. 15) They make their disciples as wicked (son of hell) as they are. (vs. 16-22) They swore and didn't keep their word (they lied).

(vs. 23) They tithed of mint and anise and cumin but neglected to be righteous (justice), merciful, and faithful. (vs. 24) They STRAIN OUT A GNAT AND SWALLOW A CAMEL! (Made big issues out of small ones and ignored the big ones.) (vs. 25 -28) They washed the out side and look good and appear righteous, but inside were inwardly full of extortion and self-indulgence, uncleanness, hypocrisy, lawlessness, and dead men's bones. (vs.29 -32) They built and adorned tombs of great past leaders and taught loyalty toward them. While, at the same time, they killed God's people themselves. (vs. 34 -35) They murdered those very ones they represented "between the temple and the altar."

JESUS USED TITLES

At first glance, it seems that Jesus didn't focus on titles. HOWEVER, even the demons called Him the "Holy One" (Mk. 1:24; Lk. 3:34, 8:28-31). This One Who fully lives in us is known by numerous titles.

He is: the Wonderful Counselor; Mighty God; Everlasting Father; Prince of Peace (Isa 9:6); The Bridegroom (Mark 2:19-20; Matt 9:15; Luke 5:34-35; John 3:29); The Son of Abraham (Matt 1:1); The judge of the living and the dead (Acts 10:42); The spiritual rock (1 Cor 10:1); The beloved (Eph 1:6); The cornerstone (Eph 2:20); The head of the church (Eph 5:23); The image of the invisible God; The firstborn of all creation (Col 1:15); The One Mediator between God and humankind (1 Tim 2:5); The blessed and only Sovereign; the King of kings and Lord of lords (1 Tim 6:15; Rev 19:16); The author and finisher of our faith (Heb 12:2); The shepherd and guardian of our souls (1 Peter 2:25), The Amen, the faithful and true witness, the origin of God's creation (Rev 3:14; 3:7); The I AM; The Lion of the Tribe of Judah; the root of David (Rev 5:5); The root and the descendant of David; the bright morning star (Rev 22:16); and the list goes on and on.

Jesus, Who is our example of humility, was and is Master, Savior, King, and Messiah. He alone is the One Who is to come. When we PATTERN our church correctly, Jesus is the center and we encircle HIM. We begin to LOOK LIKE HIM.

Jesus is only addressed WITHOUT a title of respect once in the four canonical gospels, and that single occurrence was spoken by the penitent thief at the nearby cross who said, "Jesus, remember me when you come into your kingdom" (Lk. 23:42).

JESUS FREQUENTLY REFERRED TO HIMSELF BY TITLES: He claimed to be God. Several times He said He was the I AM (*ego eimi,* Mt. 14:27; Mk. 6:4; Jn. 6:20), the Son of God, Son of Man, Son of David, Christ, Alpha and Omega, etc.

> TITLES DID NOT TAKE AWAY THE SERVANT NATURE OF JESUS. We are to be LIKE Him.

Using relational designations of ministry function does not necessarily prevent us from being "meek and lowly" (Matthew 11:29). As we said, Jesus used titles and He is our servant example.

From countless ancient Jewish, Greek, and Latin sources it can consistently be shown that to address one's superior (one's teacher or mentor) by name and not by title in his presence, or even in his absence, or even after his death was considered very bad manners. The ancient rule governing the use of titles as the form of address was widely observed in antiquity.

 In ancient Jewish culture, being addressed by a first name was considered a breach of decorum bordering on insult.

- Sarah called Abraham "lord," (1 Pet. 3:6).
- Joshua called Moses "Lord." "*Adoni Moshe kela'em* - My Lord Moses, destroy them."
- Gehazi most likely lost his inheritance (II Kings 8:5) because he had referred to his teacher, Elisha, by name. It was common to not even speak people's name. "And Gehazi said, My lord, O King, this is the woman, and this is her son, whom *Elisha* restored to life" (2 Kings 8.5).
- Jesus is addressed "by His first name alone" only once in the four canonical gospels, and that was by the thief beside him at the cross (Lk. 23.42), "Jesus, remember me when you come into your kingdom." All other addresses to Him are accompanied with an appositive description, or title such as Son of Man, Lord, etc.
- Early leaders called James "The Just."

BEING CALLED A "CHRISTIAN" IS A TITLE

What? Did you ever think about how neither Jesus nor the Father called believers "*Christians*?" It's true! God calls us "SONS!" The name by which the Jerusalem church believers were associated was "Nazarene." In Paul's trial before Felix in Caesarea, Tertullus accused Paul (Acts 24:5), "He is the ring leader of the Nazarene sect." The Jews called the believers by the TITLE "Nazirite," which means "consecrated," or "holy ones of God," or "separated ones."

In Antioch in about 60 AD, these believers were called "Christians" (1 Pet. 4:16). Again, King Agrippa said to Paul, "Are you so quickly persuading me to become a *Christian*?" (Acts 26:28)

QUESTION: *WHY is giving respect important? What difference do titles make?* For many, using titles is a matter of respect. Why quibble about this subject? Why, I can speak of spiritual titles without recognizing their *authority* in my spiritual life. I don't have a problem saying "San Antonio, Texas" (Saint Anthony), or "San Fernando Valley," or even referring to "Mother Theresa." Yes, I call him "Pope Benedict" - how about you? I called my nun friends "Sister" – all the time – even in private (so do their families). We can give honor to people without giving them personal *authority* in our lives. In fact, my family celebrates Christmas without approving of a mass for the infant baby Jesus.

Every day we encounter people – and that meeting creates lasting impressions. A *faux pas* in the manners with a business client can keep the applicant from climbing the corporate ladder. There are many people who equate an employee who casually uses their first names as being at the same league as someone who would slaughter the English language by saying "irregardless" – instead of "regardless."

Those who have been well brought up will wait for permission. That's why they excel in leadership. An older person or one leading a ministry should always be referred to by the last name until given permission. Only when they say, "Oh, you can call me John" should that be changed.

> *We can have close relational bonding and still maintain proper respect.*

In the book and TV miniseries "Roots," the African slave Kunta Kinte faced the humiliation of having his given name changed completely. Although he didn't want it changed, he was whipped until he complied to his new Anglicized name of Toby. Through many beatings, his culture and familiar heritage was changed through a name change that he didn't want! This generation is doing much the same thing – calling people what they don't want to be called.

To many apostolic leaders, their first name is a personal point of boundary. It is as personal as their home and kids. If someone violates their comfort level, it may be construed the same as intruding inside their home without permission. It is presumptuous to assume that we can just call people whatever we want. They will usually tell you what they prefer.

"Every action done in company ought to be with some sign of respect, to those that are present." – George Washington

"The elders who direct the affairs of the church well are worthy of DOUBLE HONOR, especially those whose work is preaching and teaching" (1 tim. 5:17). Again, remember that the word "HONOR" means to prize, to fix a high valuation upon; by implication, to revere, to esteem, to dignify, to give money.

> *Did you know that animals cannot give respect, honor, esteem, or disrespect?*

RESPECT is a responsive affiliation or rapport which includes giving polite and courteous consideration, deference, acknowledgment, and significant value. The word RESPECT comes from the Latin word *respicere*, which means "to look back at" or "to look again." A person who is respected is one who is looked at again – and in the light of that perception, perceived differently from others.

Central to clearly knowing someone is the ability to see them beyond the filter of our personal opinions.

Irreducibly, people can demonstrate respect by their attitudes and actions such as politeness or manners. Giving esteem and/or respect is a behavioral response. It is the conscious rational decision to acknowledge and intentionally respond to someone by expressing regard to them. Respect and honor go hand in hand.

HONOR means to esteem in the highest degree.

The custom of giving "honor" is not just old fashioned – it still has great purpose. HONOR is a major theme of New Testament Scripture. Some examples follow:

HONOR your father and mother. Without it, we make the commandments of God of no effect (Mat. 15:4-5; 19:19; Mk. 7:10; 10:19; Lk. 18:20; Eph. 6:2).

Believers HONOR God with their lips, but their heart is far from Him (Mt. 15:8).

We should HONOR the Son as we HONOR the Father (Jn. 5:23).

Jesus said that He did not receive HONOR from men. "How can you believe, who receive honor from one another, and do not seek the honor that comes from the only God?" (John 5:39-45).

Jesus says He HONORS the Father (Jn. 8:49). He said if He HONORED Himself, it is nothing. "It is the Father Who HONORS Me" (8:54-55). He said, "If anyone serves Me, the Father will HONOR them (12:26).

Paul says that glory, HONOR, and peace comes to everyone who works what is good in the Lord (Rom. 2:10).

"Cling to that which is good. Be kindly affectionate to one another with brotherly love, in HONOR giving preference to one another (Rom. 12:8-11).

Render to all their due.... HONOR to whom HONOR (Rom. 13:7). (The Message Bible translates this verse as "HONOR your LEADERS.")

We are to bestow great HONOR on those who think to be less HONORABLE we bestow greater HONOR. God "composed the body, having given greater HONOR to that part which lacks it." If one member is HONORED, all the members rejoice with it (1 Cor. 12:23-26).

Paul says that our ministry must not give offense in anything. Among the ideals listed, is HONOR (2 Cor 6:3-8).

Each of us should know how to possess our own vessel in sanctification and HONOR (1 Ths. 4:4).

HONOR God (1 Tim. 1:15; 6:16). HONOR widows (1 Tim. 5:3). Give elders double HONOR (5:17). Bondservants should count their masters worthy of HONOR (6:1).

Cleansed believers are vessels of HONOR (2 Tim. 2:20).

The son of man is crowned with glory and HONOR (Heb. 2:7; 2:9).

"And no man takes this honor to himself, but he who is called by God, just as Aaron was" (Heb. 5:4).

That believers tried in fire be found with... HONOR (1 Pet. 1:7).

HONOR everyone, HONOR God (1 Pet. 2:17).

Husbands HONOR their wives (1 Pet. 3:7).

HONOR to God (Rev. 4:9; 11; 5:12-13; 7:12; 19:1; 21:24-27).

USING A TITLE

If you have an emergency trip to the hospital, seeing that "doctor" gives you a HOPE OF BEING HELPED. You really don't want just anyone stitching up that injury in your arm! The title "doctor" shows you that he (or she) has prepared him/herself for many years to help you. Why do you use their title? Because titles give you confidence that they actually knows what's happening! Doctors go to school and work hard to receive significant training. Calling them "doctor" gives you some hopeful assurance that because of preparation, that person is CAPABLE of doing a good job.

Doctors generally have greater ability and training in this area of your health than you do – and you have a choice to cooperate with their advice or not.

Honoring those in authority builds our confidence in their ability.

There seems to be substantial Scriptural precedent in the possibility of referring to ministries by title. In the Epistles, the apostles designated themselves by their title (Rom. 1:1; 1 Cor. 1:1; 2 Cor. 1:1; Gal. 2:8; Eph. 1:1; Col. 1:1; 1 Tim. 1:1; 2 Tim. 1:1; Titus 1:1; 1 Pet. 1:1; 2 Pet. 1:1).

Paul invariably introduced himself as an apostle. In the English language, word order is significant and we follow the sequence of words to understand meaning. This is not the case with Greek. The word is order is quite flexible and is not a strict grammatical function.[1] That means we really don't know the order of these words, it could well have been translated, "I, the apostle Paul," OR "I Paul an apostle." The apostle John also referred to himself with a job function (title), as "The elder" (2 Jn. 1).

At the same time, we must also notice that Paul also refers to himself several times just by his name, "Paul." Luke mentions Paul by name more that 120 times in the book of Acts and never addressed him as the "apostle Paul." Peter calls Paul, "Our beloved brother" (2 Pet. 3:14).

1.May, Neal W., "It's Greek to Me!" Sept. 1997

- Paul calls himself a "servant" in two epistles (Peter says he's a servant in one). In Philemon, Paul also calls himself as a "prisoner."
- The term "apostle" is not used by James, John, or Jude. They called themselves "servant" twice and "elder" twice.
- The Apostle John called himself, "Your brother and companion in tribulation" (Rev. 1:9).
- We can conjecture here that titles are not consistently used, but even so, the frequency of using titles is far greater than not.

 The point may well be made that it doesn't matter whether YOU use a title or not– it's what the person YOU ADDRESS prefers.

Recognizing and calling out one's ministerial function appears to occur throughout the Old and New Testaments. Actually, the New Testament uses the term "apostle" 74 times, Teacher - 14, Prophet - 8, Evangelist - 3, Pastor - 3. The title "apostle" is used more than any other "title" in the New Testament. They apparently functioned effectively in full "*authority*" whether they used the title "apostle" or not.

They tried, as Church Father Cyprian stated, "to quickly learn what was necessary to have a simple faith" (ANF 5.455). Remember, the first church had no Parallel Bible translations, no computer Bibles with seven dictionaries and six concordances – in fact, they had no access to a Bible in their homes. But this one thing we know. Their simple faith particularly included RESPECT. They called each other "Saints."

Countless Jewish, Greek, and Latin sources show that it was very bad manners to ever call one's teacher or mentor by name and not by title. A few examples of expected formality are mentioned here:

- Photographs from SEPULCHER INSCRIPTIONS on epitaphs at the catacombs as early as the second century show the consistent use of titles. From the earliest times from Germany to Nubia, we find the door-keeper (*ostiarius*), the grave digger, the lector, the evangelist, and bishop, etc.
- The Essenes were addressed as "Just" or "Righteous" as an honorific title. Their relationships were formal. Spiritual consideration would not allow students to address a teacher by name.
- The Gemara, Kiddushin 31b prohibits addressing or referring to one's Torah teacher or parent by name, even after their death.
- The Gemara, Sanhedrin 100a, declares that one who addresses a teacher by name is an *apikores* (one who is no longer restrained by divine law).

- Jewish students were forbidden to call their teacher by name, even when the teacher was not present, or even after he died. In fact, they couldn't say the NAME – even the name with the title. It was the title only.
- Mishneh le-Melekh, in his Parashat Derakhim, Derekh Anavim, no. 15 (p. 67), finds Talmudic support for the principle that a teacher may be addressed by name if that name is coupled with an appropriate honorific.
- Saint Benedict's writings includes the following two precepts (Reg. 4-68-69): Let the juniors, therefore, respect the seniors, and the seniors love the juniors... let the seniors call their juniors brothers (*fratres*) and the juniors address their seniors as fathers (*nonnos*)." (*Domnus et Abbas*)
- The Qur'an gives believers the honorific title of "People of the Scripture" (Al-Ankaboot, 29:46).

Our resisting all usages of titles may cause us to miss some of the essential cohesive concepts of unity that made the early church great.

SUMMARY

1. Jesus' remarks were not forbidding the use of titles, but it opposed the taking or giving of legislative *authority* that was not rightfully obtained or deserved.

2. Undue self-promotion and vain pride is prohibited.

3. God's impartiality accepts all people without favoritism – even though he has repeatedly given special calling and favor to many Biblical heroes throughout history.

4. Recognizing the capacity in which the Lord has assigned a person to serve is a customary functional designation. It is no more "partial or elevating" to address a person by an appropriate title than it is to list his name in the church sign outside, in the bulletin, or on the letterhead as the pastor, etc.

5. The overriding principle is to treat all people including spiritual leaders with respect – that could well mean referring to them by their title – especially if they are older and more seasoned than you. That is, if they themselves have adopted a title and are walking in that realm of *authority*. (We're not talking about some misleading Sanitary-Engineer type title).

6. Respect must not be restricted by such things as wealth, race, gender, or class.

7. We do well to be respectful and positive toward others and to give admiration rather than striving, being reserved, or critical.

*Using a title does not mean that we consider ourselves
infallible oracles of God.*

8. Imagine what would happen if every Christian really understood themselves to be a "CHOSEN RACE, A royal PRIESTHOOD, A HOLY NATION, A PEOPLE FOR God's OWN POSSESSION..." How can there be any striving when we are all royal priests? With different functions!

9. Honorific titles should not be used to perpetuate the "clergy-laity" division. When rightly used, they can more greatly bond us together in closer covenant relationship. They say "I see who you are in the Lord and receive you as that!"

10. We see that there is really not a problem with titles, but a PROBLEM WITH ATTITUDES. God selects leaders and then equips them with the necessary abilities needed to show the way as SERVANT GUARDIANS – operating in differing function.

*Titles should not be used to draw attention to yourself,
but to call you to humility and service. Titles should be
the call into servanthood (Mat. 23:11-12).*

We are in desperate need of reform in order to convey our thinking on such fundamental issues as the nature of the church and even how local church leaders should be addressed. The study of the New Testament church and the history of the very early church provides much evidence for addressing congregational leaders with functional titles. However, we should also consider some of the other common and functional terms such as "brother," "beloved," "fellow-worker," "laborer," "saint," "slave," "bond servant," "prisoner," "fellow-soldier," "steward" and "friend."

 Titles merely acknowledge the capacity and function that a person already walks in as a Godly assignment.

Using titles or not is a "personal style." It is a preference. We should be able to call people what they desire to be called. If they prefer a "nickname," let's use it! If they don't want one, why use it? Titles are used by the captain of a ship and the coach of little league.

Remember, the way you address people matters. When writing or speaking to someone, please pay attention to the way they introduce themselves. Please don't shorten their name because it is easier or because you think it makes you friendlier. It doesn't. It has the opposite effect — it tends to make you appear to them as self-centered and assuming.

In the future, if you have opportunity to be trained by leadership – enjoy that time and guard against becoming familiar. Realize that you are valued as important, or they wouldn't be spending time with you. Guard your heart. Every believer needs to find someone to respect. Regardless of how much learning, qualifications, diplomas, or stature they have, they still NEED to relate to others who can and will speak into their lives. No matter who you are, you need to ALLOW leadership *authority* to unlock your individual and collective future. People who carry God's *authority* help provide the essential order and direction that enables believers to mature and find answers. Delegated leaders mentor by the SINCERITY of their teaching, redirecting, correcting, and encouraging with spiritual and natural insight.

 Since we all have the choice to select which leaders will be involved in our lives, we better do it carefully and with RESPECT. It is one of life's most important decisions.

Therefore, from now on, WE REGARD NO ONE ACCORDING TO THE FLESH (2 Cor. 5:16 NKJV).

At the Triumphal entry into Jerusalem, when Jesus walked under the waving palm branches and heard the singing of "Hosanna," He spoke in ancient Aramaic, "Oh, Jerusalem, you missed My visitation" (Lk. 19:44). Our very God incarnate groaned that those who watched Him approach His death had missed the reason that He came. Perhaps on the grander scheme of importance, this time God's big concerns would be that we NOT MISS who Jesus really is IN US.

Lord, You give us Your Name. The Word says that You are our Brother – we don't know how to lay hold of that! Just to ponder it is staggering. We adore You. Lord, and we pray that we might not miss this visitation of Christ IN US. We honor how You exhibit Yourself in our brothers and sisters. We stand amazed at how you give us Gift Offices and allow us to lead. Fill us with Your very being, Your likeness, Your Name, and your authority.

BOOK #3 -- Guarding Your Authority

God's Authority is missing because

IT MUST BE GUARDED

We have studied about WHY AUTHORITY IS MISSING in the church today. This section concerns the pitfalls of ministry – which also result in loss of authority.

Jeremiah was an avid bird watcher. In the previous sections of "Apostolic Authority" we have see how birds tell us about how to govern in this new season. Essentially, Jeremiah said, "You know, that stork has more discernment than God's people" (Jer. 8:7). He says, "Birds understand the will of God because they know WHEN to move and WHERE to go." Now, we can be as wise as the stork. We can understand what God's will is. We can know when to move and where to go next.

If we want to live as leaders in authority, we will have to modify the present thinking that the Jesus who lives within us is not as great as the One Who is to come. We must deliberately embrace Him as LIFE. The Gospel of the finished work requires that we live as an example of the finished work.

As we gain authority as we realize the increasing necessity to guard our authoriy.

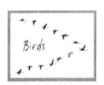

The arctic turn has been tracked with satellite radar as flying over 20,000 miles a year. Some cranes are capable of migrating as far as 2,500 miles per year, and the barn swallow 6,000 miles a year. The great albatrosses have life spans of up to fifty years and some are calculated to have flown over five million miles during its lifetime.

We tend to overlook the fact that any serious ministry must be trained to overcome many difficulties. Just as Jesus was subject to difficulties, we must also learn to have victory over life's obstacles.

We spoke in the first section of "Apostolic Authority" how the APOSTLES WERE STRONG AND TOUGH! Difficulties did not hinder the Apostles from establishing churches in the various countries they visited. If you ever have a chance to travel along the route of Paul in Asia Minor, you would be totally amazed at the gigantic mountains he traversed. The distances. The difficult weather in northern Turkey winters. It's absolutely staggering to consider these trips on horseback and on foot. Ministry isn't easy.

Apostolic ministries will be tested, tried, and proven. The Bereans tested Paul's word by the Scriptures they had. No one is infallible. True ministers are never afraid of being examined and even admitting mistakes.

- Paul described apostleship by saying that God has set forth the apostles last... "We are weak, we hunger, thirst, are naked, are buffeted, have not sure dwelling place, we labor with our hands, we bless when we are reviled, we are persecuted and suffer. We are defamed as the filth and offscouring of the world" (1 Cor. 4:10-11).

- Paul described his life, "I've worked much harder, been jailed more often, beaten up more times than I can count, and at death's door time after time. I've been flogged five times with the Jews' thirty-nine lashes, beaten by Roman rods three times, pummeled with rocks once. I've been shipwrecked three times, and immersed in the open sea for a night and a day. In hard traveling year in and year out, I've had to ford rivers, fend off robbers, struggle with friends, struggle with foes. I've been at risk in the city, at risk in the country, endangered by desert sun and sea storm, and betrayed by those I thought were my brothers. I've known drudgery and hard labor, many a long and lonely night without sleep, many a missed meal, blasted by the cold, naked to the weather. And that's not the half of it, when you throw in the daily pressures and anxieties of all the churches.... I feel desperation in my bones" (2 Cor 11:23-29, MSG).

Being an apostle is always difficult, and many will bring accusation against them. The bottom line is that faultfinding people will find something wrong with everyone.

> **We must go through the "process" to arrive at our destiny.**

Paul spoke boldly...but many who heard became obstinate and publicly maligned the Way (Acts 19:8-19, NIV).

They were persecuted (Thes. 2:15).

Crowds questioned their *authority* to do what they did (Acts 4:7).

They were accused of being "MAD" (meaning crazy, Acts 26:24-25).

Authority seems to increase in proportion to our ability to overcome difficulty...

Leadership is often emotionally complicated: many suffer extreme loneliness, isolation, and unjust accusations from those to whom they once were close. Overcoming hindrances and obstacles are part of how we become broken from the opinions of others and finally develop the character that doesn't quit. We must endure. Strengths come through overcoming sufferings, rejections, failures, betrayals, and challenges.

It is what we overcome that we remember.

TENDING AND GUARDING YOURSELF

There will be those who follow the corrupt desire of the sinful nature and despise authority (2 Pet. 2:10).

Operating in *authority* gives leaders a vitality that we call "charisma." *Charisma* is a FORCE of attraction that is embodied within the character of a leader. The influence of *authority* can be "felt."

People recognize a strong leader by their personality. When true leaders walk into a room the atmosphere changes. The demonstration of *authority* is observable – it can be seen. It is seen as a spiritual force. *Authority* releases a flow of spiritual energy that brings life to those who will receive it. *Authority* brings change.

Authority releases a flow of words with spiritual substance that delivers LIFE (Jn. 6:63). The greater the scope of influence (metron), the greater the force of the words spoken.

Authority releases a PRESENCE of the Lord that influences others for good.

Because of these dynamics concerning *authority*, there are many potential problems. The question was recently asked, "DO MOST MINISTERS AND MINISTRIES END WELL?" We certainly want to think that most ministers end well and are happy with their life. But the answer is NO. Many say that 80% of all ministers end up critical, disillusioned, and cynical. They usually tend to put others down to justify their own failures.

There have been lots of anointed Christians – why did so many fail? Obviously, they meant to do well. What are the patterns that we can observe and learn to avoid? How did they miss their assignment? Where were their mistakes? Can we learn from them? There are critical truths to learn at this juncture in time.

QUESTION: Do you see increasing and daily evidence of growth and self-discipline in your life? Do you guard yourself?

> Leaders must establish a willingness to change and a sense of urgency that is necessary to reach this new generation.

Are you willing to change many of the ideals that you hold dear? Things are moving fast these days. This generation is totally different from the one we were raised. it's just hard to keep up with it! We all have to hold our doctrines with an open hand and allow the Lord to enlarge our understandings.

What was right yesterday can change tomorrow. Leaders must embrace *inevitable* change, *integral* change, and *innovative* change.

If we try to control everything that happens, it will never grow beyond the extent of our comprehension and philosophy. Isn't it time the church became larger than our limitations? Isn't it time vision becomes larger than our plans and schemes? Usually, we just need to "let go" and let the Holy Spirit be in charge. Just trust the Lord in His ability to do what we can't. He wants us all to change.

WHY IS MAINTAINING AUTHORITY DIFFICULT?

"But ask the animals, and they will teach you, or the BIRDS OF THE AIR, and they will tell you" (Job 12:7 NIV).

The failure of most ministries can invariably be traced to the fact that their personal relationship with Christ became replaced by "other things." It may be the business of church, personal ambition, management, establishing procedural guidelines and precedents, trying to maximize efficiency, organizing, people pleasing, etc. Every failures was largely due to losing the focus of the Call. What we can learn is that there are priorities to be set, some invitations to be postponed, and our lives guarded first and foremost.

As stronger ministries emerge, we must make firm attitude adjustments based on the emerging revelation concerning spiritual *authority*. This requires putting aside much of our past and current ideas as well as doctrinal old and dysfunctional wineskins. It is time to arise into what Christ fully offers us – with defined function and with distinctively defined spheres.

Some of today's stage actor preachers are immature in their expression of God's character and nature. Some actually expect others to kiss their ring! Then there's the kind of leader who avoid confrontation and do-si-do all around the issues of sin, allowing everyone to just sashay through their lives with the wrong set of values.

Most downfalls are the result of a lack of maturity, ignorance of what it takes to lead, and the lack of stabilizing emotions.

Those in leadership and/or ministry face an ever present opportunity to lose the strength of their *authority* from false flattery, believing what others say about you, taking credit for what God has done, etc. There are countless chances to be falsely affected by the admiration of others. Common thought patterns of those who fall could be:

1. "I really do deserve more than I have." This sense of entitlement often causes leaders to get into ethical and moral compromise. "I deserve to be happy. I have worked for this and this money is really

mine." This misplaced sense of entitlement to positions of authority and benefit cannot be taken, but must be given.

2. Ability to compartmentalize and put on hold. We've learned how to preach a funeral and then handle tremendous emotion pressure in one compartment. We hear and handle confessions of gross sin in another compartment of our lives. We love our families, we teach the teens, etc. We've learned to prioritize and leave many problems on the mind's shelf – waiting for another day to solve them. In many ways this compartmentalization is helpful and necessary, but it could cause us to defer personal and family needs as well.

3. Justification – We make excuses that what we do must not be too bad. We love Jesus. AND, AFTER ALL, WE HAVE MIRACLES!!! But remember. They had miracles in the wilderness while Israel walked in circles. Miracles can still happen – but miracles don't justify or validate sin.

4. Unbelief (Mt. 17:19-21). It's not happening anymore, so it must not be true.

5. Aligning with a peers who are filled with unbelief (Mk. 6:4-6).

6. Unchecked sin that continues (Gal. 4:9; Jn. 8:34,35).

7. Demonic deception (hindrances, attacks etc.) (2 Cor. 2:11).

Take heed. Pay attention. Watch the input of media, movies, and magazines. Don't leave the TV on while sleeping – much can unconsciously enter the ear-gate as well as the eye gate. Media communicates and acts out the desires and deeds of the flesh (Gal. 5:19-21). Over viewing can desensitize us to evil and deaden our spiritual appetite. Watching too much news can cause distortions.

Did you know that the rental of X-rated movies in hotels is higher in pastor's conventions than any other convention. If you have this tendency or weakness in this area, go to someone with whom you can be accountable.

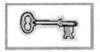 Respect and protect the anointing on your life. It is costly. Don't have familiarity with your own anointing. Remember Sampson didn't know when the Spirit left him. Treat the Gift of your life with reverence and care.

NOBODY SAID IT WAS EASY

My own personal lament and great passion is to help ministers GUARD THEIR AUTHORITY. Overseeing churches and ministries these days can be a most complex job! Not only do you have to come up with inspirational ideas several times a week for great talks – you must have a cutting edge on Present Truth (what the Lord is saying today). You must be able to use the Gifts. There must be correct vision and you must be able to sustain it within a workable plan. There's always the priority of raising up leaders.

Then, there's the complicated community issues and problems like zoning regulations and community boards. Leaders have to understand finances, logistics, networking, dealing with other local ministers, and sociological trends. They need to constantly worry about promotion and fund raising. They are concerned with being more relevant. Where are the available centers to send hurting and hungry people for help beyond what you can provide? How can you help your congregation get out of debt and get better jobs? What are the demographics of your neighborhood? Real Estate.The list goes on.

The most frequent dangers of the Apostolic are (1) building excessive structure, (2) overly competitive drive,(3) empirical misunderstandings, (4) an inordinate preoccupation with money, (5) and desire for personal ambition, status, and influence for wrong motivations, (6) the fatigue of caring.

July 19, 2006 Barna Group study says that 61% of pastors have no close personal friends. 1/6 of all pastors feel under appreciated. One in five say they have "very difficult family situations." 35% are depressed and suicidal.

Because the church has been so strongly mixed with present day society, we have produced a group of emotionally immature believers. Anyone who has been in ministry very long knows that sheep bite! Very few Bible Schools teach how much people can disappoint and hurt us. And... because we don't know it, we allow accusations to weaken us, and we lose the force of our *authority*.

 The right amount of inward pressure exerting outward upon a spacecraft keeps it from imploding.

Endurance builds greater authority.

Be steady. TRUTH always brings conflict. Peace comes from subduing and conquering (having your foot on the throat of) the enemy.

Always look toward the vision and not at the distraction. Keep the end in view. Perceive it and receive it. Don't let go of the dream! Put value on the pursuit that God called you to accomplish.

Problems are not the end of the destination – they are stepping stones to get there. There are no shortcuts – overcoming the obstacles will get you to your assignment.

Migrating birds always face predators.

 You'll never see the manifestation of your calling if you are weary and faint. ENDURE INTO YOUR DUE SEASON WHERE YOU WILL REAP (Gal. 6:9)

Many ministries don't finish well because they gave up. They didn't overcome. They lost their vision.

UNWILLINGNESS TO MIGRATE

Be sure to always be teachable and ready to move to greater under-standings and truths. Move forward and stay relevant. Don't justify staying with traditional methods that fail to produce Biblical results:

- Good leaders are able make necessary changes – rather than being bound by improper church government structure.

POWER STRUGGLES DISCOURGE AND WEAKEN AUTHORITY

This is a huge problem in almost every church. Leaders encounter conflict and confrontation from those who battle for his/her position. All power struggles are a challenge for *authority*. These challenges often come from co-workers, trusted leaders, or their members.

- Korah led 250 Levite leaders ("chosen in the assembly, men of renown," Num. 16:2) to rebel against Moses. We can learn from how Moses handled this problem, "He fell on his face" (Num. 16:4). God had the answer.
- Leaders must not allow negative ideas to impede their vision, direction, or character. Leaders must fly above negative situations.

 All leaders will have those who challenge their place of *authority*. King Solomon said "...composure allays great offenses" (Ecc. 10:4). The PRESENCE of composure is the ability to be stable, still, and anchored in purpose. Confidence and respect must be earned. After all is said and done, the congregation measures the leader by his confident responses to the accusation – rather than by the accusation itself.

The set leader must never avoid or abdicate the responsibility to oversee the overall ministry.

STRESS and BUSINESS STEAL AUTHORITY

Says the stork to the wind, "I'd really like to know

Why people are so anxious and rush and worry so?" kjs

I recently attended a pastor's conference where the minister had a Word of Knowledge that someone had high blood pressure, and asked if he would come forward. Well, every single person in the audience responded!!! There's obviously something wrong with what we are doing. Ask yourself – have you ever thought of quitting? Often? Regularly? Do you have times of rest?

Stress causes 38% of ministers to be depressed – and these are the ones who admit it. Many are suicidal. Stress causes heart attacks and cancer – plus many more diseases.

Most in ministry suffer from horribly bad diets and lack of exercise. Ministry by nature is sedentary. Stress coupled with apathy can cause vulnerability.

The professionalizing of ministry is killing the ministers who are trying to do it all themselves. The more "business like" and efficient we try to become, the more we become spiritually weakened. The demands of our time are probably disproportionate to a healthy lifestyle. Our assignment must become to re-prioritize and re-calendar our lives. It's not time management – it's life management. BUSYNESS CAN NEGATE YOUR AUTHORITY

> Emotional and physical health comes as we create boundaries and make emotional room. We must give the Holy Spirit back His job!

"Beware of the barrenness of a busy life." Corrie Ten Boom

 Over business causes a failure to maintain good physical/mental health.

We need to understand our personal limitations and recognize our own exhaustion. The frantic over-busyness and demanding lifestyle of ministry generates draining exhaustion. Jesus gave harsh rebuke when He said, "Martha, Martha, you are worried and bothered about so many things, but only a few things are necessary, really one... for Mary has chosen the good part, which cannot be taken away for her" (Lk. 10:41-42). Mary sat at His feet.

"... I tried keeping rules and working my head off to please God, and it didn't work. So I quit being a "law man" so that I could be God's man. Christ's life showed me how, and enabled me to do it. I identified myself completely with him. Indeed, I have been crucified with Christ. My ego is no longer central. It is no longer important that I appear righteous before you or have your good opinion, and I am no longer driven to impress God. Christ lives in me. The life you see me living is not "mine," but it is lived by faith in the Son of God, who loved me and gave himself for me. I am not going to go back on that" (Gal. 2:19-21, MSG).

Over busyness can destroy the anointing. Beware of the temptation to try and administrate everything out of learned habits above that of serving out of love and genuine care.

Business can cause stress. Stress blocks creativity. Continuous stress causes people to relax their value system.

We must maintain steadily focused diligence toward our mission without the business of constant distractions.

Healthy leaders pace themselves.

AMBITION THWARTS OUR AUTHORITY

Life is a pursuit of destination.

Ministers generally desire to reach certain goals... their heart is for the Kingdom. Problem is that somewhere along the line many get confused. A "Superman" mentality or a continually "Mr. All-fired-up" person who races at a hectic pace to get on a pedestal can become extremely injurious.

Trying to move in a capacity to which you are not called, can cause the greatest problems. A leader's maturity should match the position he seeks to fill. Many have been defeated because of this reason.

Over ambition causes over confidence in past victories.

Over ambition causes inaccurate appraisals of situations.

Over ambition causes leaders to not expect problems and ambushes. They are unprepared for the long haul. They tend to make wrong choices in defining moments.

Over ambition causes a sentimental attachment to old tactics and methodologies. It brings an inability to migrate properly. Successful leaders are willing to respond to change and adjust accordingly to present day paradigms.

Over ambition causes leaders to mis-appraise their potential.

Know when and how you are defined. Too many leaders are operating in the wrong function... pastoring when they should be a counselor; traveling in ministry when they should be working in a secular market; trying to build a church when they should travel as an evangelist. It causes us to get lost and doubt. Too many believe their own press reports.

Each of us needs to know what our true assignment really is. We must not overestimate our abilities. Burn out happens when people try to stretch past the "measure of grace" upon their lives.

The origin of a wrong motive is self. Selfish carnality gives false impressions and devises useless

> Refuse to be satisfied with vicariously posturing as one in great authority - or by trying to be the charismatic "Mr. Wonderful."

strategies. SELFISH AMBITION can consume us and prevent a sincere love for God and His people.

Within minutes the disciples were bickering over which one of them would end up the greatest! We must truly open our hearts to receive an ACCURATE PERSEPECTIVE OF OUR MINISTRY POTENTIAL. Disenchanted leaders may wrestle with reality and the limitations of their calling. Self esteem is found only in being all we are supposed to become in the Lord.

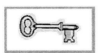 Great leaders maintain a sober estimation of their own abilities.Overestimating our ministry causes us to be frustrated when others don't validate us like we expect.

As the "great theologian" Clint Eastwood once said, *"A man's gotta know his limitations."*

OVER-CONTROL SMOTHERS OUR AUTHORITY

The development of codependent relationships causes fellow workers to be constantly fearful of making the wrong decisions. Resentment begins to build among the Body due to the leader's over control. Look for things that you may try to over control. Do you allow others the freedom to learn and even fail?

THE LACK OF MONEY DISTRACTS OUR AUTHORITY

This problem is huge. Because leaders are generally not clear about prosperity, they aren't able to teach it properly. This new Breed of ministry will challenge the custom of all giving. The tithe will become more properly used. It won't be going just to the local church and local pastor– but rather shared for the support of other 5-fold trans-local ministries that cross pollinate the Body as well.

God has pleasure in the PROSPERITY of His people (Psa.35:27). We were created for His pleasure

Of course, prosperity is a study all it's own. Nehemiah 13 tells us that the Levites weren't getting paid and had to go back to the fields. So it unfortunately is with many ministries today. We must learn to rightly divide this topic. Elders are worthy of double "honor" (the first definition of this word means money, 1 Tim. 5:17). Apostolic ministries must have money in order to disperse it for Kingdom benefit.

"LEADERS who know their business and care keep a sharp eye out for the shoddy and cheap" (Prov. 20:8).

- "But if it's only money these LEADERS are after, they'll self-destruct in no time" (1 Tim. 6:9, MSG).

- Apostles make certain that they are never a burden or take kindness for granted. Their purpose is to lay up a store house for their children in the faith (2 Cor 12:14-15). Their first motivation is to help other people. In doing that, they should be supported and cared for.
- Ministers shouldn't have to live on handouts (Mat. 10:9), THEY SHOULD RECEIVE AMPLE RECOMPENSE FOR THE WORK. This new apostolic breed is often brilliantly entrepreneurial.
- "A workman deserves support, his living and his food" (Mat.10:10, NIV).
- "Give a BONUS to LEADERS who do a good job, especially the ones who work hard at preaching and teaching" (1 Tim. 5:17).
- Apostolic leaders should also try to have independent income sources. They always work hard to make themselves "an EXAMPLE of how you should follow us" (Matt. 20:25-28; 2 Thes.3:7-9)."
- Believers laid money at the apostles feet for the distinct purpose of HELPING THE BODY and to be distributed to the poor (Acts 4:25).
- "LEADERSHIP GAINS AUTHORITY and RESPECT when the voiceless poor are treated fairly" (Prov. 29:14, MSG).

HAVING NO SONS MEANS YOUR AUTHORITY AND INSIGHT DIE WITH YOU

We've talked about this since the beginning of the book. One of the main reason for failure in ministry is because leaders never raised up SONS (not gender defined) in ministry. That means they did not duplicate themselves and therefore no one can carry on their dream. In their latter years, they are alone, with no ministry family who will continue building into what they had poured their lives (Ps. 78:4-5).

 Ministry Sons are ministry fruit. It is one way that leaders are measured.

In his twilight years, John the Apostle said, "I have NO GREATER JOY than to hear that MY CHILDREN WALK IN TRUTH" (3 John 4). Apostles pursue and build eternal relationships with SONS (Mal 4:5-6). We fulfill the dominion mandate of reproducing ourselves (be fruitful and multiply and fill the earth). These are the ones who will carry our bones.

What are we leaving behind? Programs? More administration? We must have a community of personal relationships with specific SONS.

QUESTION: Do you speak generationally? You need spiritual sons.

Our relationship with SONS activates their inheritance!

Our natural children don't call us by our first names.

Fathers and mothers have sons

The reason birds migrate is to reproduce.

One of the greatest apostolic objectives in our migration should be TO PROPAGATE AND RAISE UP spiritual SONS (children - male and female).

Job 39:13 marginal rendering in RSV state, "Her pinions and feathers are like the stork's." This obscure verse seems to point out the stork's respectful affection for her young, while the ostrich is indifferent toward her young.

The Message Bible of Psalm 45:16 commands us, "SET YOUR MIND NOW ON SONS— you'll set your sons up as princes all over the earth." This word was a resounding command inside of me. "SET YOUR MIND NOW ON SONS!" This is a new MIND-SET.

Don't spend your life serving an institution – God is into relationships and people! Invest your time and life into individuals. The POWER of this apostolic move is that it doesn't stop with the individual (your vision doesn't end when you die), but it is passed down through SONS.

> Apostolic leaders need to consider important issues through a Biblical lens – rather than depending upon what is happening now.

Raising SONS who are rightly connected to walk with us helps them to imitate and inherit our similar abilities. We teach them to seek trans-ferable principles not just methods. It is imperative that we build up and extend our SON-SHIP relations. We need to have parents and be parents (not coverings). A spiritual parent functions in an essential role in our rebirth in Christ.

A parent cares for your soul. Building SONS causes the Kingdom to become a corporate possession. We move from singularity of purpose to corporate community. COMMUNITY diminishes the primacy of our personal efforts and celebrates the perpetuation of the distribution to the whole.

Apostolic leaders develop relational covenant and ways to teach their sons and daughters how to duplicate and exceed them. Those of apostolic grace can release and impart it to their sons. Much like throwing rocks in a lake... and watching the concentric ripples of circles form –impartation causes a ripple effect to those we mentor. Those coming behind us to complete the restoration need to be equipped, blessed, and released.

Look for those who's heart beats covenantly with you. Teach them to be strong and fearless. Train them to reproduce relationships. Expect them to join in the work with you (Lk. 10:1-2).

Ask them for a commitment of their time. Become a mentor and model and teach legitimate ministry. Spend time with them. Meet on a regular basis. Affirm them. Teach them how to study, how to pray, how to respond, how to deal with difficulties, and how to be committed. Teach them to possess the gates. Show them how to win! Encourage their unlimited potential. Know their situations at home and work. Strategize with them as to how to solve these issues. Teach them to differentiate between "The Work of the Kingdom" and "Church work." Give them a big vision.

Leaders must impart to SONS the ability to release their personal gifts. Commission them publicly. Release them into defined authority. Equip them. Teach them their value and uniqueness. Send them out in teams on specific assignments – open doors for them. Know that you have the "authority to deliver" those who belong to you.

Use them above others. It is a devaluing experience when a senior leader chooses to embrace a talented newcomer over those who have been positioned with him over the long haul. There will be reactions and hurt feelings of violation of trust if/when the previously established order of relationship is displaced. A wise leader values faithful trusted relationships.

FATAL ATTRACTIONS DESTROY YOUR AUTHORITY

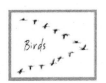

Birds that are continuously exposed to POLLUTION develop endocrinal and sexual abnormalities. Even if they migrate, pollution can greatly limit their ability to reproduce. Also, many birth defects result. Other birds of prey threaten their lives.

As of this writing, it is thought that *avain* flu is nurtured in these places of non-migrating poultry farms. When migrating birds stop by these locations, they accidentally pick up the disease and carry it with them on their routes.

God gives His extraordinary Gifts to mere human beings. Sometimes, those humans fall short. Just a quick look at the ministries that have failed shows us the POLLUTION of some deadly attractions. We've heard that it's "Gals, glamour, and glitz!" But these days it's not just the men that fail. It can probably all be summed up in ambition, greed (excesses), and immorality. Isn't that what the Bible says? It's the sin of the flesh, the pride of life (1 Jn. 2:16).

Beware – many leaders hope to slip right through without repentance or conversion.

Numerous ministry scandals have rocked this nation. It seems that a majority of leaders are characterized by the loss of respect for life and morality. Ministries of opportunity, sexual promiscuity, homosexuality, and even pedophiles are allowed to minister in some pulpits.

One of Paul's greatest concerns was to keep his flesh under control. He said, "I keep under my body and bring it into subjection" (! Cor. 9:27). Subjection in this context means "lead one's flesh about as a slave." Paul demanded that his flesh be the instrument through which he preached the gospel. He went on to say that he kept his body under subjection "Lest that by any means, when I have preached to others, I my self should be a castaway." Castaway means to become disapproved, discredited, or disqualified.

- A minister's reputation influences the souls of the saved and unsaved. The future of others is at stake.
- Demas was a greatly loved and respected leader (Col. 4:14) who is mentioned again in 2 Timothy 4:10 as to have forsaken Paul and escaped into the world.

Peter warned, "God is especially incensed against these TEACHERS who live by lust, addicted to a filthy existence. They DESPISE INTERFERENCE FROM TRUE *AUTHORITY*, preferring to indulge in self-rule. Insolent egotists, they don't hesitate to speak evil against the most splendid of creatures (angels)... trying to slander others before God."

Take time to read this verse again. They are, *"Brute beasts, born in the wild, predators on the prowl. In the very act of bringing down others with their ignorant blasphemies, they themselves will be brought down, losers in the end. Their evil will boomerang on them. They're so despicable and addicted to pleasure that they indulge in wild parties, carousing in broad daylight. They're obsessed with adultery, compulsive in sin, seducing every vulnerable soul they come upon. Their specialty is greed, and they're experts at it. Dead souls!*

They've left the main road and are traditionless... There's nothing to these people — they're dried-up fountains, storm-scattered clouds, headed for a black hole in hell. They are loudmouths, full of hot air, but still they're dangerous... they themselves are slaves of corruption, for if they're addicted to corruption—and they are—they're enslaved"
(2 Pet. 2:12, MSG).

We are cautioned to "take heed lest we fall" (1 Cor. 10:12).

Our *AUTHORITY* is vulnerable to attack in many ways. Early in ministry we need firewalls placed into position to protect ourselves. It's still our job to tend and guard our garden (our soul and mind) (Gen 2:15-17, Is. 58:11 NKJV). We must work diligently to protect against deception and safeguard the anointing that resides. The garden is the place where we need to have victory.

"Don't dissipate your virility on fortune-hunting women, promiscuous women who shipwreck LEADERS" (Prov. 31:3, MSG).

Moral Failure. How can it happen? TAKE NOTE: Even David, the one after God's own heart, committed adultery and murder. And, it didn't happen until he was fifty years old! Without doubt, he was at his potential peak of life! But regrettably, he became weakened by being overly comfortable in his position of luxury and rulership.

David's daily choices brought him into sin. Look once again at the story we all know so well. It wasn't a one time fling – David continued in sin with Bathsheba for nine months. It was only after Nathan exposed adultery and murder that David repented - he didn't admit his sin until he was caught. It was the jolt of his sin being made public that brought remorse.

After David married Bathsheba, their baby became sick. David spent much time fasting and praying. When the baby died, the scripture says that he comforted Bathsheba. But, the sin didn't stop there. HIS PROBLEM PERPETUATED INTO THE LIFE OF HIS SONS. David never addressed his sin with his very own children and they later reproduced it. Absolom ended up wanting to kill his own father.

PEOPLE PROBLEMS WEAKEN AUTHORITY

"Prayer, meditation, and temptation make a minister." Martin Luther

PEOPLE CAN STEAL OUR AUTHORITY. WE FACE A WORLD THAT REBELS AGAINST *AUTHORITY* of any kind. The pendulum of freedom has swung too far the other way. Now, the church is full of many stubborn believers who refuse to regard any *authority* or be advised on how to live. They question, find fault, accuse, ridicule, and make excuses for their own behavior so they don't have to follow anyone. Familiarity and lack of respect abound.

Some leaders constantly try everything to make people happy. They try to appease them by doing everything. We try seeker sensitive meetings in order to not offend. We try home meetings for more personal relationships. We try more outings. Better ambiance. More programs. More sensationalism, etc.

Meanwhile, much of the church seems to be sleeping during the midnight cry – they have become insensitive to the genuine presence of the Lord. They are overdosed with their own problems. There are too many options for them. The Lord told Samuel that the people had rejected God and not Samuel (1 Sam. 8:7).

Certain issues require different types of oversight, with different instructions and clear boundaries. The goal however, is to see the Lord mature and raise up a company of believers who are creative and functional. It's not a baby child that we're awaiting – but a grown-up MAN-child. Sometimes, it's difficult to wait for others grow (when it seems that nothing is happening). But if we give them the same confidence that God gives them... it will most generally and eventually happen.

Years ago, I saw Kenneth Hagin preach at a convention – and I'll never forget it. He stopped in mid-sentence and pointed to me saying, "Stop counseling." Then he went back to his service. Later, he stopped again and said to me, "I said stop counseling and preach harder! People try to grab hole of your neck and suck you dry. Preach harder..."

Needy people want to create a never-ending vicious relationship of co-dependence upon counseling and ministry. This will eventually destroy the minister and take away ministry.

Preach harder. Spend more time developing leaders. Mature people with person vision need very little counsel. Raising mature sons releases resurrection power upon this earth. We must teach sons to be self-governed and highly motivated. We eventually learn to only counsel those in direct son-ship and train others to take care of the rest.

 Surrounding yourself with continuous counseling sessions concerning people engaged in evil mischief can negatively affect your soul.

MOSES: Moses was charged to deliver a people. He brought them OUT OF Egypt – but he couldn't BRING THEM INTO the Promise. He failed because he allowed people's problems to be his own! Moses succumbed to complaining people who longed for leeks and quail. Now don't gloss over this. He was meekest man on earth – and anger consumed him. People continually challenged and attacked Moses. "Just speak to the Rock," God said. But, in anger, Moses hit that rock! Moses did not conquer the influence of other people. The control of others upon a leader's emotions allows ground for failure.

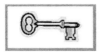 The maintenance of authority requires a continual garrison of our emotions and a right positioning for wise choices. As the famous saying goes, "Choose who you loose!"

As soon as Moses descended the mountain and came near to the camp, there they were molding an idol. Enraged, Moses broke the tablets that God had written with His own finger (Ex. 32:19).

- Anger stops the anointing and favor. Then you can't govern anymore. Deal with it, or you will miss out too.
- Don't let people stop you. Develop persistence and keep on keeping on. OVERCOME.

The trials of our flock are continuous. Seditious and undermining behavior plagues the church. Many people don't want to be corrected and they avoid accountability. The surge of the "independent streak" in people has brought a tremendous resistance to accepting any accountability. They usually seek to validate their self-conceived opinions and actions rather than correct them.

- Many times people turn bitter and accusatory toward leadership and the church rather than realizing their own responsibility because of their wrong decisions.
- Some people are predators who come to church seeking connections for their personal business down lines, resources, or positions of influence.
- Because believers are sometimes drawn to the excitement of the Gift Office (anointing), they create superhuman expectations about their leaders. Then, when they get too close, the sin of familiarity moves in causing them to find flaws and make them public.
- Don't let the carnality of others harden and disillusion you.

Preach more about corporate destiny and less about just individual destiny. All Biblical prophecies are corporate. Preach and build generationally.

CAREFULLY MAINTAIN RELATIONSHIPS BETWEEN LEADERS AND THOSE WHO ARE LED

Anytime you have competitive "familiarity" – you can count on contempt being very close at hand. Like the pecking order in a chicken coop, people begin taking liberties with you. If you offend them, they often strike out. Don't doubt – there is something about the fallen nature that wants to find fault with leaders (I.E. I don't want you better than me, so anything that I can do to make you seem more equal is my assignment). Judging makes those who assume they are an "underling" to feel more worthy.

DANGERS: Over familiarity can easily happen with leaders who are very outgoing and enigmatic in personality. It often happens that the emotional devotion on the part of certain believers can become fanatical. If their expected facade should fade, their leprous response could affect their whole church. Organizations exclusively build as personality driven familiar groups often crash.

When hurt believers start to develop overly familiar "relationships" with the leaders, their "ego begins to "sum-up" the leader (JUDGING and evaluating them). They unconsciously LOOK for faults because they want to "feel" equally important (she doesn't do her dishes, he is not organized enough, he hurt my feelings, etc.).

Like it or not, the church is full of these kind of carnal attitudes and ASSUMPTIONS that basically are go back to wanting to be "NUMBER ONE." (Personal power because every chicken want to "rule the roost.")

CORRECTION: Apostles can have accurate prophetic revelation that God cannot fulfill because of the leader's inability to deal with people and problems! We must be able to move past people problems, past betrayal, and past offenses. An imperative question for apostolic leaders to ask themselves is, "How do we solve these issues without emotionally clouding the vision?"

> We must be able to go the distance to enter in! True apostles are able to MAINTAIN the vision in spite of opposition, find the field, and "pay the price."

> Once we realize what is happening, we can prepare ourselves to NOT be victims. Be confident that God will take care when others fail us.

We must act

without

reacting.

The writing of Jeremiah shows that he knew this problem first hand. "I never joined the party crowd in their laughter and their fun. Led by you, I went off by myself. You filled me with indignation. Their sin had me seething. But why, why this chronic pain, this ever worsening wound and no healing in sight?" (Jer. 15:18, MSG).

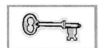

All leaders can expect verbal accusation and betrayal. We must be healed and not minister out of our wounded places.

NEED FOR APPROVAL

"If your greatest goal is to please people, become an entertainer; If you want to be a great leader, expect to have those who oppose you." Bishop Joseph Matera

Leaders MUST be motivated by Godly vision. They must not be dependent upon daily acceptance and affirmation. Those driven by a need for recognition and approval will live an emotional yo-yo life of alternative depression and exhilaration. Their inability to lovingly confront people as necessary will cause them excessive disappointment.

The need for approval causes a halt between appeasing the opinion of others and obeying the voice of God. Preaching will become guarded and unfocused when trying to please people.

Vision must always win over needing recognition, wanting friends, or needing others to like you. Leaders must not vacillate over making precise and correct decisions – regardless of popular opinion. The number one common trait of great leaders is the ability to solve stressful problems. Respect comes from holding onto God's principled standards and codes.

Approval seeking causes a lack of establishing strong core values and principle based ministry. Emotionally based leaders tend to establish more lenient forms of governmental structure. Sustained consistency in leaders posed toward vision will engender security and trust from the believer and in turn causes them to maintain respect toward their leader.

Rightful affirmation comes from obeying the Lord.

INABILITY TO HANDLE CRITICISM: Ask yourself, how do you react when people don't agree with you? Are you quiet and withdrawn or do you attack? Check for a locked mind, unaddressed culture barriers, carnal responses, victim mentality, territorial possessiveness, laziness, emotional outbursts, prejudices, pride, anger, unredeemed attitudes and beliefs, false self perception, etc. Why do you respond like you do? Do you need to change? How? If you learned bad habits, you can learn good ones. Fortunately, you CAN teach an old dog new tricks!

GOSSIP: Don't! When in doubt, be quiet like the stork! Having no syrinx muscles, storks are mute. They produce a clattering noise by snapping their bills.

CONSEQUENCES OF FALLING

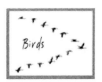

Birds do get lost sometimes, thrown off course by huge storms, fierce winds, or other weather conditions. Sometimes very young birds, or very old birds, or those who started too late in the season may become confused and stray.

The sins of the LEADER HURTS their FLOCK. When David counted the census, his sin of trusting numbers brought "guilt upon Israel" which became a plague (1 Chr. 21:3 NIV). Leviticus says that if the anointed priest sins it brings guilt on the people (Lev. 4:3). Zechariah says that if the Shepherd falls, the sheep can be scattered (Zech. 13:7). The sin of an anointed apostle brings oppression upon those who are joined in any way to that ministry. Wounded followers then carry a cloud of heaviness and a cynicism that affects future relationships.

Moral failure causes guarded distrust. Proverbs tells how unresolved sin caused "shades of the dead there (specters haunting the scene of past transgressions)" (9:18). This guilt by association can "haunt" the lives of those around you as well as yourself.

The entire tenth chapter of first Corinthians tells us why Israel had to wander in the wilderness. Grumbling and unbelief cancelled their journey to the Promise. Our greatest warfare (a personal Armageddon) is in our garden (soul). It's in the Garden where we can watch the birds and discover when to migrate.

> "Do not say, I am being put through an ordeal by God." As GOD CANNOT PUT ONE THROUGH AN ORDEAL, (occurs only here in scriptures—rare word – emphatic - "trail or intensive difficulty") AND HE HIMSELF PUTS NO ONE THROUGH AN ORDEAL! Rather each person goes through ordeals by being dragged along and hooked ON BAIT BY THEIR OWN WANTS AND WISHES. Then wants and wishes conceive (get pregnant) and give birth to sin (has a baby), and sin when it grows up, produces death (becomes a real killer) (Jms. 1:13, The Source Bible).

Most things don't start wrong. Addictive behavior traps us and we can't get out. Unchecked lust is insatiable. The unrestrained progression of our own carnal desires leads to death. We don't just suddenly wake up one morning and want to be a dope dealer or a prostitute. Ministers don't just suddenly commit adultery. The horrible consequences result from seasons or years of bad and unrestrained thoughts. Subtle secret sins grip sooooo strongly that they prevent us from responding properly in repentance. Who can you talk to? Ask yourself, is it time now to make your heart right?

 We must learn to handle vain imaginations. Paul precisely addressed the issues of immorality by saying that all temptation is common to man and God is faithful to deliver (1 Cor. 10:13). Anybody can fall. It's not an accident when we allow ourselves to be vulnerable to temptation.

> Clergy spousal abuse is now an unspoken pandemic.

> Divorce rates among Christians are the same or greater than the secular world. How can we take cities if we can't win our families? Can our ministry exceed the health of our family?

Guard your Garden.

Ask yourself, "What fills my waking thoughts?" Beware of thoughts like, "She is very spiritual and my wife is not." "Maybe God is bringing this woman into my life because something will happen to my wife very soon." "He should have been my spouse." "I can be released from my marriage vow because we weren't Christians when we married."

Think about the consequences if you yield to these temptations. Make a list. What should we do to protect ourselves? What is your potential for greatest destiny? Do you KNOW your potential for greatest failure? What are your weaknesses? What do you do when you are all alone? What you believe is what you do. Your personal viewpoint determines your public performance. The old adage is true: Faith is your belief in action.

CHECK LIST FOR BEING UNGUARDED:	
Discouragement	Financial weakness
Inability to be taught	Not knowing how to rest
Tiredness, boredom	Lack of intimacy in your family
Needing a continuous adrenaline rush	Thinking that people are always challenging or criticizing you
Disappointment over unanswered prayers	Making hasty and unwise decisions
A unyielding need for affirmation in your life	Addiction
Lying	Lack of priorities
Fantasy or compulsive immoral thoughts	Isolation and self-dependence. Wanting to escape and not fellowship with people
Excusing little sins and habits	Addictive thoughts about someone other than your mate.
Exclusiveness, thinking you are better than others	Innocent flirtations
Undo disappointment about not reaching goals	Deception or private interpretation of Scripture (no one understands me)
Aloneness, loneliness, no friends	Victim mentality and life is unfair
Rejection or envy	Not sleeping or eating correctly
Unresolved hurt and offense	Stressful lifestyle, feeling emotionally drained, discord
Arrogance	Unguarded ambition. A preoccupation with position and success
Lack of right prioritizing	Lack of Godly devotion and worship

Gal 6:1-5 If someone falls into sin, forgivingly restore him... If you think you are too good for that, you are badly deceived. (if you think you're a big shot when you're really no one, you are deluding yourself (s). Make a careful exploration of who you are and the work you have been given, and then sink yourself into that. Don't be impressed with yourself. Don't compare yourself with others. Each of you must take responsibility for doing the creative best you can with your own life. (MSG)

 Never forget: When your life backs up your message, people will listen to your words. If your life does not back up your message, you forfeit your authority to speak into their lives.

Leaders Often Walk Ahead and Alone

Leaders MUST MAINTAIN a certain DETACHMENT from circumstances and problems and not get personally involved. They remain "seated."

SEATED AUTHORITY: This term implies that we have found our rightful place of rule and have come to rest. Governmental authority comes easily to those who sit. Sitting in heavenly places" gives all believers the "BIRD'S EYE VIEW" of the problem.

 The authority we can exert on earth is directly proportional to how well we abide in heavenly places (Eph. 1:20-23).

Attempting to have "buddy type" relationships between the leader and each believer is virtually impossible and could cause obligatory or assumed expectations for entitlement that could hamper future effectiveness. Apostolic leaders can't have close friendships with everyone, anymore than they should "Lord over them."

- Even though all people are equal in the sight of God, the flock should not expect "PEER" level relationships with their LEADERS – who must lead, guide, and guard them.
- Leaders are not called (nor is it possible) to be "best friends" with everyone they lead. Not all relationships are not meant to be "close." There are distinctions between developing a mentoring relationship and having a peer relationship. Mutual respect brings growth while unrestrained familiarity tends to divide.
- Leaders cannot give their life to everyone. Jesus gave His life FOR everyone but not TO everyone. He concentrated on the twelve.

People respond to leaders with clear focus on direction and vision. Strong leaders must govern through right positioning of their soul. Jesus often went off to be alone with His Father. Yet, He wanted His apostles to KNOW HIM and fully receive from Him (Mark 6:5).

> Leaders often receive
> Divine answers
> because they embrace
> their responsiblity
> to maintian
> proper boundaries.

Sometimes, Jesus taught the multitudes, sometimes the seventy, sometimes the twelve, sometimes the three, sometimes the disciple whom He loved (John). Relationships can not be expected to be equal. Leaders cannot live isolated lives from the people to whom they minister. But, they must often seek the Lord alone.

Many times as a pastor I would fly to nearby places and just "get away." It always seemed that distancing myself from the problems brought immediate answers to what had seemed impossible. Distancing allow us to get a true "bird's eye view" and stay "one step ahead." It keeps us from being too side-tracked by unnecessary personal involvements.

Necessary boundaries may be misunderstood by others. Be sure to communicate love and acceptance.

> Don't allow familiarity to rob from your anointing.

Strength of conviction is essential. When leaders position themselves in a focused direction of firmly leading, a corresponding energy will move them toward answers, new ideas, ordered thoughts, purpose, open doors, and significant results.

- The intentional lowering of a leader's esteem because he/she didn't do what members might want, violates their ability to accomplish their destiny.
- Leaders must not allow themselves to be the available doormat – any more than they should arrogantly rule over others with superior attitudes.
- Great leaders do not try and "kill themselves" to please others. They have a mental resiliency to interpersonal issues.

 Leaders must establish peer level accountability relationships.

PERCEPTIONS DO CREATE REALITY

Of the four things most amazing is, *"The way of an eagle in the sky"* (Prov. 30:18-19).

One of the best pieces of advice I've ever learned is to reserve Divine secrets for just myself. That means to have a private reservoir. Never allow the Word to become commonplace. Seek the Lord for yourself and not just to have another message to preach. In fact, keep some treasure inside and DON'T TELL IT. It's private – between you and the Lord. This keeps us advised of the readiness of the hour and keep us ready to soar at any given moment.

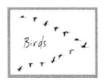 Birds lovingly and willingly live in great freedom together and still can exist without self-centeredness or desire to impress. Flight is not of self-effort but of soaring toward obtaining greater understanding of our incredible salvation. They spread their wings to capture the wind. Their amazing flight plan is ours.

The fulfillment of destiny comes through migrating toward the achievement of our God-given assignments on earth. We can't finish the course if we are derailed, distracted, disorganized, or fatally attracted!

Apostolic people build on principles and values rather than gifts, hype, and personality.

True destiny is accomplished through right choosing and proper execution of Godly character.

 PERSONAL VALUES and CHARACTER: If you desire to lead in the greatness of God's full authority, you must nurture true character. Religion generally considers the outward and physical but ignores the inner values of the heart.

Determine what lies at the core of everything you are as a person. What are the unifying principles and core beliefs of your character? Who are you? Values are what you stand for and believe. Values are the axle around which the CIRCULAR WHEEL of ministry turns. Correct standards should govern your life and determine your friends. There is no more powerful message than one backed up by a Leader's lifestyle.

Take care of the anointing. TEND and GUARD it.

> The dependablity of your AUTHORITY comes through your personal value system.

Each of us must regard and respect the Gift Office and authority that has been given us. Honor the Christ in yourself. "Good LEADERS abhor wrongdoing of all kinds; sound leadership has a moral foundation" (Prov. 16:12 MSG).

"GOD loves the pure-hearted and well-spoken; good LEADERS also delight in their friendship" (Prov. 22:11 MSG).

"Like the horizons for breadth and the ocean for depth, the understanding of a good LEADER is broad and deep" (Prov. 25:3 MSG).

"Leadership is a combination of strategy and character. If you must be without one, be without the strategy." Gen. H. Norman Schwarzkopf

ACCOUNTABILITY

"Perhaps nothing in our society is more needed for those in positions of authority than accountability." Larry Burkett

Accountability is a popular buzz word, but only a few leaders actually practice it. Our challenge is to develop accountability and stop applying bandages on top of gangrenous wounds. MOST ministry problems can be corrected by creating an accountability system. We need protective voices around us that are not impressed or intimidated by our Gifts.

> Through accountabililty, we develop our capacity to maintain and expand God's authority (exousia) in our leadership.

QUESTION: In time of trouble where will you go? To whom are you accountable? The importance of accountability must be reiterated over and over. You are not in ministry alone – you are part of others.

Establish the criteria for an ongoing system of safeguards and structure evaluation – how will accountability be accomplished? What will happen?

Determine an expected protocol concerning how to deal with future problems. An independent board should be in place to deal with improper moral issues.

There is a price to bridge into relationships of accountability. Honesty about everything in our lives.

Pursue mentors, they will not always pursue you.

Prepare to ask provoking questions.

 Accountability is a relational subject and not an organizational issue.

Changing behavior changes results. Maintaining Godly character demands constant external balances. We must willfully determine to constantly readjust our internal character. That means no façade. It means no lying and no stealing. It means honesty, morality, faithfulness, dedication, dependability, accountability, loyalty, teachableness, and uprightness – all these are sources of Godly *authority*.

Apostles of Jesus PERSONALLY live in the resurrection life of God.

An apostle lives for the truth of Godliness (Titus 1:1). Their assignment is to live "God like" in character and help reproduce godliness in others.

* Growing Godly virtue is the key that unlocks doors to full *authority* that were previously closed to you. Find an accountability system – someone who will push you and confront your weaknesses. Be transparent to someone.
* Adjust your confession.
* People can follow and commit to those of strong character and integrity. No one can fully commit to razzmatazz.

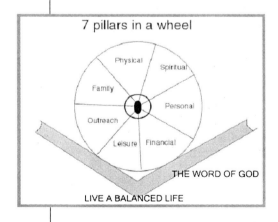

7 pillars in a wheel

Physical
Spiritual
Family
Personal
Outreach
Leisure
Financial
THE WORD OF GOD
LIVE A BALANCED LIFE

BALANCE YOUR LIFE – TAKE HEED!

"We are what we repeatedly do. Excellence then, is not an act, but a habit."
Aristotle

Balance your life and enjoy all the important things along with ministry.

Ministers live in glass houses. That means we must be willing to live a life that is pleasing to God and others. We must live naturally by example and not by demand. We must be wise with the company we keep. We need much wisdom to embrace the characteristics that move us more deeply into effective apostolic oversight.

Paul admonished Timothy, "Take heed to yourself." That word "heed" means "to grab hold of something very tightly – and get a firm grip on it." Your personal life must become significant enough to protect with all your might! Don't let your *authority* be weakened with clogged pipes. Keep the pipeline open.

So much emphasis is put upon the message we bring – but the message is not enough! It must have a credible voice. Our voice must resound with legitimate *authority* (*exousia*) so that others may recognize it. Not words of fancy wisdom.

The maintenance of integrity and moral values must be strongly self imposed by willing obedience – such as consecration, morality, and humility. Be committed to good character no matter where you are.

Keep marriage holy. Invest in your children and families. Stand for those in your family.

Fix yourself first. You'll know when your ready – because then righteous leading will be easier.

Birds sing for JOY. They sing sweet melodious songs because it is their nature to sing. They don't sing to advertise their ministries. They don't sing to express their own pleasure. They sing because the are created to sing. We have that one thing in common with birds! We both sing. We were created to sing in worship. We must praise God with understanding (Ps. 47:7). We must commit to a systematic prayer, meditation, and daily worship. Stay there until you SEE with God's perspective and love.

> *"Praise the Lord from the earth... wild animals and all cattle, small creatures and flying birds... let them praise the name of the LORD"*
> (Ps. 148:7, 10, 13).

Confront yourself with the reality of your specific calling. Review your prophetic words. Review your vision.

Have special relationships that allow you to have wholesome fellowship on a peer level. Make friends in different age levels so that when you become older there will be friends left.

Make certain you have an accountability structure in place where you have someone to talk to about anything.

Be led by the Spirit in all that you do. Pant after the Lord. Weep with others. Stay tenderhearted (Eph. 4:32).

Get your mind off yourself and love God with all your heart, mind, and soul.

Stay away from gossip. (Proverbs 29:12 MSG), "When a LEADER LISTENS to malicious gossip, all the workers get infected with evil."

"Everyone tries to get help from the LEADER, but only GOD will give us justice" (Prov. 29:26).

Determine to not be distracted by confusing doctrines. Know nothing but Jesus and Him crucified. KNOW HIM as He is today!

Allow Jesus to be revealed WITH IN you – not just by telling others (Gal. 1:16) about Him. It's about BEING not DOING. The governing apostle becomes THE message and not merely the transmitter of a message.

Overcome the intense crucible of difficulties and the struggles of life. Years of extreme training and learning should precede your being sent out.

Steward the mystery of CHRIST IN US, the hope of glory (1Cor. 4:1).

Determine to do the greater works of Jesus and not just talk about them.

"Love and truth form a good LEADER; sound leadership is founded on loving integrity" (Prov. 20:28, MSG).

View leadership as a temporal gift that does not make you superior.

Build communication skills that mentor and empower.

Accurately access your gifts and influence.

Build an effective sphere of influence with faithful relationships.

Craft knowledge that is not just a lot of schooling but connects to the Holy Spirit and also uses common sense.

Build endurance. "That you may be invigorated and strengthened with all power according to the might of His glory, (to exercise) every kind of endurance and patience (perseverance) with joy..." Col. 1:11 AMP).

Be decisive – Indecision takes away our energy and momentum. Success comes through decisiveness.

Be bold and determined – Only those with daring purpose can adequately lead people to maturity and completion.

Allow experience to be honed by time, not be blown by winds of doctrine.

Create a positive attitude that overcomes all interferences and hindrances.

Learn listening and motivational skills that build others.

Commit to the success of others rather then self accomplishment (1 Cor. 10:24, 1 Thes. 5:15). If we bless others, then we are also blessed.

Develop the capability of being corrected and trained in successive revelation. Be a disciplined learner.

Assume the ability to apologize when wronged. Walk in love and forgiveness toward all.

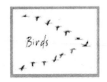 REPENT: Always show a fervency to quickly repent when necessary. Birds show REPENTANCE. Look at Jeremiah 8:6-7 again – it's all about repentance! "...They do not say what is right. No one repents of his wickedness asking 'What have I done?' ... Even the stork in the sky knows her appointed seasons... but my people do not know the requirements of the Lord." Four times the Lord God warned the stubborn people. Four times he repeated, "I looked." He looked for those who would be His. Those who would be light. Those who would obey His warnings.

Decide to quickly forgive others when you are persecuted, mistreated, or grieved.

Give yourself honest self-evaluation and diagnostic assessment.

Daily maintain the passion for true worship. Keep a captivated heart that continuously searches for Truth.

Be honest with your inner and outer life. Have self discipline in appearance, work habits, and personal life.

Take personal initiative toward responsible self government.

Sustain and preserve the big vision and clear sense of direction.

Build your intellectual interests.

1 Timothy 3:1-11 gives us these qualifications: Be a person of good report, blameless, temperate, sober, serious, given to hospitality, not a striker, not greedy, patient, not a brawler, not covetous, house and children in order. Not a novice. Be sincere, not double-tongued, not given to much wine, pure of conscience, proved, self-controlled, and faithful in all things.

Anointed apostolic *authority* strives to prepare a people to be LIKE HIM – not just preparing to speak another sermon. Be able to say as Paul did, "Follow me (imitate me) as I follow Christ (2 Thes. 3:7,9).

"A leader leads by example, whether he intends to or not." Unknown

- Know what you want.
- Find someone else who has already done what you want.
- Learn from them and do what they did.

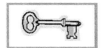 We must have permission and authority from God to speak for God. That only comes through the character and likeness of Christ IN US.

"Good LEADERS motivate, they don't mislead, or exploit" (Prov. 16:10, MXG).

"Good LEADERS cultivate honest speech; they have advisors who tell them the truth" (Prov. 16:13, MSG).

"We don't expect eloquence from fools, nor do we expect lies from our LEADERS." (Prov. 17:7, MSG).

It is a privilege to share this information with you - we are only beginning to soar together in order to see the formation of the future church.

Dr. Kluane

DR. KLUANE SPAKE is a learned theologian who walks in the Spirit. This ministry helps believers grow up and mature until they are able to realize, enjoy, and activate the things that Jesus died to give. Through this ministry, thousands and thousands of people have been healed, strengthened, and challenged to be all they can be in Christ.

Doctor of Theology

Doctor of Naturopathy

Member of the International Coalition of Apostles (ICA)

An Ecclesial Board Member for the International Christian Wealthbuilders Foundation, Ap. John Kelly

Faculty for Vision International University, Dr. Stan DeKoven

International Conference Speaker

This ministry is a bold and pioneering voice that confronts issues and dilemmas of today's church by providing scholarly insight and Spirit filled activation and solutions.

Dr. Kluane Spake has been in ministry for over 25 years. She founded and pastored a successful church in Guam for fourteen years. She understands the needs of the LOCAL PASTOR and local church.

She travels world-wide preaching/teaching at local church services, conferences, and pastor's meetings.

FOUNDER OF JUBILEE ALLIANCE, an apostolic network of 5-fold ministers (www.jubileealliance.com) which is based on relational peer-level association that provides apostolic mentoring and accountability to churches, leaders and ministries.

AUTHOR. Thousands of people have been challenged and changed by these books and numerous articles. Dr. Spake also sends out two monthly newsletters, Right-Dividing, and Jubilee Alliance.

CONTACT US

Mail: P.O. Box 941933
Atlanta, GA 31141

www.kluane.org   www.jubileealliance.com

electronic, mechanical, photocopy, recording, or any other without author's permission.

CREDITS & THANKS:

Special thanks to Dr. Melanie Martin Trip for meticulously editing the first book portion. Dr. Stan DeKoven for encouragement. Also credit to Rev. Terre Penn for editing the second two book portions.

1. *McClintock and Strong Encyclopedia,* Electronic Database. Copyright © 2000, 2003 by Biblesoft, Inc. All rights reserved. "Authority in Religion."

2. See my books "*Understanding Headship*" and "*From Enmity to Equality*" for a personal thirteen-year study of the word *kephale,* and complete analysis of the topic of "submission."

3. In the Greek version of the O.T. the word occurs only once (2 Kings, 14:6).

4. Various John Kelly lectures

5. & 6. See "*Connecting*" for study on "image and likeness."

7. See my book "*Melchizedek*" for information on this city.

8. Ibid, "*From Enmity to Equality*"

9. Click, Bill, "*Function & Form In The Apostolic & Prophetic*" Part 7, bibledesk.com

10. www.jealvarez@worldnet.att.net

11. See my book "*Connecting*" to understand how the Garden is our soul.

12. Lightfoot, "*Galatians*", London, 1896, p. 93

Barklay, Mark T., "*Avoiding the Pitfalls of Familiarity*" Mark Barclay Ministries, 1997

Boswell, Dr. James, Sr., "*Reformation of the Existing Church into the Kingdom of Jesus on Earth*" self published. Idea for delegated authority illustration, various points.

Clements, Kirby, "*The Second*," self-published by author, Jan. 1995, and personal conversations.

David T. "*Dominion Authority*" Albury Press, Christian Publishing Services, Inc.Tulsa, Ok. pg.14.

Eberle, Harold R., "God's Leaders For Tomorrow's World," Worldcast Publishing, Yakima, WA 2003" Posing of the soul"

Early, Tim, "*The Apostolic Dimension,*" internet (sent, strategy, dates, terms, *ecclesia*)

Fowler, Joshua, "*Access Granted*," self-published by author, 2002

Godwin, William, "*The Enquirer,*" written in 1797 (page 86).

Hook, Cecil, "*Religious Titles*" not known.

Mattera, Bishop Joseph, ideas and quotes from "*10 Points for Set Leaders*" "*Why Jesus Had Authority,*" approval, and various other writings

Peacock, Dennis, "*Doing Business God's Way*," REBUILD, 2003

Posey, Michael, talk on ministry failures, Chicago, 2006

Stott, John, "*The Birds Our Teachers*" Essays in Orni-theology, Candle Books, 1999

Tetsola, John, "*The Reformers*" magazine, winter '07

Yoder, Barbara, "*Mantled with Authority*" Wagner Publications, 2003, "mantle" concepts.

WEBSITES:

http://www.5solas.org/media.php?id=79

http://www.abu.nb.ca/Courses/Pauline/Soter6.htm Pauline Soterology

http://www.amazon.com/gp/offer-listing/B000RW1APA?ie =UTF8&condition=new&tag=dealtime-kitchen-mp-20&creative= 380345&creativeASIN=B000RW1APA&linkCode=asm jet formation

http://www.answers.com/topic/urk

http://www.bibleresearch.org/index.html

http://bibletools.org/index.cfm/fuseaction/Topical.show/RTD/cgg/ID/385/Respect.htm

http://www.biblewheel.com/Art/Art_Wheel.asp, Icon, Gilgal, wheel, etc.

http://www.birding.about.com/library/weekly/aa090401b.htm

http://www.come-and-hear.com/sanhedrin/sanhedrin_100.htm)

http://www.dictionary.reference.com/search?q=revolution
http://www.en.wikipedia.org/wiki/Bird_migration

http://www.en.wikipedia.org/wiki/Dignity, respect, original apostles

http://www.foundationsforfreedom.net/Topics/Parenting03_Authority.html

http://www.geocities.com/davidjayjordan/TwelveWomenApostlesofJesus.html

http://www.indygear.com/props/ark.shtml picture of priests altered

http://www.jewishvirtuallibrary.org/jsource/Environment/birds1.html, Zech. 5:9-113

http://www.livingbiblestudies.org/study/JT60/002.html, the stork

http://www.members.aol.com/excognito/candles.html 2 Cor 10:8

http://www.newadvent.org/cathen/07365a.htm, confronting leader

http://www.oaspub.epa.gov/gedri/pack_edri.studys?p_studys=Field+Study

http://www.plato.stanford.edu/entries/respect/

http://www.rfiusa.org, Polis, John, internet articles,

http://www.santasusanna.org/images/StPaulCatacombs.jpg, susanna image

http://www.smallvoices.net/svj_vol_3/authority.htm

http://www.scripturecatholic.com/apostolic_succession.html

http://www.theexaminer.org/volume5/number5/titles.htm

http://www.the-tribulation-network.com/dougkrieger/unsealing/
unsealing_by_chapter.htm, Zech. 5:9-11

Vine's Expository Dictionary of Biblical Words, Copyright © 1985, Thomas Nelson Publishers

Thayer's Greek Lexicon, Electronic Database. Copyright © 2000, 2003 by Biblesoft, Inc. All rights reserved.

Most art work is original by Dr. Kluane Spake – some using Microsoft clip art, Google clip art, and google images

html.calendar.&h=429&w=334&sz=22&hl=en&sig2=GcjyIlGhd5m2nHPbL6FEdw&start=4
&um=1&tbnid=cGDJMwYyp5gb (arrowhead)

http://pippahunnechurch.com/humblepie2.gif

www.thefreedictionary.com Farlex, proton image

BIBLE TRANSLATION

NIV, KJV, NKJ: PC Bible Software.

THE MESSAGE: The Bible in Contemporary Language © 2002 by Eugene H. Peterson.

Biblesoft's New Exhaustive Strong's Numbers and Concordance with Expanded Greek-Hebrew Dictionary. Copyright © 1994, 2003 Biblesoft, Inc. and International Bible Translators, Inc.

International Standard Bible Encyclopedia, Electronic Database Copyright © 1996, 2003 by Biblesoft, Inc.

Thayer, The New Thayer's Greek-English Lexicon of the New Testament\(Peabody, MA: Hendrickson Publishers, 1981), p. 225.

THECLA information from my book "From Enmity to Equality" with bibliography below:

 Ramsay, "Church in the Roman Empire," pg. 375.

 Elwell, Ellis Enterprises, Compactdisc, ordination.

Rhoodie, Eschel, "Discrimination Against Women," (McFarlan and Company Inc. 1989) pg. 410.

 Kroeger, Catherine, various talks

Howe, E. Margaret, "Women and Church Leadership," (Zondervan Publishing, Grand Rapids Michigan) pg. 39.

Picture of Thecla from unknown photographer, postcard bought in Turkey.

Full-color diagrams of the authority being in a circle presentation are available online as an E-book that you can put into computerized projection or overhead transparencies, and then you can use them to teach this subject.

CONTACT Dr. Kluane

877-SPAKE-99   spake@mindspring.com

Mail: P.O. Box 941933 Atlanta, GA 31141

www.kluane.org   www.jubileealliance.com

www.kluane.org/store

Other books by Dr. Kluane

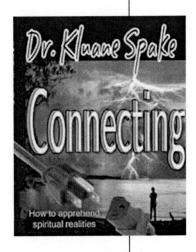

LaVergne, TN USA
09 March 2011
219473LV00004B/29/P